BLACK PANTHER

Paradigm Shift or Not?

A Collection of Reviews and Essays on a Blockbuster Film

Edited by
Haki R. Madhubuti and Herb Boyd

BLACK PANTHER
Paradigm Shift or Not?

Third World Press Foundation
Publishers since 1967

thirdworldpressfoundation.org
facebook.com/ThirdWorldPress

Cover Design: Lance Tooks & Craig Barnes
Library of Congress Control Number on file
ISBN: 978-0-88378-409-9

Printed in the United States of America

DISCLAIMER
The views expressed in the essays throughout this book are not necessarily the views of Third World Press Foundation.

DEDICATION

Wesley Snipes   Danny Glover

Safisha Madhubuti (Dr. Carol D. Lee)

In memory of and more:
Walter P. Lomax Jr., M.D., Maxine Graves Lee, Gwendolyn Brooks,
Malcolm X, Ossie Davis, Dudley Randall, Hoyt W. Fuller,
Barbara Ann Sizemore, Margaret Burroughs, Richard Wright,
Charles Burroughs, Ruby Dee, Derrick Bell, W.E.B. Du Bois,
Paul Robeson, John Henrik Clarke

I work for
My children, grandchildren, cultural children
and
all children

HRM

CONTENTS

INTRODUCTION

CHAPTER 1
"BLACK PANTHER" AND THE INVENTION OF "AFRICA"
Jelani Cobb |1|

CHAPTER 2
BLACK PANTHER IS A MUST-SEE
Christina Greer, Ph.D. |6|

CHAPTER 3
BLACK PANTHER HAS TEACHABLE TOOLS FOR ORGANIZERS
Omowale Adewale |8|

CHAPTER 4
IS BLACK PANTHER THE BIGGEST PARADIGM SHIFT OF ALL BLACK
MOVIES EVER?
LM Arnal |12|

CHAPTER 5
LIES CAN'T GET US WHERE WE NEED TO GO!
Abdul Alkalimat |14|

CHAPTER 6
BLACK PANTHER AND THE DEGENERATION OF BLACK PUBLIC
AND POPULAR DISCOURSE
Rayfield A. Waller (The Panopticon Review) |16|

CHAPTER 7
REAL WAKANDA–BATTLE OF ADWA, SEARCHING FOR HEROES &
LIBERATORS, AND THE POLITICAL ECONOMY OF BLACK PANTHER
Milton G. Allimadi |20|

CHAPTER 8
WISHING FOR WAKANDA, MAROONED IN AMERICA: Movies and Matters of
Reflection and Resistance
Dr. Maulana Karenga |26|

CHAPTER 9
BLACK FEMINIST MEDITATIONS ON THE WOMEN OF WAKANDA
Robyn C. Spencer, Ph.D. |30|

CHAPTER 10
IT'S ALL ABOUT THE MONEY
Fred Logan |34|

CHAPTER 11
BLACK PANTHER: A Nuanced Film for a Nuanced People
C. Liegh McInnis |37|

CHAPTER 12
BLACK PANTHER: REFLECTIONS ABOUT THE MOVIE
A HISTORICAL AND MYSTICAL SYMBOLISM PHENOMENA
Aminifu R. Harvey, MSW, DSW |47|

CHAPTER 13
BLACK PANTHER: VIEW FROM THE COMICBOOK GEEK DEN
Todd Steven Burroughs |52|

CHAPTER 14
AN ECONOMIC ANALYSIS OF BLACK PANTHER: Separating Myth from Reality
Patrick Delices |56|

CHAPTER 15
IMAGE MAKERS REVISITED: QUEST FOR A NOBLE BLACK SUPER HERO
Useni Perkins |71|

CHAPTER 16
WILL THE REAL WAKANDA WAKE UP?
Molefi Kete Asante |74|

CHAPTER 17
AFRICA AND WHAT WE KNOW:
The Visceral Response of Black People to Black Panther the Movie
Michael Simanga |80|

CHAPTER 18
WHAT IS AFRICA TO ME NOW?
Greg Tate |83|

CHAPTER 19
YOU'RE PRETTY (AWESOME) FOR A DARK GIRL:
Beauty, Power and Strength in the Movie Black Panther
Marita Golden |85|

CHAPTER 20
THE BLACK PANTHER FILM HAS MERITS AND DEMERITS
Norman Richmond |89|

CHAPTER 21
BLACK PANTHER: Race and Representation
Diane D. Turner, Ph.D. |94|

CHAPTER 22
BLACK PANTHER AND THE BLACK PUBLIC SPHERE
Keith Gilyard |101|

CHAPTER 23
DETERMINING A NATION
Allyson Horton |104|

CHAPTER 24
BLACK PANTHER IS A MILESTONE IN
AFRICAN AMERICANS' SEARCH FOR HOME
Peniel E. Joseph |107|

CHAPTER 25
GOOD PANTHER, BAD PANTHER
Paul Street |110|

CHAPTER 26
DID YOU EXPECT SOMETHING DIFFERENT AND
MORE RADICAL FROM HOLLYWOOD? WHY?
Dr. Eric Curry |119|

CHAPTER 27
THE BLACK PANTHER: Archetypal and Symbolic Conversations About
Carol Lee |124|

CHAPTER 28
BLACK PANTHER: More Than Just A Wrinkle in Time, It Wrinkles Time
Eugene B. Redmond |132|

CHAPTER 29
WAKANDA IS A BEAUTIFUL IMAGE, BUT WE DO NOT NEED A KINGDOM: A
Critique Of the 'King And Queen' Narrative Underlying The Film, "Black Panther"
K. Tutashinda |135|

CHAPTER 30
BLACK PANTHER MEETS PINK PANTHER
Michael Dinwiddie |142|

CHAPTER 31
TERRA FIRMA
Temple Hemphill |146|

CHAPTER 32
THE MASS APPEAL OF 'BLACK PANTHER'
Monica Moorehead |148|

CHAPTER 33
THE AWAKENING
Angela Kinamore |148|

CHAPTER 34
BLACK PANTHER–REAL AND REEL
Bill Ayers |155|

CHAPTER 35
WHO ARE BLACK PEOPLE–REALLY?
Dr. Patricia Williams Diaw |158|

CHAPTER 36
THE AFROFUTURISM BEHIND 'BLACK PANTHER'
Brent Staples |164|

CHAPTER 37
BLACK PANTHER—WE NEED A HERO!
Thabiti Lewis and Don Matthews |166|

CHAPTER 38
POWER TO THE PEOPLE!
Sadiki "Bro. Shep" Ojore Olugbala (s/n Shepard P. McDaniel) |169|

CHAPTER 39
A POWERFUL BLACK PANTHER AND A SUBTLE WHITE SHADOW
Nicole Mitchell Gantt |172|

CHAPTER 40
WOULD-BE WAKANDA: The Black Panther and the Paradox of the Congo
Ewuare X. Osayande |178|

CHAPTER 41
BLACK PANTHER: The Film - Bobby Seale's and the Inner Office Staff's Review
Original Black Panther Bobby Seale |183|

CHAPTER 42
TAKE THE A TRAIN TO WAKANDA:
The Trailblazing Paths of Luke Cage and the Black Panther
L.A. Williams and Lee Bynum |188|

CHAPTER 43
VIBRANIUM AND GAGUT
Clemson Brown |193|

INTRODUCTION

Just when we thought the *Black Panther* film had provoked every conceivable angle, every possible literary and cultural perspective, a minister friend wanted to add another one. Minister Clemson Brown of Brooklyn, a noted documentarian and a passionate follower of Dr. Gabriel Oyibo, a physicist who has proposed a unified theory of everything — GAGUT (God Almighty's Grand Unified Theorem) — said that the precious metal vibranium of Wakanda is comparable to GAGUT.

Rather than attempting to explain the intricacies of Professor Oyibo's theorem, we will leave that to Minister Brown. Our point here is that there are so many intriguing and interesting ways to view the *Black Panther* film, and nothing underscores this better than the diverse contributors assembled here. We are reminded of the proverbial nine blind men asked to describe and define an elephant by holding different parts of the animal's anatomy. The contributors represent a broad spectrum of our political and cultural matrix, and they evoke every theme from Afrofuturism to Kemet, anticipating and probing some of the outcomes of the film while taking stock of its reflection on ancient African concepts and modalities.

The moment we saw how the film was lining up folks at the box office, raking in the bucks, and stimulating a range of often differing views, we knew a book would be helpful in placing the film within both a cinematic and historical context. In many respects, we were reminded of the controversy that emerged after the publication of the late Dr. Manning Marable's biography of *Malcolm X*. At that time, along with Dr. Maulana Karenga and Dr. Ron Daniels, we gathered a collection of different reviews and opinions and published *By Any Means Necessary – Malcolm X: Real, Not Reinvented*.

As the title indicates, *Black Panther: Paradigm Shift or Not? – A Collection of Reviews and Essays on a Blockbuster Film*, the book, like the previous endeavor mentioned above, we allow the contributors to voice their own impressions, whether pro or con, or a little bit of both as so many of them concluded. Obviously, there was bound be a lot of overlapping, a repetition of views, something we discovered in our Malcolm project. That was inevitable and in some instances it merely shored up and embellished a point of view, giving it a popular, undisputed resonance.

Our aim from the very inception of the anthology was to get it out while *Black Panther* was still in the theaters. And with it now being shown in Saudi Arabia, thereby launching cinema in a country that had forbidden films for nearly forty years, there's a renewed global momentum. Even so, speed was less a primacy than to have a miscellany of compelling observations; while many of the reviews have already been published, others were requested from a number of prominent activists, intellectuals, and film scholars. Given the time we imposed to publish the book, several commentators, and they should be conspicuous by their absence, were unable to meet the deadline. Perhaps there will come another book to add to what we have completed here and provide a further excursion into the film's portent and reverberations.

It certainly has reverberated — and as we go to press the film has already exceeded the billion dollar ceiling and this does not include the foreign take. Yes, Black Panther has surpassed all expectations, breaking box office records and raising the bar higher than a mountain in Wakanda. But the film's magnitude, the impact it's had in spheres here and abroad is something our contributors will disclose, and maybe, just maybe you can arrive at a conclusion of whether the film is a paradigm shift or not. Is this time to celebrate or recalibrate our plans for liberation?

If you decide the film is a complex mix of excellence, fantasy, and a way to stay "woke," then count yourselves among the multitude who warmed the seats, enjoyed the beats, and wished for a real Black Panther and Wakanda.

Jelani Cobb provides us a real African gateway to the past through the "Door of No Return," on Goree Island, off the coast of Senegal. Before delving into the film, he summons the wise counsel of such notable thinkers at Edward Blyden, Marcus Garvey, Queen Mother Moore, and John Henrik Clarke, and then postulates that "If the subordination of Africa had begun in the minds of white people, its reclamation, they reasoned, would begin in the minds of Black ones." For Cobb, *Black Panther* is "a redemptive counter-mythology," flipping the script on Tarzan and Edgar Rice Burroughs. "Most filmmakers," Cobb asserts, "start by asking their audiences to suspend their disbelief. But, with Africa, [Ryan] Coogler begins with a subject about which the world had suspended its disbelief four centuries before he was born." Cobb repeatedly and cogently remind us of a real Africa, although he insists that "Marvel has made a great many entertaining movies in the past decade, but Ryan Coogler has made a profound one."

Christina Greer is glad she chose to see the film on the opening weekend because she had a chance to experience what appeared to be "a cultural event." In her estimation the film is a "must see," mainly for the full range of Black expression on screen. "Some of the most interesting roles were given to Black women, who served as women of strength and not merely damsels in distress to aid the Black Panther," she notes. "They were not seen as women in despair, solely love interests, the long suffering woman in the wings or any of the other various tropes allotted to women on screen. Their sense of strength was fueled by conviction and not anger, and their love of themselves, their comrades and their country allowed a multifaceted interrogation of the ways in which Black women have served and continue to serve as moral compasses and backbones of democracy." *Black Panther*, she concludes, is a movie "for us" and "by us."

Among the many teachable moments that abound in *Black Panther*, according to

Omowale Adewale, is that "we must be careful in not fusing Black Panther the Marvel comic book with a Black Panther who is a former member of the Black Panther Party, formed to gain self-determination for Black people in the U.S. Seasoned organizers know best how to navigate this discussion or engage in community action to help shine light on political prisoners." This is a very important distinction, particularly for that generation of viewers who have little understanding of the history and legacy of the Black Panther Party. Several of our commentators make note of this fact, but Adewale makes it plain, and he illustrates another point that may have been missed by many filmgoers, but not by vegans such as Adewale. When M'Baku (Winston Duke), leader of the Jabari clan, states "We are Vegetarian," for Adewale it "highlights that huge, muscular men can abstain from animal flesh and still obtain necessary levels of protein. Also, it's a dog whistle to the Black community's unhealthy eating of animal flesh, causing high rates of heart disease and cancer."

If Adewale is mindful of what we ingest, Abdul Alkalimat's caveat addresses what our minds consume, and being bedazzled and hoodwinked by Hollywood. "Our situation is so dire," he opines, "that we will reach out for this Hollywood fantasy as if it can be helpful, healing, and a lens through which to view history. There is dialogue about freedom, but in no way reflects the past or gives positive advice for us. Lies can't get us where we need to go." Alkalimat also has some pointed comments about Killmonger [Michal B. Jordan], a friendly associate with the CIA. "The reference to the actual Black Panthers, meaning the child of Wakanda (aka Killmonger) who grew up in Oakland, is a sort of gangster living a Fanonian fantasy that violence will change the world. He, too, is the son of a member of the royal family. This guy was trained by the CIA and begins the film in alliance with a white South African fascist. The big lie is that to be a Panther one has to be of 'royal blood,' and not simply a victim of the system who stands up to fight back." Moreover, Alkalimat warns, "People see the film and feel good, but isn't that what people say about first getting high on drugs. We know how drug addiction turns out. This film is dangerous and we must be vigilant against culture used to control and oppress."

L.M. Arnal's review, in several ways underscore Alkalimat's warnings and concludes even stronger with this charge that the film is "the Oscar of all Scams!" Where, he contends, is "the thirst for justice" in the film and why no concerted attack on "systemic racism"? Arnal is unequivocal that "Hollywood is a cliché machine whose strongest function is to create ideologies, sets of beliefs to live by. And the well-being of Black people is still not on their very conservative agenda." He ends with a question: "Wakanda or wake up right now! Which one will you choose?" That is a question that resounds throughout the collection.

Arnal's analysis is given further impetus by Rayfield Waller who declares that *Black Panther* is just a movie "based on a comic book by multinational, corporate sell out Stan Lee's Marvel Comics conglomerate—it would do well to not lose track of the source." Waller, again reminding us of Arnal's "masquerade...minstrel show" riffs on the film, writes that the film is not the point "we are. Are we willing to buy into one of the most destructive and negative developments in American cinema (many critics say the Marvel regime's supremacy is in fact ruining cinema through its degrading of complexity of plot, adult theme, and complexity of characterization) simply because a monopolist Marvel movie is doing it now in Blackface?"

Milton Allimadi picks up where Jelani Cobb left off, with a definite concern to bridge the gap between the African motherland and the Diaspora, a subtle under current in *Black Panther*. This, he believes "are the keys to Pan-African empowerment. Can you imagine Africa's tremendous resources — its 1.2 billion people, its hundreds of trillions of dollars' worth of mineral and natural resources, and its possession of two-thirds of the world's untapped fertile agricultural land — leveraged with the $1 trillion in Black annual purchasing power in the United States?" With such wealth, Allimadi continues, "the Global African world would be second to none. That is the vision that Killmonger (Michael B. Jordan) had for Africa's Wakandas." In a reference to the real world of African wealth, he posits that the "Congo's combined mineral riches is estimated at $27 trillion--that's one African country alone. Wakandans has what amounts to vibranium--in the form of rich deposits of uranium, gold, diamond, copper, cobalt, and coltan; the latter is used in all cell phones and other electronic products." Allimadi takes exception to the film's depiction of the CIA. "How is it possible for the director, Ryan Coogler, to permit this storyline even in a film about a fictitious African country given what the CIA did to some of Africa's heroes, real life T'Challas such as [Patrice] Lumumba, [Kwame] Nkrumah and [Nelson] Mandela?"

Like Allimadi, the venerable Maulana Karenga insightfully places Black Panther in a cinematic and political context, noting that "it is good to remember that no matter how long we stay in the theater and no matter how many times we return to cheer, clap and dance in the dark, sooner or later the lights will come on, and we will have to exit and confront the off-screen, cold-water reality of America." Karenga, through his years of fighting for freedom and liberation, knows first-hand the "cold-water reality of America," and as a deeply informed scholar and historian, he dutifully consults the ancestors when faced with contemporary problems. When it comes to the media and its messages, Karenga turns to Malcolm X who, as he says, "taught us to reject and resist the power and manipulation of the media, a weapon used constantly in the war to win the hearts and minds of our people and other oppressed and turn them against themselves and others." The film, he adds, comes at a most dangerously propitious time "when the attacks on African people, Black people, on the continent and in the diaspora, have taken a wild and openly racist turn. And the film becomes an alternative narrative for many to the rampant racist reductive translation and claims of who we are."

One of the most poignant and pertinent discussions on the role of women in *Black Panther* flows effortlessly from the mind and words of Robyn Spencer. Her feminist analysis bristles with fresh insight, taking care to offer an inclusive overview tactfully folded in lines like these: "Scholars of Black women's intellectual history have pointed to the ways that racism and sexism combine to easily dismiss Black women as 'doers,' rather than thinkers." Spencer is emblematic of the doer and thinker and she, like Karenga, is very much aware of the film's arrival in the national debate and neo-fascist tinge of the Trump administration.

| xiii |

"There is no better time to launch critical conversations about what liberation could look like; connect new people to pre-existing organizations and political networks; re-center aesthetics in freedom making projects and have some frank transnational diasporic dialogue," Spencer relates. "Perhaps the best thing about Black Panther is that it grounds these conversations in intergenerational soil."

When it's all said and done, if Fred Logan is right, *Black Panther* is all about the money. The financial component, the enormous cash turnover, both at home abroad, more than confirms Logan's premise as Marvel Studio—"and they produced the film, not Black folks" Logan charges—grosses capital well beyond the expenditures. Logan, a true student of film, particularly African and third world productions, argues another point, another Hollywood omission. "Independent black cinema is replete with images and portrayals of Black women that are light years ahead of the Marvel Comic Black women," he writes, echoing Spencer's superb summary. "The astounding captivating images of Black women in Julie Dash's 1991 groundbreaking film *Daughters of the Dust* set new cinematic standards for African American women. This epic cinema also recognizes and cherishes indispensable cultural links between continental Africans and African Americans that stand autonomous of the European American cultural hierarchy. For this reason, the motion picture establishment has never sought Julie Dash for a full length theater film."

In many ways, C. Liegh McInnis's extensive discussion is as nuanced as *Black Panther*, which is at the heart of his commentary on the film. We agree with his verdict that Black Americans do not comprise a monolith, and McInnis interrogates this premise with precision, noting the historic binary of contending ideologies, from Booker T. Washington and W.E.B. Du Bois to Dr. Martin Luther King, Jr. and Malcolm X. These contentious moments, the internecine rivalry drives the narrative in Black Panther, but McInnis thoughtfully reminds us that "one leaves Black Panther not discussing good versus evil or the right and wrong way to respond to white supremacy but making sure to engage in discourse that includes the complexity of what it means to be African and African American in a world smothered by white supremacy and how that unique and complex understanding colors or impacts one's choice of how best to respond to inhumanity and injustice."

As if commenting on and extending McInnis's dichotomy, Aminifu R. Harvey, opens his review with an epigraph—"Harmony is the union of opposites." Before he delves into ancient Kemetic modes and a learned exposition of African rituals, Harvey establishes an important historical fact, a brief but compelling exegesis of the Black Panther Party that is only signified in the film by the Oakland, California location where it was founded and a photo of a Panther member on the wall. Harvey draws a number of striking parallels between the present and the edicts of the past, and uniquely cites a very symbolic moment in which Okoye (Danai Gurira), the leader of the all-female corps, Dora Milaje, during a confrontation with an attacker expresses her disgust with European standards of beauty. "When the conflict starts," Harvey writes, "she throws off the wig and clothes to prepare for fight – transition and such symbolism as African descent women should throw off their

European-isms and be their natural African self." Harvey uses this scene to expound on a legacy of warrior women, including such modern day freedom fighters as Amy Garvey, Fannie Lou Hamer, and Judy Richardson.

Few writers have the expertise, the authority to plumb the realm of comic books like Todd Steven Burroughs, and here he offers brief but informative bios of the African American writers and artists involved in the history of Marvel's *Black Panther*. While it is rewarding to know the background of Stan Lee and Jack Kirby, the creators of *Black Panther*, Burroughs shows his true colors and knowledge of the genre with his short profiles of Christopher Priest, Reginald Hudlin, and Ta-Nehisi Coates, three Black writers employed by Marvel to continue the evolution of the character. His point by point recitation on which writer created which character has pertinence as well. This history is profoundly significant and is a set piece for his ruminations about the overall purposes of the film. "Marvel's Black Panther is about race, mainstream superhero comics and the Black American imagination within the backdrop of American history and world history," Burroughs explains. "It's about the limitations of white liberalism and the power of Black-centered but white-controlled American popular culture; ultimately, it's how 20th century white liberalism had to yield to the 21st century multicultural reality."

Political economist Patrick Delices relished an opportunity to examine and analyze the financial impact of Black Panther. When Fred Logan declared the movie was about money, Delices applies the figures, Marvel's spread sheet, the profits and dividends. "Economics," Delices begins, "is therefore associated with land, labor, and resources, not necessarily money; even though this 'Marvel/Disney film earned an astounding $652.5 million at the U.S. box office and more than $1.2 billion worldwide.' Thus, making it 'the fourth highest grossing domestic film of all time,' behind '*Avatar, Titanic*, and *Star Wars: The Force Awakens*,' as it earns the title of 'the top grossing superhero film of all time.'" The footnotes at the end of his review indicates the informants he quotes. One of the authorities essential to Delices discourse is public intellectual and scholar Edgar Ridley, and he is summoned to extrapolate on the difference between myth and reality so intricately intertwined in Black Panther. "A thoroughgoing, careful reading of history tells us that it is only when we are not able to face the realities of life that we tend to mythologize and distort anything and everything that we do not want to be true," Ridley says, evoking the ideas of the great Senegalese scholar Cheikh Anta Diop. "Symbols produce myths, superstition, and ritual, and these elements cannot be allowed to stand if we are to progress as a people. Nothing makes sense when it is carried out from a mythological point of view and when it is acted out symbolically. This is the dividing line between civilization and barbarism. We have to make the choice to live either symbolically (which is to live a mythical existence) or to live symptomatically (which means to live in a state of ultimate reality)."

Myths and stereotypes are basic to Useni Perkins' take on *Black Panther*. Hollywood, as he denotes, is replete with stereotypes and they are viciously abundant when it comes to depicting the Black experience. From *Birth of a Nation* to *Gone with the Wind*, among a gallery of other demeaning films, Perkins lists the indignities. And Black stories and characters are no better during the Blaxploitation era with the arrival of *Superfly* and *Sweet Sweetback*. "It didn't matter if some of these 'Black Super Dudes' were flawed with transgressions," Perkins avers, "the fact that they performed heroic feats against white people compensated for any lack of moral attributes they may have had. More importantly, these films filled a void in the emotional psyche of many Black people to see Black heroes on the big screen, regardless of how disingenuous they may have been." Perkins' critique of past films is a timeless one and he adds, "Granted this mythical version of a Utopia African nation, with the moral principles and technological advancements to humanize the planet, has its moments of Black pride and archival images of great African civilizations, we must be cautious not to elevate it to a height that is immune from constructive criticism. I say this not to discredit or minimize the extraordinary achievement of BLACK PANTHER but to acknowledge that art of any genre can best be assessed when it is exposed to a wide range of diverse views."

Afrocentricity pervades *Black Panther*, and who better to explore the meanings than Molefi Kete Asante. A putative founder of the concept, Asante weighs in here with his typical concern for accuracy and intentions of Afrocentric thought and tropes. "To be clear this movie does not entertain us with a Tyler Perry storyline with its simplistic and non-attempt at Afrocentric invention or reinvention," he says up front. "This film does not play to the lowest common denominator in order to jerk laughter; it is an attempt at serious moviemaking in the creation of myths that carry with them nuggets of golden wisdom." To this end with a serious assessment, Asante interprets Black Panther as a film, not a movie, thereby requiring a rigorous, thoroughgoing analysis. Even so, he advises, "I also know that in a racialized society the pitfalls of filmmaking are great and treacherous both for the creators and for the audiences." Most disturbing to Asante are the imperfections of Wakanda where, he asserts, there is no "culture of science." At the end of his deft conclusions, Asante laments: "**Black Panther** is an OK hero but where is Nat Turner, Zumbi, Thutmoses III, Ramses II, Opoku Ware I, Sundiata, Nehanda, Mansa Musa, Abubakari II, Yenenga, Hatshepsut, Frederick Douglass, Marcus Garvey, Antenor Firmin, or Steve Biko?"

There is an intuitive appreciation and jubilation of *Black Panther*, Michael Simanga proposes, feelings that are shared from one community to another across the nation. "Black people celebrate *Black Panther*, because it gives us joy, strength, inspiration and imagination, not because it is a perfect rendering of what was or what we need," he writes. "Our people are thankful for a film that gave us a moment to rest in ourselves away from the death grips of the oppressive places where we became Africa's diaspora." The film has left Simanga with a number of presumptions about filmmakers, including those involved in *Black Panther*, who "understood that ours is a fight for power, to live as full human beings, to defend against those who attack us, to build a new world. Even in mythology, Black people's human right to self-defense and self-determination are rarely presented. The film makers understood that depicting the totality of our struggle for human rights was absolutely necessary. They knew and we know that only we have the power to be who we've been and are destined to be. We know like Malcolm X knew: 'We declare our right to be a human being.'"

Simanga's imperatives are easily discerned, Greg Tate's are more challenging but no less meaningful as he takes issue with the throw down between T'Challa (Black Panther) and Killmonger, even as he riffs on what they symbolize in past differences and current despair. "Today our most current, coherent shared collective vision of ourselves as a Community — or the mythic stand-in for one — are provided by trap rap pipedreams, The Church, HBCUs and the prison-industrial complex," Tate observes. "So the imperative for taking the Utopic-invoking capacity of The Kulcha and Movement into the Virtual — especially for the babies — has never seemed more acute. But The Panther also wisely and surreptitiously speaks to the topical, zeitgeist reality of Black Lives Matter as a Black woman intellectual led Movement and the super macho pushback against that in certain throwback quarters. And in its Mandingo-beefcake Battle Royale moments it feeds a nostalgic throwback desire for balls-out hyper-masculine Black militant dick-slinging once again unleashed on the masses in the peanut gallery. But folk been jumping on Team T'Challa and Team Killmonger without considering how cunningly the tandem were conceived to represent our classic stag conundrum — that of internecine Black Siamese twins not so artfully going at The Art of War." His discussion requires a full reading.

Images are precious and potent, Marita Golden writes at the start of her essay. Her views are reminiscent of those that occur in several of the authors, most vividly in Michael Simanga's populace rendering. "Like many viewers I was astonished and reassured by what I witnessed unfolding on the screen," Golden effuses. "Astonished because I had never seen a celebration of black power in the world of politics and global power and in our personal lives, intertwined and dramatized so vividly. Reassured because *Black Panther* affirmed what I know and what poet Sonia Sanchez said, 'We a BaddDD people.' In much of African American fiction and creative representation of Black life, we suffer from a "hero deficit." Black audiences are famished for images of Black life and possibilities that are more about life than death, more about joy than pain, and that present us with Black people as heroic. This, even though we witness in our daily lives the heroic woven into the tapestry of our families and friendships, *Black Panther* gave us Black people to envy, root for, cheer on, and mostly, *want to be.*"

Along with his strong condemnation of how the CIA is portrayed in the film, the failure to even hint at the role it played in the assassination of major progressive political leaders, Norman (Otis) Richmond, accentuates a few of the economic points made by Delices and others, highlighting the disparity in pay between Black and white actors, and exorbitant reaping of cash by the corporations underwriting the film. "If you compare what Marvel and Disney have made and will continue to make our great actors and actresses were paid sharecropping wages for their splendid work," Richmond muses. "Robert Downey Jr. pocketed $50 million for his role in *Iron Man*. This is ten times what the Pan African cast of *Black Panther* made. Chadwick Boseman who played T'Chaka/Black Panther received the biggest check earning three million dollars; Lupita Nyong'o who played Nakia received one million; Michael B. Jordan who played Erik Killmonger received one million; Dania Gurira who played Okoye received one million; Daniel Kaluuya who played (W'Kabi) received $800,000; Forest Whitaker (Zuri) received $600,000; Letitia Wright who played Shuri received $500,000 and Angela Bassett $400,000." As a parting shot, Richmond quotes the prolific scholar Gerald Horne, admonishing viewers glued to the screen to look deeper to observe what's happening behind it.

Diane Turner is certainly a scholar and contributor who has peeled away the film's veneer to probe some of its deeper implications. Moreover, she taps into several of this anthology's basic aims. "*Black Panther* is a vehicle that creates dialogue about race and representation in American popular culture but also the history of Black comics. Hopefully, *Black Panther* provides greater opportunities to the talented and creative Black filmmakers, screenwriters, actors, comic writers, comic educators and comic artists and illustrators, who have been underrepresented in comics and film." Like Richmond, Turner calls on other scholars to support her African-centered critique of the film, including an extensive quote from Ytasha Womack's *Afrofuturism: The World of Black Sci-Fi and Fantasy Culture*: "Whether through literature, visual arts, music, or grassroots organizing, Afrofuturists redefine culture and notions of blackness for today and the future. Both an artistic aesthetic and a framework for critical theory, Afrofuturism combines elements of science fiction, historical fiction, speculative fiction, fantasy, Afrocentricity, and magic realism with non-Western beliefs. In some cases, it's a total re-envisioning of the past and speculation about the future rife with cultural critiques."

At the outset of Keith Gilyard's intelligent assessment of *Black Panther* is a clear-eyed view of Killmonger, which he rightfully contends is the source of much debate and controversy. Killmonger, Gilyard postulates that while the character is "certainly overconstructed as gangster, he is unreconstructed in his righteous rage. His passion to fight White supremacy is too powerful to be watered down simply because he can excel within institutions of the dominant culture." The film's pedagogical potential is also of importance to Gilyard's thinking and "given its widespread reach, *Black Panther* could be the centerpiece of a program of study both in school and throughout the Black public sphere. Potentially, it is the bridge that connects our renewed inspection of the central concepts, across disciplines of rhetoric, poetics, and politics, technology that affect how our lives are structured and suggest how they may be restructured."

To remove any word, any stanza from Allyson Horton's poem would be an injustice and rupture her searing content of remembered history, au courant tropes, inventive metaphors, no rapaphors, her "spherical illumination"
centripetal "Power to the People"
"Wakanda Forever" the *sequel?*
transmitting fierce energy moonwalking
Marvel comics into a whole new
stratos-*Fear of a Black Planet*

diasporic continuum of a soul powered
nation of Black lives that matter
in all our Afrofuturistic polyrhythmic vibrations
melanistic gradations shapes: sizes: plait-forms." Okay, so we couldn't resist excerpting just
a portion of her stimulating verse. But you have to read the entire poem to feel its total
impact.

Gilyard's take on Killmonger is given additional tincture and historical references
by Peniel Joseph, who asserts that "Killmonger's brash intelligence echoes an unsettling
combination of Malcolm X and Stokely Carmichael, updated with a burning desire to
eradicate the system of mass incarceration in the United States, end neocolonial policies
that impoverish much of the world, and ignite a political revolution that will alter power
relations between the global north and south. His anger well-earned, his desire for home
overwhelmed by a need for a reckoning that imperils Wakanda and the rest of the world."
But Joseph's main thesis is the African American quest, the "search for home," that Black
Panther embodies. At the close he invokes the film's soundtrack, the chorus of Kendrick
Lamar's song "imagines home as a world away that, on some magical nights, seem closer.
Black Panther's major achievement is to make those stars appear closer to all of us who are
still seeking a port in the storm, a way back home."

It's true that Wakanda is ruled by a warm, smart, attractive, and benevolent royalty, Paul
Street proffers, but where are the ordinary folks, the commoners and their contributions?
"The everyday people of Wakanda are backdrops at best in Black Panther," Street deplores.
"All the action in the movie revolves around the royals and their top warriors. Ordinary
Wakandans do not merit any attention. It's all about the rulers." A very considerate
class analysis pertains in Street's summation of the film and he also broaches an age-
old Hollywood tendency. The film he declares, is "another Hollywood update of white
America's longstanding distinction between the good Black and the bad Black. The good
Black pursues moderate ends in dignified and polite ways. He doesn't take to the streets.
He is respectful and respectable. He can be trusted and included. He believes in law and
order and the maintenance of existing hierarchies. He is mindfully at peace with himself
and his surroundings. He's "constructive" – "someone you can work with" to 'get things
done.'"

No dichotomy is at play in Eric Curry's review, no *good Black* versus *bad Black*, but an
opaque veil that is endemic to *Black Panther* and shields Wakanda from white intrusion
and exploitation. To make his point, Curry resorts to the African American literary canon,
invoking such visionaries as Phillis Wheatley, William Wells Brown, and the esteemed
W.E.B. Du Bois. He presumes that the director Ryan Coogler uses a similar method.
"Coogler's cinematic narrative draws on an African American literary tradition in which the
perceptual limits imposed by white supremacist culture cast a veil over the reality of Black
subjects and the possibilities in Black geographic spaces," Curry relates. "I want to draw
attention to how we might read the hidden nation and people of Wakanda as a narrative
representation of white epistemology and its self-imposed perceptual limits, what W. E.

B. Du Bois terms 'the Veil of Race' in *The Souls of Black Folk* (1903)." "Wakanda," Curry continues, "exists behind a technological veil, and this veil could be a representation of the racial contract as an epistemological agreement. In *The Racial Contract* (1997), Charles Mills looks at white supremacy as a political system, requiring 'its own peculiar…norms and procedures for determining what counts as moral and factual knowledge of the world' (17). What whites know about the world and its peoples is and has been colored by the imperatives of colonialism, imperialism, slavery, Jim Crow, and apartheid." Curry could have further illustrated this point by citing from the opening to Ralph Ellison's *Invisible Man*, whose protagonist's invisibility is mostly "because people refuse to see me."

Pan-Africanism is among the most arresting themes in Carol Lee's wide-ranging review, and in her estimation a useful prism through which to view the film. "The Pan-African focus is important because it informs themes that emerge explicitly and symbolically in the film. And this focus is important because of the centrality of relations between Africans on the continent and African descendants across the diaspora within our communities for centuries," she writes. The ballast of her erudition on Pan-African thought evolves from a corps of formidable thinkers before she presents examples of contemporary African and African-American connections, whether via the African Burial Ground or the Schomburg Center, both in Manhattan. *Black Panther* provides significant guidelines for discussion, Lee suggests, but "I don't think the popular success of this film among Black people is because it gives us answers. Rather I think its power is in helping us to imagine a world in which Black people are in charge, including at least some of the conundrums that accompany being in charge of our own destiny, namely then how do we interact with the rest of the world and with one another." In effect, she concludes, "The power of a film is not to give us answers, but to pose and help us imagine possibilities."

Poet and griot Eugene Redmond, in his inimical style, entertains as he parses Black Panther in word-play, metonym, portmanteaus, and an assortment of other literary devices. And the musical analogies are never far behind. A sample of his ingenious use of language and imagery abounds here: "*Black Panther*, after accomplishing all of the above minus the operatic soap, carries us, in 'giant steps,' beyond *Roots*—like John Coltrane's 'sheets' that go a-sound-steppin' over minstrelsy—Ntu Pre-Ancient, Contemporary and Post-Future Black Modalities'" he practically recites. "In *BP*, the Sci-fy, Marvel Comics, Euro-Surrealism and Make Believe cave under the wait/weight of Vodun-Juju-Folk Funk, Magical Realism (Dumas/Reed/Morrison) and Interpenetrations of diverse elements of the Soular System. Including Life, Death and the Yet-to-be Born/e Life." You wit it?

Several of our commentators tackle the issue of monarchy that resonates so strongly in *Black Panther*. But K. Tutashinda invests considerable space and rejection of the king and queen motif, and we are reminded of Paul Street's admonitions. "While the film is excellent entertainment filled with more positive images than almost any film ever made, the continued perpetration of the 'King and Queen ' narrative as being our greatest days needs challenging," Tutashinda decries. For Black Americans, long the victims of real and symbolic dismissals, to rejoice from the "feel good" vibes of *Black Panther* is almost inevitable. This sensation is not ignored by Tutashinda: "However, the assumption that just because we had 'kings, queens, and kingdoms,' in the past, it does not mean that we should view that or any other hierarchical living or governing arrangement as preferred or ideal in the future. Furthermore, we must challenge the personal attitude of an individual who goes around thinking 'I'm a King' or 'I'm a Queen.' This attitude could easily morph into an egoistic tirade. This is not just semantics--words have power."

Playwright Michael Dinwiddie knows fully the power of words as well as the influence of visible and hidden persuaders. He is also wary of superheroes, especially those who have emerged from the Marvel inkwell. There is no need for them in Dinwiddie's universe when he has a coteries of real role models, past and present to summon. "Frederick Douglass instantly comes to mind," he begins. "As you study his life, you realize that he freed himself—psychologically and then physically—from a slave system that had no intention of letting him go. Frederick Douglass was a real-life, human being. He was willing to risk everything. Mohandas 'Mahatma' Gandhi was a small man in stature, scrawny and near-sighted. But his vision, shaped in apartheid South Africa, was large enough to unshackle a half-billion people from centuries of colonial rule." When it comes to those imagined, fictional saviors, Dinwiddie poses "it is more reasonable to think of *Black Panther* in the ways we think of *Batman* or *The Pink Panther*. There is always a place for a fantasy life. Bruce Wayne does not exist. There is no way that people mistake Clousseau for a real person, and a cartoonish holograph can never alter a real-life struggle for wholeness and wellness. *Black Panther* helps us understand that, in a war of attrition such as the one being waged in post-Obama America, imagery can only inspire us to aspire. No fictional character will advance our struggle for justice. We must never lose sight of the fact that orange hair is fake, whether on Batman's Joker or soaring above the clouds on Air Force One."

Temple Hemphill may now and then soar with her head in the clouds, but her feet are planted solidly on "terra firma" as she terms her reflections on *Black Panther*. First there is frank confession from the scholar. "Although I admittedly have limited institutional knowledge about comic books and science fiction, I possess an affinity for 'bad as I wanna be' women," she declares. "Thus, for a decade, I have held on to a deep desire to dress up like Wonder Woman and cheer on people at the annual Bank of America Chicago Marathon. What I know for sure is Wonder Woman is a bad-ass. And, anyone attempting to run 26.2 miles fits the same category; I'm riding with them. Just as Nakia graciously supported T'Challa played by Chadwick Boseman in *Black Panther*." So, as Hemphill seems to imply, some films can touch the very core of a person's being.

Afrofuturism, monarchy, and the real not the "reel" Black Panthers are subject very germane to the political outlook of Monica Moorehead. For those who harbored notions that Huey Newton and Bobby Seale might make cameo appearances in the film, Moorehead said that was highly unlikely. Nor was there any chance that Hollywood would give a Black director $200 million to "bring forth a positive story featuring a national liberation organization." Like Diane Turner, Ytisha Womack is a valuable resource for

Moorehead on Afrofuturism, and she adds that the concept was first raised by white critic Mark Dery in his 1994 essay. "Since then it's been made universally popular by Black authors like Octavia Butler and Ishmael Reed and artists Janelle Monáe, Jean-Michel Basquiat, Sun-Ra and Jimi Hendrix."

Motivational and refreshing are two words that standout in Angela Kinamore's review. *Black Panther*, she hopes, will provide the motivation to continue what the film has launched in such a strong and positive way. And how refreshing, she adds, to see a film where the N-word does not occur. But central to her assessment of the film is its call to arms, the sound of spiritual and cultural alarms. "Now is the time to take up your Wakanda state of mind and go forth to bring out the innovative creativity and greatness within you," is her plea. "Immerse yourself in this awakening. Teach our youth on whose shoulders they stand, so they can never forget how great we truly are as a people. It is time to usher in the new day, and in the words of John Henrik Clarke, we will take that 'great and mighty walk' one last time. The film *Black Panther* has placed the ball back in our court and now we must fly with it!"

Veteran activist Bill Ayers sees a clear distinction between the film *Black Panther* and the actual Black Panther Party, ever mindful that the film makes no attempt to evoke the Party. Even so, he doesn't "underestimate the power of a cultural moment to elicit some sense of pride, history, and even agency. Of course my political head was gagging at the white CIA agent (!!!!) since they killed [Patrice] Lumumba and [Kwame] Nkrumah and lots of others, and never did ANYTHING good for Africa! I also have an abiding dislike of royalty, and I always remember Jimmy Boggs saying, 'To me a king is always a son of a bitch.' And then at the end, with all their technology and brilliance, the whole deal is to rehab buildings in Oakland? Charity not power." His listing of the Panther's Ten Point program is an important addition, helping to frame the real against the reel.

Patricia Williams Diaw asks an existential question about African American reality and then valorizes the film's form and content. "The humanity of African people is the theme entwined and embellished into the fabric of the movie's plot, in a film decrying violence, poverty, and oppression. On some level, *Black Panther* filmmakers must have realized a point discussed by Nathan Ruthstein. '[Dehumanizing practices of racism] will never be eliminated in America until its white citizens overcome their deep-seated belief that blacks are inherently inferior to whites.... Simply put, it is a matter of accepting blacks as full-fledged human beings' (1997, p. 51). Brilliantly depicted on the screen and instilled into dialogue and action is a story of struggle, honor, sacrifice, fear, anger, revenge, all human-like in quality and mood. Courageous African ancestors and millions of victims/survivors of the Middle Passage are referred to and gloriously honored by the film's existence."

Brent Staples joined several contributors in emphasizing the film's Afrofuturism, but in citing Mark Dery, the cultural critic who putatively coined the term in the 1990s, Staples extends that focus, noting that Afrofuturism describes "the work of artists who used the tools of science fiction to imagine possible futures. The list of practitioners was relatively short at the time: It included Black science fiction writers like Samuel Delany and Octavia

Butler and the fantastical Arkestra leader Sun Ra, who carried the name of the ancient Egyptian sun god and offered an allegory of salvation in which African-Americans were urged to escape tribulation by emigrating to the stars." But for the powerful Afrofuturistic intimations, Staples adds that the film's most distinction is "that it is told from an Afrocentric point of view; it breaks with the spirit of derision that has always saturated Hollywood films about Africans." So, Afrofucentruism?

The concept of Afrofuturism is given additional heft and gravitas by Thabiti Lewis and Don Matthews, which they do after noting the Black community's dire need for a hero in a time of great despair and police hostility. Afrofuturism, they proffer, "is a cultural aesthetic philosophy of science, and philosophy of history that combines elements of science fiction, historical fiction, fantasy, Afrocentrism, and magic realism with non-Western cosmologies in order to critique the present-day dilemmas of Black people and to interrogate and re-examine historical events." The film, they conclude, "is a perfect blend of Afrocentrism, fantasy, science fiction, and historical fiction that makes black folk feel good about being Black and Africa and a hero figure who cannot be killed."

Bro Shep, who is widely known for upholding the banner of Black power and the political legacy of the Black Panther Party, makes sure viewers of the film are equipped with an analysis beyond the screen. He was among a coterie veteran Panther and community activists outside movie theaters passing out flyers to inform patrons there "are real Black Panther freedom fighters from the '60s & '70s who are still unjustly in political exile and being held captive by the U.S. Government as Black/New Afrikan Political Prisoners & POWs."

"In the final analysis," Bro. Shep submits, "as the fictional Black Panther super hero continues to generate billions of 'non-returnable' dollars from the Black community; We need to seriously tap into the real Ancestral Black Panther spirit and bring about a true Revolutionary Pan-African Unity that will free the so called 'Wakanda' aka Africa and take total control of our so called 'Vibranium' aka natural resources... in order to use them for the benefit of both the African motherland and the entire Black diaspora."

A significant piece of the anthology's title was lifted from Nicole Mitchell Gantt's cogent and inventive mind. "A sense of euphoria swept through Black social media that hadn't existed since Obama's first election. Does Black Panther signal a paradigm shift in Hollywood's representation of Blackness, especially in science fiction?" is the potent question Gantt raised and then tactfully added that the film's greatest success "has been the global intensification of Black imagination. Black Panther, a crescendo to the global movement of Afrofuturism, offers a win for Black audiences, although with a closer look, one can detect Hollywood's remaining, if subtle, granular white shadow underpinning the film." She sees through the clever manipulation of the filmmakers and the producers who have "decided that playing this card of Black genius could be of mutual benefit — Black psychological empowerment in exchange for Hollywood's financial gain." It's a trade-off, a game of exploitation that has always been in play and African Americans have, without exception, received the short end of the stick, the least benefit. But Gantt is a superb musician and commentary on the film's music was what we sought and what delivered with bountiful results. Gantt concludes: "Looking at *Black Panther's* music, its brilliant score is an African diasporic kaleidoscope, containing samples of musical essence found in the South African mbira, the West African talking drum and djembe, the harp sounds of the kora, the impassioned sounds of Malian fula flutist Amadou Ba, woven with some 'bim bap' of African American hip hop, North African oud, and the soaring calls of Senegalese vocalist legend Baaba Maal, all intertwined into a compelling, yet traditional musical experience that movie-goers expect to hear."

Finding correspondences between the film and actual individuals and political circumstances resonate throughout Ewuare X. Osayande's splendid analysis. After tracing the origins of *Black Panther* via the creativity of Stan Lee, Osayande ties the realities of the Congo with the envisioned Wakanda. "Lee has long acknowledged that he conceived of the X-Men in response to the Civil Rights Movement," Osayande observes. "It is therefore not a stretch to imagine that Lee's *Black Panther* might well have been inspired by Lumumba's short-lived yet heroic leadership and the will of his people to be unfettered by the colonial yoke. But whether Lee had Lumumba in mind or not, there are significant compelling comparisons between the world of Wakanda and the Congo of our own. Some of the main characters in the *Black Panther* narrative are mirrored in the historical arc that is the Congolese saga in ways that are uncanny."

This creative comparison is nowhere better drawn than in this account: "Klaw as a Belgian mercenary responsible for assassinating T'Chaka follows the actual account of the Belgian mercenaries who were responsible for the execution of Lumumba in the Katagan bush in January 1961," Osayande relates. "In *The Assassination of Lumumba*, Ludo de Witte recounts the role the Belgian government played in partnership with the United States and British governments to 'eliminate' the prime minister of the newly independent Congo."

For tech savvy Bobby Seale, founder of the Black Panther Party, the film has relevance in several ways, and perhaps none more important than its resurrection of the real Panther Party and giving a boost to Seale's ongoing organizational activities. "Today in 2018 through 2020 with the Ryan Coogler, fantastic, marvelous, profound block buster Marvel BLACK PANTHER movie," Seale wrote, "I am still involved and speaking at higher education institutions and teaching voter electoral organizing to community organizations. I am working with various ecological/social justice/economic justice organizations and have now, since May 2, 1967 when my name suddenly became a household reference: because I led an armed delegation of thirty Black Panther people which included six sisters into the California state legislature to read for the second time my Black Panther Party's executive MANDATE number one: A statement in opposition to a pending piece of 'Mulford Act' legislation to stop me and my Black Panther Party's very legal rights to stand and observe police and state, when a policeman first said to us, 'You have no right to observe me.' WE responded with, 'No, California State Supreme Court ruling states that every citizen has a right to stand and observe police officers carrying out their duty as long as they stand a reasonable distance away. A reasonable distance, in that particular ruling, was constituted as eight to ten feet. We are standing approximately twenty feet from you. Therefore we will observe you whether you like it or NOT!' We were so legal it was a crying shame. We were reciting the law to the police and the thirty or more people standing in back of us had their minds blown. One guy said, 'Man, what kind of Negroes are these?'.... Power to the people! Thanks!"

Following a thoughtful delineation of *Black Panther*—from its utility of language, music, and costume, et al—L.A. Williams and Lee Bynum introduces *Luke Cage*. "While the Black Panther was the first black superhero, it took years before he headlined his own comic. The first black superhero with his own solo comic series was Luke Cage in 1972. There's an array of ideas and questions about black heroes, imagery, impact, and viability that will need to wait for another writing. But suffice it to say for now that there's an unprecedented number of black superheroes on store shelves and various screens these days, and most of them wouldn't exist, nor would the *Black Panther* film been made, had Cage not sustained a regular series from 1972-1986 with numerous subsequent revivals." Most rewarding between the duo is the way they interrogate each other while interrogating the film and Cage.

At the beginning of this Introduction, there was a reference to Gagut, a theory of everything formulated by a noted African physicist Gabriel Oyibo and in these pages explained by one of his devotees, Minister Clemson Brown. There is no easy exposition of Gagut, but Brown has found an accessible entry into the complex theory via vibranium. "While vibranium is a fictitious mineral substance, and Wakanda is a fictitious place somewhere on the continent of Africa, the movie 'Black Panther' conjured up a mirror for us as a people to explore our ancient past and present day reality," Brown writes. "The noun '*vibranium*' and the verb vibration are connected in origin. 'Vibration' meaning the movement of energy and vibranium meaning a change in energy from one state to another. The ancient Africans understood the nature of energy, that it could not be created or destroyed. They understood that this energy moves throughout the universe from infinity to infinity in waves. These waves move so fast that they are present all over the universe at the same time. There is nothing in the universe but this energy expressing itself in varying speeds. All things constitute this energy." Add melanin to Oyibo's equation and the convergence with "Black Panther" becomes even more interesting and intriguing.

As you can see from this veritable cornucopia of perspectives, *Black Panther* has evolved from cinema into semiotics, quantum theory, historiography, and is currently having an impact on fashion and the automobile industry. Along 125th Street in Harlem vendors are displaying tote bags embroidered with Wakanda spelled out in shiny rhinestones. There are T-shirts with the names of the characters from the film, and one jeweler has necklaces and rings which he swears are made of vibranium. The book stores are crammed with an assortment of *Black Panther* memorabilia to say nothing of the collection of books chronicling the history of Marvel Comics and the evolution of T'Challa/Black Panther.

There appears to be no end to the film's popularity, and there is sure to be a sequel, if not a prequel, extending the appeal of the superhero into another generation, into that Afrofuturism realm that more than one of our contributors have cited.

Our writers have voiced their impressions, their views on the film, but the final assessment belongs to you. If we compile enough responses it might necessitate a second volume of reviews and commentary, and that would be in keeping with the film's Panthermania, the film's way of prowling its way into the national discourse.

II. Follow the Money

Ask the average and not so average Black person in America how he or she would identify him or herself culturally and politically, and in listening to his or her answer, you will find yourself in a maze of acute confusion and ignorance. We all say or do that which we have been taught to say or do, not an original thought, but nevertheless true. One's insight regarding Africa and its people—"at home and abroad" has seldom been truthfully or accurately inculcated from birth, preschool, K-12, college or university in the world. This is a political, cultural and economic fact. Enter "Wakanda Forever":

forgetting and bypassing Tarzan, Jane, Jungle Jim, Bomba, Sheena, She-Woman, King Kong, and many of the Marvel and other imperialist/white supremacist definitions of Black people, African Americans or people of African ancestry. For us, Black critical thinkers, following the money can be a starting point for serious political cultural and economic discussions around Black realities on the continent of Africa and in the Diaspora. That is our aim with this book clearly acknowledging that the film gives us an opening to serious deliberations on the culture, politics, technology and science within the Black world and the role that Black people play in it.

We, the unpromised, the forgotten many, the people with a leadership whose numbers defy logic and are unexplainable when measured against Black people's acute suffering, disrespect, disproportionate incarceration, betrayals, impoverishment, exist locally and internationally as an undefined disconnectedness that Black/African people experience each second of each minute, hour, and day. Like most people of all cultures, Black people have a unique relationship to film, and the images displayed on the large and small screens. The unpredicted phenomenon of the film *Black Panther* opened many Black people in the United States to the reality that we are indeed Africans, even make believed, but real with unlimited possibilities, powers, ideals and most of all imaginations.

The acceptance, better yet the celebration of the film *Black Panther* by Black people worldwide has been unprecedented. Black women, men and children of all economic classes found a topic that demanded interaction, analysis, debate and loud explanations, exhortations by way of voice, song, dance, cultural expression and clothing. The celebrations were not only because all the lead actors were Black—the director and screenwriter are Black, and much of the production crew, workers, extras are Black, and all involved in a film that transcended the Black community. *Black Panther* introduced much of the Black Diaspora to science-fiction, speculative fiction or as Nnedi Okorofor's editor describes her work "magical futurism."

Along with Okorofor, there are three several Black science-fiction writers that must be acknowledged as pioneers in this genre. They are Samuel R. Delany., Octavia Butler, and the multi-talented scholar, lawyer and advanced thinker, the late Derrick Bell. However, it is *Black Panther*, the movie that has captured the conversation this year and the lead writer on an entirely new line of *Black Panther* Marvel Books, Ta-Nehisi Coates, is the internationally respected author of the best-selling *Between the World and Me* (2015). It is certain that Wakanda will live to appear in Black Panther 2 and possibly 3.

Nevertheless, the final decisions are always in the hands of the producers and owners of the franchise, who are mostly white. Nate Moore is an executive producer and he is Black. Stan Lee and Jack Kirby created *Black Panther* in 1966 in issues of *Jungle Action*. The company soon brought into the creative mix the only Black artist to work at Marvel in the early days. His name was Billy Graham and according to *The New York Times* (3/11/18), he was known as "the irreverent one." Mr. Graham initially worked on *Luke Cage* and was moved to *Black Panther* staying with the company for about six years, leaving in 1976.

The Walt Disney Company owns *Black Panther*, which was a part of the Marvel deal which Disney paid $4 billion for in 2009 (Forbes 2/18). *The New York Times* reports that Disney's strongest quarter in two years went "well past Wall Street's expectations for profit and revenue growth, thanks in large part to the success of *Black Panther* (5/09/18)." The paper goes on to report:

> For the quarter, Disney reported net income of $2.94 billion or $1.95 per share, an increase from $2.39 billion or $1.50 a share, in the same period a year earlier. Analysts had expected per-share profit of $1.69. Disney's revenue totaled $14.55 billion, a 9 percent increase; analysts expected $14.08 billion.
>
> The strong results for the second fiscal quarter, which ended March 31, were driven by Walt Disney Studios, where operating income soared 29 percent, to $847 million. The biggest contributor was Ryan Coogler's *Black Panther* which has collected $1.34 billion worldwide since its record-breaking February release. Sales of *Star Wars: The Last Jedi* on DVD and video-on-demand services also helped. (*New York Times*, May 9, 2018)

It is obvious that Black people's primary contribution, even if we do not know it, is as consumers. This was best illustrated as a bankable fact when week after week *Black Panther* sold out in most of the theatres in and around Black communities across the country. In fact, Black churches, schools and fraternity and sorority organizations across the nation bought out complete showings of *Black Panther* for community viewing by their parishioners, students and members. Very seldom, if at all, has this ever happened for any other movie. The real strength of Black consumers was confirmed when ABC owned by Disney cancelled *Roseanne* within 24 hours after the star Roseanne Barr tweeted that Valerie Jarrett, who is Black and a close friend as well as advisor to former President Barack Obama and First Lady Michelle Obama, was birthed as a result of the mating of "Muslim brotherhood and *Planet of the Apes*." The president of ABC Entertainment, Channing Dungey, first Black person to be president of a major broadcast network stated that Barr's tweet was "abhorrent, repugnant, and inconsistent with our values and we have decided to cancel the show." Barr is nationally known as a white supremacist who not only attacks Jarrett, but also Ambassador Susan Rice. Another reason that the show was cancelled is that *Roseanne* was estimated to make about $40 million in the new season and *Black Panther* had already made over $1.34 billion in less than two months. In this case, we can easily see that money talks and everything else walks. As consumers, Black people's economic contribution to Disney's bottom line mattered more than making excuses for Roseanne Barr.

Black Panther continued with this amazing run when it became the first commercial film opening in a movie theater in Saudi Arabia in April. And, it has continued to break records as it goes into DVD and home movie sales. The major question for all of us should be—after over a billion and a half dollars in 2018 ticket sales on a movie that was produced, publicized and distributed for around $200 million, how much of the billion dollars plus earned on the film touches any part of the national Black community? Very little.

As we complete the editing of this book, *Forbes* magazine published its annual richest people in the world edition. Out of the top twenty billionaires in the world, each worth a minimum of $39 billion, only two are non-white. No African Americans or Black people are among the world's richest. There are 585 billionaires in the United States whose worth is $3.1 trillion with Jeff Bezos as the richest man in the world leading with $112 billion dollars.

Two of the richest Black people in the U.S. are Robert Smith at $4.4 billion and Oprah Winfrey at $2.7 billion. When will the big payback come to the "little people," those without hope or happiness who view film as life's escape? The overwhelming numbers of Black people unable to leave the South Side of Chicago, the Bronx, Eaglewood-California, or all of Detroit. We are not writing about James Brown's "The Big Payback," or Trump's crime family misuse of the nation's treasury. We are questioning the rightness of Black struggle in a time of outrageous hoarding of wealth by the top 1% of the nation, who are all white. The owners of Disney are a part of that 1%.

History is the best teacher if one reads, studies and incorporates into one's life the truth of one's own stories, inventions, visions, real tales, victories and defeats; all while realistically looking at and accessing one's own community, leadership, development and strategies in 21st century America.

Always look for the ultimate decision makers. Most people make choices within the decisions of other people, primarily, unknown people. They are the people writing the unwritten rules, who pay the creative people to create on their terms, on their avenues, in their studios, before and behind the cameras, and we must not forget that they too are the ones writing the cue cards, running the Teleprompters. They determine action, non-action and supply words and images that drive the emotional narrative tearing at the heartstrings of the young, and uninformed. Is *Black Panther* in many ways white Panther in Black face? Where is Frantz Fanon when he is needed the most? We, today in America, and much of the world are experiencing terrorism of the mind, a complete imperial domination of our intelligence. Seldom does one walk any urban areas, university campuses or large gatherings of people and see the most present carrier of new media—the cell phone—occupying the brain of its users. Our loss of the critical ability to realize that we are being fed an "African or Black reality" is one that is not solely of our own making and is clearly divorced from the real world; therefore, the creators are correct in calling this film science-fiction or speculative fiction. However, the amount of money that *Black Panther* has made and will make in the future is not fiction nor will such revenue impact the larger Black/African universe.

1

"BLACK PANTHER" AND THE INVENTION OF "AFRICA"

Jelani Cobb

In Ryan Coogler's "Black Panther," the hero and his antagonist are essentially dueling responses to five centuries of African exploitation at the hands of the West.

The Maison des Esclaves stands on the rocky shore of Gorée Island, off the coast of Senegal, like a great red tomb. During the years of its operation, the building served as a rendezvous point for slavers trafficking in a seemingly inexhaustible resource: Africans, whose very bodies became the wealth of white men. A portal known as the "Door of No Return," leading to the slave ships, offered the forlorn captives a last glimpse of home, before they were sown to the wind and sold in the West. For nearly four centuries, this traffic continued, seeding the populations of the Caribbean, Brazil, Argentina, Mexico, and Central and North America, and draining societies of their prime populations while fomenting civil conflict among them in order to more effectively cull their people. On the high seas, the vessels jettisoned bodies in such terrible numbers that the poet Amiri Baraka once wrote, "At the bottom of the Atlantic Ocean there's a railroad made of human bones."

I visited Gorée Island in 2003, with a group of Black academics, just days after George W. Bush had come to the island and offered platitudes about the cruelties of human history but stopped short of apologizing for the United States' role in the transatlantic slave trade. Residents of the island greeted us in the markets like long-lost kin. We repeatedly heard some version of "Welcome home, my Black brothers and sisters!" But, later, over dinner, a Senegalese guide casually informed us that we were neither their siblings nor even distant kin to Africa, implying that the greetings in the market had been merely a clever sales tactic directed at gullible Black Americans who travel to the continent in search of roots, as if they were abused foster kids futilely seeking their birth parents. "You are Americans. That is all," she said. This exchange took place fifteen years ago, but I can still recall the way her words hung in the air, like a guilty verdict. The policy of "No Return," she suggested, applied to distant descendants, too.

There is a fundamental dissonance in the term "African-American," two feuding ancestries conjoined by a hyphen. That dissonance—a hyphen standing in for the brutal history that intervened between Africa and America—is the subject of "Black Panther," Ryan Coogler's brilliant first installment of the story of Marvel Comics' landmark Black character. "I have a lot of pain inside me," Coogler told an audience at the Brooklyn Academy of Music, on Wednesday night. "We were taught that we lost the things that made us African. We lost our culture, and now we have to make do with scraps." Black America is constituted overwhelmingly by the descendants of people who were not only brought to the country against their will but were later inducted into an ambivalent form of citizenship without their input. The Fourteenth Amendment, which granted citizenship to all those born here, supposedly resolved the question of the status of ex-slaves, though those four million individuals were not consulted in its ratification. The unspoken yield of this history is the possibility that the words "African" and "American" should not be joined by a hyphen but separated by an ellipsis.

Our sensibilities are accustomed to Marvel films offering clear lines of heroism and villainy, but "Black Panther" dispatches with its putative villain, Ulysses Klaue, a white South Africa-based arms dealer, halfway through the film. Chadwick Boseman's T'Challa, the Black Panther and the King of Wakanda, confronts Erik Killmonger, a Black American mercenary, played by Michael B. Jordan, as a rival, but the two characters are essentially dueling responses to five centuries of African exploitation at the hands of the West. The villain, to the extent that the term applies, is history itself.

Wakanda is a technologically advanced kingdom in Central Africa that was never colonized by any Western power. T'Challa, the noble leader of an unvanquished people, upholds the isolationism that has always kept the kingdom safe; Killmonger, driven by the horrors that befell those who were stolen from the continent, envisions a world revolution, led by Wakanda, to upend the status quo. When Killmonger arrives there, after the death of King T'Chaka (the father of T'Challa), he sets in motion a reckoning not only with his rival but with broader questions of legitimacy, lineage, and connection. Black Panther, as Ryan Coogler pointed out in Brooklyn, has been an inherently political character since his inception, during the Black Power era of the 1960s. He is a refutation of the image of the lazy and false African, promulgated in the white world and subscribed to even by many in the Black one. Coogler told Marvel up front that his version of the story would remain true to those political elements. It is shot through with the sense of longing and romance common to the way that people of a diaspora envision their distant homeland.

Like the comics on which they are based, the Marvel movies, in general, have not shied away from political concerns. "Captain America: The Winter Soldier," released in 2014, grapples with ideas of preemptive warfare, drones, and the surveillance state, as elements of the war on terror. The first "Iron Man" film, from 2008, addressed war profiteering and arms contractors at a time when the United States was still heavily involved in Iraq.

Yet nothing in Marvel's collection of films is or could be political in the same way as "Black Panther," because, in those other stories, we were at least clear about where the lines of fantasy departed from reality. "Captain America" is a fantastic riff on the nation's idealism, filtered through the lens of the Second World War, a historic event whose particulars, however horrific and grandly inhumane, and are not in dispute. "Black Panther," however, exists in an invented nation in Africa, a continent that has been grappling with invented versions of itself ever since white men first declared it the "dark continent" and set about plundering its people and its resources. This fantasy of Africa as a place bereft of history was politically useful, justifying imperialism. It found expression in the highest echelons of Western thought, and took on the contours of truth. In 1748, the Scottish philosopher David Hume wrote, "I am apt to suspect the Negroes, and all other species of men... to be naturally inferior to the whites. There never was any civilized nation of any complexion other than white." Two centuries later, the British historian Hugh Trevor-Roper wrote, "Perhaps, in the future, there will be some African history to teach. But at present there is none, or very little: there is only the history of the Europeans in Africa."

Africa—or, rather, "Africa"—is a creation of a white world and the literary, academic, cinematic, and political mechanisms that it used to give mythology the credibility of truth. No such nation as Wakanda exists on the map of the continent, but that is entirely beside the point. Wakanda is no more or less imaginary than the Africa conjured by Hume or Trevor-Roper, or the one canonized in such Hollywood offerings as "Tarzan." It is a redemptive counter-mythology. Most filmmakers start by asking their audiences to suspend their disbelief. But, with Africa, Coogler begins with a subject about which the world had suspended its disbelief four centuries before he was born. The film is a nearly seamless dramatic chronicle of the threat created when Killmonger travels to the African nation he descends from. Yet some of the most compelling points in the story are those where the stitching is most apparent. Killmonger is a native of Oakland, California, where the Black Panther Party was born. (In an early scene, a poster of Huey P. Newton, the co-founder of the Party, hangs on a wall, next to a Public Enemy poster.) In an impeccably choreographed fight sequence, T'Challa and General Okoye, the leader of Wakanda's all-female militia (brilliantly played by Danai Gurira), alongside Nakia, a wily Wakandan spy (played by Lupita Nyong'o), confront a Boko Haram-like team of kidnappers. At the same time, it is all but impossible not to notice that Coogler has cast a Black American, a Zimbabwean-American, and a Kenyan as a commando team in a film about African redemption. The cast also includes Winston Duke, who is West Indian; Daniel Kaluuya, a Black Brit; and Florence Kasumba, a Ugandan-born German woman. The implicit statement in both the film's themes and its casting is that there is a connection, however vexed, tenuous, and complicated, among the continent's scattered descendants. Coogler said as much in Brooklyn, when he talked about a trip that he took to South Africa, as research for the film: after discovering cultural elements that reminded him of Black communities in the United States, he concluded, "There's no way they could wipe out what we were for thousands of years. We're African."

There is a great deal more that differentiates "Black Panther" from other efforts in the superhero genre. The film is not about world domination by an alien invasion or a mad cabal of villains but about the implications of a version of Western domination that has been with us so long that it has become as ambient as the air. When Shuri, Wakanda's chief of technology and the irreverent younger sister of T'Challa, is startled by a white CIA agent, she says, "Don't scare me like that, colonizer!" When I saw the movie, the audience howled at the inversion, "colonizer" deployed as an epithet rather than a badge of cultural superiority. In addition, Marvel has been criticized for failing to center a film on any of its female characters, but it is the female characters in "Black Panther" whose ideas and determinations dictate the terms on which the rivalry between the male protagonists plays out. T'Challa engages with his female counterparts as equals; Killmonger kills two women and assaults a third. Their political positions may be equally compelling; their ideas about gender are not.

Coogler's commentary on the literal tribalism of the African diaspora, his devotion to a glorious vision of Africa, and, most provocatively, his visceral telling of the pain of existing as an orphan of history—as seen in the story of Killmonger, whose separation from Africa is not simply historical but also paternal—is striking but not unique. The narrative of Africa as a tragic tabula rasa in world history exists in dialogue with another version, equally imaginary, but idealized, and authored by descendants of those Africans who passed through the Maison des Esclaves and the other structures like it. In 1896, after Ethiopian forces defeated an invading Italian army in the Battle of Adwa, Black people across the globe celebrated the country as the last preserve on the continent free from the yoke of colonialism, and a sign of hope for the Black world—the Wakanda of its day. In the 1930s after Mussolini invaded Ethiopia, Depression-era Black Americans and West Indians scraped together pennies to send to a country they had never visited to fund the resistance. In the late nineteenth century, the West Indian educator and diplomat Edward Wilmot Blyden envisioned and promoted a kind of Black Zionism, in which people of African descent in the West would return to work on behalf of African redemption. What Blyden, and what Marcus Garvey—a Jamaican who, in the nineteen-twenties, organized a global pan-Africanist effort to end European colonialism—and what the organizer Audley Moore and the scholar John Henrik Clarke, and what the entire lineage of that pan-African tradition insisted on was a kind of democracy of the imagination. If the subordination of Africa had begun in the minds of white people, its reclamation, they reasoned, would begin in the minds of Black ones.

I understand this story intuitively and personally. In my twenties, I consumed volumes of African history and histories of the slave trade, seeking out answers to the same questions that Coogler asked in South Africa, a fugitive from the idea that I descend from a place with no discernible past. I dropped my given middle name and replaced it with an African one, in an effort to make transparent that sense of connection. On Gorée Island, I patiently listened to the guide's argument, before pointing out to her that we were conducting our conversation in English, in a building constructed by the French, in a country that had been a colony of France, and that the issue was not whether Black Americans retained any connection to Africa but whether history had left anyone on the continent still in a position to pass judgment on that question. Superheroes are seldom tasked with this kind of existential lifting, but that work is inescapable in the questions surrounding Wakanda and the politics of even imagining such a place. Marvel has made a great many entertaining movies in the past decade, but Ryan Coogler has made a profound one.

Jelani Cobb is a staff writer at The New Yorker and the author of "The Substance of Hope: Barack Obama and the Paradox of Progress."

2

BLACK PANTHER IS A MUST-SEE

Christina Greer, Ph.D.

I've never been one to rush out to see the movie "everyone" is talking about. I rarely go to the movies, to be honest. However, "Black Panther" seemed like more than just a movie and more like a cultural event for Black people in 2018. So I made it a point to view the movie during the opening weekend in the theaters, and I am so glad I did.

Very rarely do Black movie goers get to experience a full range of themselves on screen. Some of the most interesting roles were given to Black women, who served as women of strength and not merely damsels in distress to aid the Black Panther. They were not seen as women in despair, solely love interests, the long suffering woman in the wings or any of the other various tropes allotted to women on screen. Their sense of strength was fueled by conviction and not anger, and their love of themselves, their comrades and their country allowed a multifaceted interrogation of the ways in which Black women have served and continue to serve as moral compasses and backbones of democracy.

Indeed, this movie is a Disney movie about a comic book hero, so I do not want to ascribe too many interpretations to the film. However, what makes "Black Panther" transcend just another action hero movie is the way Black people across the Diaspora have responded to the film in this particular moment. The feelings of joy, pride, sense of action and love of one's people across geographic space are just some of the reasons this movie has resonated with movie goers both young and old, comic book diehards and those who have never watched a Marvel or superhero film in their lives.

Esthetically "Black Panther" is first-rate. The costume designs nod to varying cultures, tribes and designs across the continent of Africa. Couple that with a cast that hails from across the Diaspora and "Black Panther" becomes a movie "for us" and "by us." With the incredible financial success of "Black Panther," Ryan Coogler, the rising young director from Oakland, has inadvertently opened doors for young Black directors for years to come. All of these factors contribute to the unprecedented excitement about this film.

It is my hope that Hollywood has taken notice (and has been put on notice). Blacks in film (in front of and behind the camera) are more than capable of creating films that everyone wants to see. They are capable of creating art that touches the masses both inside and outside of the United States. They have been ready for the world stage for decades. Finally, the opportunity arrived and "Black Panther" more than exceeded the challenge.

Christina Greer, Ph.D., is the 2018 NYU McSilver Institute Fellow and an associate professor at Fordham University, the author of "Black Ethnics: Race, Immigration, and the Pursuit of the American Dream" and the host of The Aftermath on Ozy.com. You can find her on Twitter @Dr_CMGreer

3
BLACK PANTHER HAS TEACHABLE TOOLS FOR ORGANIZERS
Omowale Adewale

The film "Black Panther" garnered $900 million at the box office since the President's Day weekend opening and during Black History Month. The goal of colossal film openings is to make gigantic stacks of cash. It's no secret, mega-parent company Disney and Marvel wanted to make money. It's capitalism and no country does it like the U.S.

Yet, there are eight reasons why "Black Panther" is not your everyday Hollywood blockbuster and exists as a revolutionary masterpiece for organizers to educate the African Diaspora.

AFRICAN ART, CULTURE AND CUSTOMS

As a Black community organizer for approximately 20 years, one of my most significant and difficult tasks has always been to transform the everyday community member into a community organizer. We need to replenish human resources and develop sisterhood and brotherhood among our African people. Toward that end, Black people must know that they are African people. Being Black is not limited to having melanin.

"Black Panther" accomplishes this objective in the opening scene by identifying African artifacts and noting that Europe stole Africa's art and culture. Erik Killmonger plays coy with the museum curator as she describes the different artifacts that he questions her about. He then corrects her on the last piece, although it was from a fictional country, it underscores the point that Africa has rich art and culture for millennia.

Of course, the entire film is rife with African art through the wardrobe and set design. In addition, there is the circle of elders and younger men and women from the Wakandan families. Black Panther gives the Black community the visual of seeing African families as a unit.

A DIFFERENT TYPE OF HOLLYWOOD DIRECTOR

Let's take a back step for a minute to learn who the genius behind "Black Panther" really is—Ryan Coogler, the co-writer and director. In a *Vanity Fair* video interview, Coogler goes off the usual Marvel Comics script to interweave the concept of liberation and Pan-Africanism. Pan-Africanism is the ideology of activists and organizers that unites members of the African Diaspora. It is hopeful to hear Coogler explain to viewers, "The Pan-African flag is red, black and green." The clothes color combinations of Nakia, Okoye and T'Challa is not by accident.

Coogler first debuted as director and co-writer of "Fruitvale Station" (2013). The Oakland-born director beautifully transformed a budget of $900,000 into $17.4 million in sales, which is why he was tapped by Marvel executives in the first place.

"Fruitvale Station" was based on Oscar Grant III's last day on earth and his untimely death at the hands of a white police officer on the Fruitvale Station platform in Oakland, Calif., in 2009. Coogler chose to humanize the whole person of Grant and briefly share the problems of police-profiling and the slew of powerful protests against police murder that followed Grant's death.

BLACK WOMEN ARE THE MOST VALUABLE ASSET

There are numerous signs that indicate the filmmaker decided to not create Black actresses out of stereotypical caricatures only to exist as love interests. First up, Shuri, acted by Letitia Wright. She is the young genius who is responsible for the advancement of the modern Wakandan society. Shuri oversees the production and design of the military machinery and arsenal. She is also prepared to fight whenever necessary.

Lupita Nyong'o plays Nakia. It is pivotal to point out that Nakia is already prepared to fight for Black women on the continent of Africa and she is internationally connected. She is the Black revolutionary you thought you envisioned in Erik Killmonger. Nakia believes in and promotes the idea that Wakandan society can utilize its resources to help others. She is the most resourceful and unattached for the most part.

General Okoye, played by Danai Gurira, is the powerful leader of the Dora Milaje, a warrior society of Black women. She is clearly fierce, but the most intriguing and revolutionary part of the movie comes when she declines Nakia's request to follow her when T'Challa is dethroned and thrown off the cliff. This scene is translated as (1) Black women recognizing that they are stable beings able to keep the continuity of the regal tradition and (2) Black women do not have to follow men (Black or otherwise) to be great.

Black women caused none of the drama that ensued in Wakandan society or the world, but they stand guard as always to restore everything in its rightful place.

BLACK PEOPLE, GO VEG!

For a vegan who abstains from consuming any animal products, it was shocking and liberating for M'Baku, leader of the Jabari clan, played by Winston Duke, to state, "We are vegetarian." The point highlights that huge, muscular men can abstain from animal flesh and still obtain necessary levels of protein. Also, it's a dog whistle to the Black community's unhealthy eating of animal flesh, causing high rates of heart disease and cancer.

Erik Killmonger's path isn't revolutionary.

Sorry, y'all. You can't helm the Mother Elder up, slay the Wakandan shaman and threaten to destroy the most advanced African society with the goal of uniting African people. However, Killmonger, acted by Michael B. Jordan, did a tremendous job of illustrating how not to unify African people and how traumatic it is living under white colonialism. When Ross says, "Killmonger is one of ours," he means he is bred by the U.S. and utilized as an incredibly sharpened knife for the purposes of imperialism. Therefore, he is not capable of being a leader of any African people.

BE AN ORGANIZER LIKE BLACK PANTHER

Before making this point, we must be careful in not fusing *Black Panther* the Marvel comic book with a Black Panther who is a former member of the Black Panther Party, formed to gain self-determination for Black people in the U.S. Seasoned organizers know best how to navigate this discussion or engage in community action to help shine light on political prisoners.

T'Challa was able to unite the Jabari clan with his clan and the other clans of Wakanda. He did not cape for Ross the CIA agent when the Jabari clan shut down Ross. T'Challa, the Black Panther, was able to understand that although Killmonger was wrong in his actions, he had excellent points and a right to be angry. The interpretation is that so-called Black Americans must comprehend that there are Africans in Africa who love us and understand our collective history.

T'Challa also relied heavily on all the Black women, all while fighting to change the ideologies of Wakanda's former leaders.

WHITE PEOPLE, BE ALLIES

Ross, played by Martin Freeman, did blow up the last jet that was heading to the Western world. Ross was instructed and taught by Shuri.

White folks have a job if they are to be allies, and that is to take direction from the Black and POC organizers to set the world right today. White allies are key to stopping racism, imperialism and colonialism. They must relinquish the resources that were stolen by their forefathers.

THE AFRICAN DEBT IS RIDICULOUS

African debt is around a quarter of a trillion dollars. This debt is a game played by the World Bank, the International Monetary Fund and the G-8 nations that provide funds to Western companies to work on projects crafted by U.N. partners. This reality makes the ending incredulous.

After film credits begin rolling, T'Challa addresses the U.N. to offer the world assistance. It is difficult to witness because it intends to give the world more access to Africa's natural resources.

However, it is one of the most realistic scenes in *Black Panther*. Africa gave the world life and civilization, technology and deposits daily wealth through diamonds, gold, coltan, rubber, etc. Now, Africa wants to do more. At this point, I see this scene as T'Challa representing an Africa finally setting the terms of conditions.

Omowale Adewale is a vegan boxer and Grassroots Artists MovEment G.A.ME executive director.

4
WHY IS BLACK PANTHER THE BIGGEST PARADIGM SHIFT OF ALL BLACK MOVIES EVER?
LM Arnal

Have you wondered why so much promotion has been lavished on this studio production (gathering by the way the youngest pearls of Black cinema), and worldwide? At least the fact that a big studio embraced such a project should have made you think. What's the message? What BS is hiding behind it?

Here it is, my brethren, in a nutshell:

Black social case kid with strong revolutionary message is a big threat to money, white of course—even if here it has been given Black faces. It is an Orwellian tale, indeed.

Who is Wakanda? Wakanda is peopled by Oreo Cookie duplicated ad nauseam; it is Oreo-cookie Land as a matter of fact—or what Malcolm would have called "the house brothers," whereas social case kid is the "field brother." Thus, Wakanda elite have the money, the knowledge, the power and most importantly, they share knowledge with white dude. By the way, white dude talks Black and he lets you handle everything because, of course, he is Mr. Nice Guy. (By the way, have you ever seen a white dude taking a bullet for a sister? I haven't—not in this world we live in.)

Doesn't it seem to you that Wakanda is the Western World with a Black face—like a masquerade, a new minstrel show, every Black man's hope, deep inside?

So, of course, you have again symbols of dependence —Mr. Nice guy will of course help oreo-cookie peeps. The second addiction, which I had already noticed in "Blade," is a drug. Here it is some ancestral blueish hallucinogenic thang they drink, as if they could not summon enough strength within. And of course, the third addiction is prayer—this time to the ancestors. Of course, you have the ridiculous gear that Marvel heroes always wear: the one-piece suit that makes men's asses real tight. They even threw in some martial arts to try to make it look real. Come on, peeps!

Yeah they sold it to you fine, this one! You've got gotten. You've been played! So who cares if all the cast is Black? Down the line, we've gotten bamboozled one more time.

Watch out people. What they want is to make the struggle wrong.

Of course social kid, the Black monster (even defined as such by king of Wakanda), is given as a product of your own doing because his uncle abandoned him, which erases all the real bad conditions of systemic racism, and you were so excited that almost everybody (finally!) is Black in that movie that you did not see the real message of this real killer movie. Because it is here to kill our thirst for justice. It makes justice seekers the monsters. What is really at stake here is the fear of big money, at the emergence of an educated Black intelligentsia issued from the ghetto.

The only thing I can tell you is go beyond appearances. Hollywood is a cliché machine whose strongest function is to create ideologies, sets of beliefs to live by. And the well-being of Black people is still not on their very conservative agenda.

Beware what they feed you lavishly. They would not insert money into anything that could topple the power of their chosen elite.

My thoughts go to the Black Panthers—the real heroes who fought for a cause and died in shame and bad repute. This film repackages the concept into something hollow, a farce that does not render to these dedicated fighters for Black freedom the recognition they deserve.

I still think the cast was outstanding and the cinematography impeccable. Hey, they might even give it an Oscar. I'll call it the Oscar of paradigm shifts!

And with all the promo they have created a cornucopia of products to sell you, because money has to be made again, on Black folks' dreams.

Damn, they also got me, too. And sorry to burst your little Marvel bubble! It's wake up or Wakanda!

Wakanda or wake up right now! Which one will you choose?

LM Arnal is a Black writer and painter.

5
LIES CAN'T GET US WHERE WE NEED TO GO!

Abdul Alkalimat

The *Panther* movie is out and people are going in droves to check it out. Both Black and white. This requires clear hard-headed thinking. It's not about the actors in the film and their careers. Can't blame a brother or a sister for needing a payday and a chance to make it inside the system, in this case Hollywood. It's certainly not about the capitalists promoting it on all media, as they have the dual interest of making money and controlling our consciousness to prevent our movement from making sure they stop making all this money. It has to be about our clear understanding of history, and how we can get free from this system.

The first thing is that they know how to go fishing. Beautiful Black people celebrating culture and positive relations. A view of traditional Africa that defies all logic and historical experience but gives Black people a view of the past that can be imagined as the technological future. This fits the imaginative rethinking of ancient Egypt as an answer for our future. Our situation is so dire that we will reach out for this Hollywood fantasy as if it can be helpful, healing, and a lens through which to view history. There is dialogue about freedom, but in no way reflects the past or gives positive advice for us.

Lies can't get us where we need to go.

Let's take a quick look at this film. It is a replay of the conflict of the 1960s between cultural nationalism and revolutionary nationalism, the US organization of Karenga and the Panthers of Huey Newton and Bobby Seale. The story is about who is going to control the Kingdom of Wakanda. The point of conflict is the Panther as a metaphor for a Black liberation change agent. The cultural nationalist is the King of Wakanda, who uses their special natural resource plants to become the Black Panther. He is a friendly associate with the CIA. The reference to the actual Black Panthers, meaning the child of Wakanda (aka Killmonger) who grew up in Oakland, is a sort of gangster living a Fanonian fantasy that violence will change the world. He too is the son of a member of the royal family. This guy was trained by the CIA and begins the film in alliance with a white South African fascist.

| 14 |

The big lie is that to be a Panther one has to be of "royal blood," and not simply a victim of the system who stands up to fight back.

Another big lie is that the CIA is an ally in the fight for a better world.

The film is a commercial hodgepodge of references to other popular films:

1. A young women plays the part of the tech-savvy Q of James Bond movies
2. The space ships are a nod to Star Wars
3. The CIA agent is the star from the Hobbit movies
4. The car chases refer to the Fast and Furious films
5. Moving into Wakanda makes you think of Stargate

In 2018 we live in a moment of spontaneous movement and there is the possibility that another version of the real Panthers will likely emerge. Some original Panthers are still incarcerated and being brutalized by the system they dared to oppose. A movie like this has the bait to pull us in like fish about to be hooked by the system. People see the film and feel good, but isn't that what people say about first getting high on drugs. We know how drug addiction turns out.

This film is dangerous and we must be vigilant against culture used to control and oppress.

Abdul Alkalimat is a veteran black liberation activist, educator, researcher and a founder of Black/Africana Studies.

6

BLACK PANTHER AND THE DEGENERATION OF BLACK PUBLIC AND POPULAR DISCOURSE

Rayfield A. Waller (The Panopticon Review)

I am willing to see "Black Panther" as entertaining and exciting fantasy, as in some ways less noxious fare than usual for young Black Americans, as entertaining, though a little too cultural nationalist. However, do young Blacks really need to idealize concepts like monarchy in the name of pride? Some people are trying to ascribe the manufactured popularity of "BP" to the emerging re-interest over the last two decades that we see in 'The Mother Country' on the part of all diasporic African peoples, and on the part of beleaguered and currently re-segregated African Americans suffering from 'negative media imagery' that "BP" assuages.

Yes, it's true that African diasporic peoples are returning in appreciable numbers to our homeland, but that homeland is a place which is NOT a paradisiacal kingdom of   super Negros but is, as Wole Soyinka used to remind us, his graduate students at Cornell, "A very non-idealized and challengingly flawed absolute diversity of hundreds of states, traditions, histories, nations, tribes, villages, city states, ideologies, myths, clans, and communes."

I know three people who picked up and moved to South Africa, which has been anything but ideal thanks to the flaws of the ANC, the venality of political leadership, continued injustice for the trade union movement, and to its still lacking adequate land reform, and lack of a will to nationalized diamond and gold resources that ought to have made South Africa hands down the wealthiest Black nation on Earth after the revolution. All those lost opportunities are the things Nelson Mandela claimed to stand for. Everyone I know who went there is happy they did, admittedly. Struggle in one's own home is better than triumph in the prison founded by one's oppressor.

The problem, those who've moved to South Africa, Ghana, and Cote d'Ivoire have told me, is that one has to banish naive idealization of the homeland and deal with corruption, pollution, capitalism, misogyny and class injustice just like everywhere else one might be drawn to live. Once returning to the real African continent not as super heroes but as citizens, we will have to deal with Africa not as a fantasy of glorious esteem and muscle padding in our spandex costumes, but as a real polity demanding struggle, disappointment, sacrifice, and even critique. I'd move to Cape Town's De Waterkant, Green Point, or Mouille Point at the ocean the moment I could get a good job there, though, and say screw the US, if that were the end point of the debate.

To my alarm, though, I am finding dear friends, degreed, published, otherwise politically conscious people my age (Generation X), collapsing into overweening positivism over this little movie. This morning at the supermarket a Black man and Arab-American came almost to blows over whether "BP" is really about any real Africa that ever existed, and because the Arab-American expressed distrust that "BP" is real or even should be real, I must admit I sided silently with the Arab American brother even as he was driven out of the frozen food section to take cover in produce with angry African Americans on his heels. This irruption of discussion can take on the character of cathexis, and as Jung taught, the relative non-importance of the OBJECT of cathexis drops away in analysis, because the cathexis ITSELF and what it betrays about the psyche, is the real issue. 'Movies' as opposed to film, never deserve a great deal of critical energy, as far as I'm concerned, even when Arab Americans are sent afoot into the spinach, but along with other diatribes I've overheard a recent spate of comments I've seen and heard comparing "BP" to the film, "Color Purple" troubles me.

"Color Purple?" Time out. That is unfair to "Color Purple" (Spielberg and Meyjes, released in 1985) which was a serious film, not a movie. Comparisons to other Hollywood product from that much earlier in our history is begging the question; the issue is not that we ought to be starting out by accepting conversations about 'movies' as if they de facto reflect some desired reality, but we should be drawing a distinction BETWEEN movies (particularly capitalist Hollywood cartoon movies) and reality, both positive AND negative.

Anyone who criticized OR complemented Color Purple decades ago as a reflection of reality was given a hard time, as I recall clearly since I was involved in public debates and panel discussions about "CP" at the time, in Detroit. Most Black public intellectuals were saying something or other about "CP" that it had this or that historical significance as a film, not at history, and even those who favored "CP" kept in sight of the understanding that it was a Hollywood rhetoric. We were that conscious back then. To cite "The Color Purple" is to re-enter the realm of actual cinema (as opposed to the fantasy and wish fulfillment of "BP"). Cinema demands that we raise the level of discourse now, by taking to task all Hollywood films as clearly not comparable to reality. MARVEL Hollywood even more so. Marvel movies are not nor are they meant to be real or meant to be allegories of the real.

What's problematic about euphoria over this (bad comic book based) movie, "BP", is the way "BP" does the same thing all profit driven 'blockbuster' product is intended to do: manufacture a shift in focus from history to fantasy. We can safely say that whatever its flaws and virtues, "CP" was not primarily constructed to do that. American capitalist culture had changed immensely since "The Color Purple" was produced, shot, and released; specifically, American film has degenerated a great deal since then. Furthermore, it is not at all fair to draw a comparison between "Color Purple", a film that can legitimately be either supported or criticized history, as regional reality, as a depiction of life under southern segregation, and as an artifact that captured in many ways a failure of critical capacity in a Hollywood film that we all argued over IN THOSE INTELLECTUAL TERMS (how accurate is it, we asked, how fair? How racist? How open to interpretation of author intention, and how acceptable as an American-Jewish and Netherlandish production (Steven Spielberg- -director and Menno Meyjes–Screenplay/adaptation) instead of being a Black production? And, how representative of the Hollywood ethos was it?).

I would resist comparing "CP" to "BP" therefore, inasmuch as "BP" is not being discussed at that level, but is increasingly being discussed in a way that begs whether we are even still capable as Americans of discussing our popular art forms in terms of history, politics, economics, and even ethics (all of the things that "Color Purple" DID evoke as any legitimate cinematic work does). "BP" too frequently evokes discussions about 'positive images', 'feeling proud', 'and grandeur (?)' 'pride,' and how 'magnificent' the fictional characters are. "CP" was an adaptation of a critically acclaimed novel by one of our most gifted authors, while "BP" is an adaptation of a largely failed Marvel comic book which I collected every copy, and had long discussions with my boyhood friends about, as we cited the flaws therein. The comparison to "CP" is unfair to "Color Purple," as it is unfair to "In the Heat of the Night," "Cotton Comes to Harlem," "Guess Who's Coming to Dinner," even "Shaft," all of which were problematic as all get out, but were also challenging American filmmaking and social reality in some way or other and thus evoking Americans to have thoroughgoing debates over these artifacts as touchstones of social and political reality. These films were not confined to a superficial level of debate in terms of simplistic concepts (public relations, mass media, advertising, image, self-esteem, and let's be honest, Black Christian positivism).

These were films, even the Blaxploitation genre that were not primarily 'entertaining' though they entertained, yes, but whose primary significance as public topics was not how 'good' (OR bad) they made us 'feel', but rather how much in touch with material reality they were, and where they fit into what were then the current sociopolitical struggles we were engaging, thus they were reflective of how materially engaged we all used to be. How adult we used to be.

In the end, the movie "BP" is not the point, it's just a movie, based on a comic book by multinational, corporate sell out Stan Lee's Marvel Comics conglomerate–it would do well to not lose track of the source. The point, the crucial issue particularly in these times of peril not just for African Americans but for people of color all over this planet, is whether or not African Americans still have the guts, the critical faculties and the will toward dialectical analysis that we used to display only twenty years ago when we had serious debates over the reality and significance of Denzel Washington's performance in the film "Fallen," a strange and in many ways disturbingly unreal fantasy based in White Christian dogma about Satanic possession, but one which because it was rooted in narrative reality (unlike "BP") still drew critical, and religious, social, political, and even cinematic argument.

Black Americans were more than up for THAT kind of debate twenty years ago, before cell phones and global visual culture through internet regimes. It is telling that very little has been said so far by us about BP's cinematic techniques (which in some ways, as with "Avengers," remind me of fascist, Leni Riefenstahl), it's mise-en-scene, it's direction, it's strategic passages of cinematographic high key schemes (ala Disney), and all of the same suspect visual elements that make it just another questionable, socially revisionist Marvel movie (not unlike the VERY suspicious "Iron Man", another of Marvel's adolescent revisions of real technocracy, and real geopolitical, post-colonial issues as fantasy and wish fulfillment).

African Americans have never been of the sort that we would disregard the larger social and political issues of American cinema ITSELF while being narcissistic about our own place in a specific film. "BP" is not the point, WE are. Are we willing to buy into one of the most destructive and negative developments in American cinema (many critics say the Marvel regime's supremacy is in fact ruining cinema through its degrading of complexity of plot, adult theme, and complexity of characterization) simply because a monopolist Marvel movie is doing it now in Blackface?

Rayfield A. Waller is a poet, cultural critic, labor activist, and political journalist who is a professor of literature, history, Africana Studies, and the social sciences at Wayne State University and Wayne County Community College in the postindustrial city of Detroit, Michigan.

7
REAL WAKANDA-BATTLE OF ADWA, SEARCHING FOR HEROES & LIBERATORS, AND THE POLITICAL ECONOMY OF BLACK PANTHER

Milton G. Allimadi

I have major beef with *Black Panther* but I start my political economy review on a positive note.

As a Pan-African, I love the possibilities for mutually beneficial constructive cooperation between Africans on the motherland and Diaspora Africans suggested in *Black Panther* the movie. It comes towards the very end when T'Challa (Chadwick Boseman) travels with his sister (Letitia Wright) from Wakanda to Oakland, California, and tells her of his plans to invest in the Black community.

He had been thinking of the passion and anger that drove Erik Killmonger (Michael B. Jordan), who is no villain at all; Killmonger raged about his "abandonment" in America but he meant it in a very bigger way. If Africa could realize its power, sisters and brothers wouldn't be victims of police brutality and mass incarceration here and poverty in Africa. It's not coincidental that in Hollywood in order for a character to be permitted to speak Truth to Power he or she must appear as an evil person.

I've always believed that joint projects between the motherland and Diaspora– are the keys to Pan-African empowerment. Can you imagine Africa's tremendous resources – its 1.2 billion people, its hundreds of trillions of dollars' worth of mineral and natural resources, and its possession of two-thirds of the world's untapped fertile agricultural land– leveraged with the $1 trillion in Black annual purchasing power in the United States?

The Global African world would be second to none. That is the vision that Killmonger had for Africa's Wakandas.

In our real world, embezzlement of vast fortunes in public funds has stunted development in Africa. Widespread rape of Africa's resources by multinationals also continues to create Western billionaires. What if instead of being siphoned off to Swiss banks through the decades the $5 billion stolen by Congo's Mobutu and the nearly $4 billion by Nigeria's Sani

Abacha had been invested in Black-owned banks and businesses and institutions in the United States? This is the question Killmonger – in the real world – would pose.

Black Panther not only suggests Pan-African cooperation, it practices it in the real world. The mega-budget production which cost $200 million to make – and has already grossed $427 million – has a predominantly Black cast that brings together Diaspora African and African actors and actresses. From here, they include Boseman, Wright, Jordan, Forest Whitaker, Angela Bassett, Daniel Kaluuya, and Winston Duke, and others; from Africa, Lupita Nyong'o, Danai Gurira, and Florence Kasumba, and others.

Might this *Black Panther* template not be used for other collaborative enterprises – in business, science, education, politics and other artistic endeavors? This would make Killmonger smile.

So why hasn't this strategy – Pan-African collaboration– which has been preached since the era of Booker T. Washington, Marcus Garvey and W.E.B. Du Bois been put into effective play? The truth is that a wedge exists between continental Africans and Africans in Diaspora. This is not surprising given the centuries of demonization of both Africans and Diaspora Africans in Western literature (This is the subject of my book "The Hearts of Darkness, How White Writers Created the Racist Image of Africa").

On the silver screen, Hollywood traditionally caricatured African Americans as non-achievers inclined to a life of leisure or criminality. Africans have been (and are) cast as backward "tribesmen" constantly engaged in senseless wars.

When Africans use the word "tribe" there are no negative connotations; not so, when Western scholars and writers dismiss Africans as "tribal" as the late Ugandan author and educator Okot p'Bitek observed in "African Religions in Western Scholarship."

Malcolm X, the charismatic Black Nationalist and freedom fighter, in "You Can't Hate the Roots of a Tree without Hating the Tree," summed up the impact of demonization: "...the colonial powers of Europe, having complete control over Africa, they projected the image of Africa negatively. They projected Africa always in a negative light: jungles, savages, cannibals, nothing civilized. Why then naturally it was so negative it was negative to you and me, and you and I began to hate it. We didn't want anybody to tell us anything about Africa, much less calling us 'Africans.' In hating Africa and hating the Africans, we ended up hating ourselves, without even realizing it..." Malcolm practiced what he preached. He attended an Organization of African Unity meeting in Cairo in 1964 and traveled to several African countries, meeting leaders like Julius Nyerere, Jomo Kenyatta, Tom Mboya, Milton Obote, Kwame Nkrumah and Sekou Toure.

While Malcolm discussed the inferiority complexes created in African American communities by demonization, some Africans who were lucky to attain some education during colonial rule also developed similar disorders. Here is Frantz Fanon describing the behavior of Africans and Diaspora Blacks whom he met in Paris, in "Black Skin, White Masks" his classic work: "We have known, and unfortunately still know, comrades from Dahomey or the Congo who say they are Antillean; we have known and still know, Antilleans who get annoyed at being taken for Senegalese...It's because the Antillean [thinks he] is more 'evolue' than the African—meaning he is closer to the White man.."

Black Panther, the movie, is the kind of production that contributes towards combating the inferiority complexes that bedevils many Black people all over the world. Many more major productions with empowering storylines are needed.

The timing of *Black Panther's* release couldn't have been better, coming weeks after Donald Trump, America's most blatantly racist president of the modern era declared Africa to be a collective of "shithole" countries. (In truth, the Orange Racist lies—he knows of Africa's riches. During the UN General Assembly last September be boasted that his friends were making money in Africa).

In fact Africa continues to sustain and build the wealth in the Western world – as it did during the colonial regime, as Walter Rodney showed in "How Europe Underdeveloped Africa." The World Bank's neo-liberal economic dictate ensures that African countries will never industrialize and compete with the West as China has managed to do. African countries will continue to supply raw materials and consume the much more expensively sold manufactured products from Western –and now Asian–factories.

Yes, *Black Panther* presents an idealistic and fantasized Africa, where a monarch with superpowers fights to preserve his kingdom, Wakanda's, independence. What's wrong with that? Black Panther does for millions of Black youth what Superman, Spiderman, Batman and other superheroes have done for youth –especially White ones– for decades. It allows them to think big, beyond earthly shackles–this can be psychologically and emotionally transformative.

I myself, like hundreds of millions of Black youth, while growing up was a victim of the White-Hero-Complex. This is because they were the only heroes offered.

Here's my own evolution: I first came to the United States around age five when my father was appointed Uganda's ambassador to the U.S. and to the United Nations.

One day, in 1971, I recall how all the adults at home were speaking in hushed tones. Then one of my relatives told me that there was bad news from Uganda. I was told a "bad guy" named Idi Amin, who commanded the army, had ordered tanks in the streets and said he was now running the country. My first reaction was to imagine superman flying to Uganda, smashing up the tanks and sending Amin fleeing.

It was when my family lived in Tanzania, exiled from Uganda during Amin's regime, that I developed a Pan-African consciousness. One day, I was about 12, walking in the streets of Dar es Salaam the Tanzanian capital when I saw something shocking – a painting of a Black Jesus Christ on a bookstore display window. How could this be? I wondered. That initial thought quickly turned to why should it be otherwise? The incident sparked my interest in challenging representations of Africans and questioning received or prevailing "truths."

The National library in Dar es Salaam became my home. I read books, Tanzanian newspapers and publications from around the world. My new heroes included: Tanzania's President Nyerere; Ghana's Nkrumah; Congo's late Patrice Lumumba; Zimbabwe's Robert Mugabe and Joshua Nkomo; Guinea's Amilcar Cabral; Mozambique's Samora Machel; Angola's Agostino Neto; and of the then-incarcerated South African global icon Nelson Mandela.

Tanzania was home to liberation movements still fighting for independence in African countries still under European rule.

I read magazines, newspapers and books at the United States Information Services (USIS) and the British Council Library. I learned about Dr. Martin Luther King, Jr. and "The Autobiography of Malcolm X."

There were no Black comic superheroes – it did help that the Pan-African fighters for liberation were real-life superheroes. I prayed for them to crush Ian Smith in what was then Rhodesia and the racist regime in South Africa.

But young people need superheroes in comics as well. The closest such superhero was Lance Spearman, a crime-fighting Black detective in a South African produced picture-book. I was no longer satisfied with Ian Fleming's James Bond. So at the age of 12, I wrote my first novel about a Tanzanian super-spy. I don't know whatever became of that manuscript.

When Amin was overthrown in 1979 my family returned to Uganda and I came to the U.S. the following year. Later, Black Panther became my hero. I read the recent series by Ta-Nehisi Coates. I can totally relate to the euphoria of T'Challa coming to the Big Screen. The potential impact on Black youth – all youth actually because it's good for Whites to also imagine and accept Black superheroes – can't be underestimated. Especially in the United States where Black boys are so demonized.

Let me now discuss the major beef I have with *Black Panther* that I declared upfront.

The storyline about a CIA agent becoming a hero by fighting on behalf of T'Challa and the people of Wakanda is blasphemous to all Pan-Africans. It's outrageously insensitive. It's abhorrent.

How is it possible for the director, Ryan Coogler, to permit this storyline even in a film about a fictitious African country given what the CIA did to some of Africa's heroes, real life T'Challas such as Lumumba, Nkrumah and Mandela?

Congo's combined mineral riches is estimated at $27 trillion – that's one African country alone. Congo has what amounts to vibranium – in the form of rich deposits of uranium, gold, diamond, copper, cobalt, and coltan; the latter is used in all cell phones and other electronic products.

Just as with Wakanda the outside world has always coveted Congo's riches.

In the 19th century King Leopold of the Belgians seized Congo and murdered 10 million Africans while plundering the resources. At the Berlin Conference of 1884-1885 when European powers partitioned Africa in a meeting not attended by a single African the maniacal Belgian king declared his eagerness to get a slice of the "magnificent African cake."

When Congo won its independence from Belgium in 1960, Lumumba became Prime Minister. All he wanted was for Congo to get a fairer slice of the profits from exports of its riches. The CIA worked with the Belgians to have him deposed in three months. The following year he was murdered and the notorious thief and dictator Mobutu was installed in power and supported by the U.S. for 37 years.

Did Coogler not see Raoul Peck's "Lumumba" the compelling movie about his brutal murder, and the destruction of Congo and of Africa's hopes? Lumumba was a spell-binding human being. When Dave Chappelle's mother Dr. Yvonne Seon heard him speak in Harlem in 1960 when she was only 22–yes, the Dave Chappelle of comic fame– she volunteered and went to work in Congo. She left soon after Lumumba's murder.

(Tragically today Congo is still exploited for its riches, including coltan. In recent years as many as 6 million Congolese have been murdered. Western corporations no longer need European colonial governors or armies. They use neo-colonial leaders –Nkrumah warned of sell-outs such as these in "Neo-Colonialism: The Last Stage of Imperialism"– like Gen. Yoweri Museveni and Gen. Paul Kagame in neighboring Uganda and Rwanda, respectively. These two basically rent their armies to invade and plunder; they and some Western multi-nationals are beneficiaries of the loot).

One of Lumumba's mentors was Kwame Nkrumah who led Ghana to become one of Africa's first countries to win independence from Britain in 1957. During Ghana's independence celebration he declared: "Today, from now on, there is a new African in the world! Our independence is meaningless unless it is linked up with the total liberation of Africa. That new African is ready to fight his own battles and show that after all, the black man is capable of managing his own affairs." Indeed it was Nkrumah's passion to help liberate the other African countries from colonial rule that contributed to his demise. He also tried to industrialize Ghana –this is the only way for Africa to break dependency from the West and to create prosperity. Nkrumah also was overthrown in 1966 with the involvement of the CIA.

An African hero whom many consider to be Africa's T'Challa of T'Challas, Nelson Mandela, was also a victim of the CIA. In 1962, it was the U.S. spy agency that provided the South African intelligence services a tip about Mandela's hideout when he was underground and fighting the racist regime; this led to his arrest and later trial, conviction and 27 years' incarceration. Who knows, with Mandela actively involved in the struggle from outside apartheid may have collapsed earlier.

If these African giants – Lumumba, Nkrumah, and Mandela – were alive today, what do you imagine they would think about a film that transforms a CIA agent into a hero on behalf of Wakanda an African nation, albeit imagined, of high science, technological achievement and wealth?

I now close out my commentary on *Black Panther* on an uplifting note– about a real story that deserves a movie (and yes, I've been working on a script for the last few months).

Wakanda takes great pride in its independence and for having never been conquered. In Africa, the real life version of Wakanda was Ethiopia, also referred to as Abyssinia before the 20th century.

When Italy invaded Ethiopia with an army of 17,000 commanded by five Italian generals it was defeated within a matter of hours during the great Battle of Adwa on March 1, 1896.

A real life Black Pantheress, Empress Taytu Betul, carrying a sword and rifle, personally commanded an army of 6,000 men and fought for her beloved country. Her husband, Emperor Menelik II, commanded even much larger armies, together with other Ethiopian generals such as Ras Alula Aba Nega – referred to admiringly because of his skills by contemporary European writers as "Africa's Garibaldi" after the legendary general who played a key role in Italy's reunification – Ras Mikael of Wollo, Ras Mengesha, and Ras Makonnen.

While in Rome, before heading to Africa, the Italian commander Gen. Oreste Baratieri promised to return with Menelik II in a cage.

But when the dust settled Empress Taytu and Emperor Menelik and their Grand Army were leading about 2,000 captured Italian soldiers as prisoners of war. They were forced to march on foot more than 350 miles back to the Ethiopian capital, Addis Ababa –"little flower" – which had been founded by Taytu herself.

On the battleground Taytu and Menelik left more than 7,000 dead enemy soldiers, including 2,918 Italian non-commissioned officers and men and 261 Italian officers. Two Italian generals, Giuseppe Ellena and Giuseppe Arimondi, were killed and another one, Matteo Albertone was captured. Gen. Baratieri fled with his surviving troops and generals. Baratieri himself was later tried for "cowardice" by a court-martial.

The Ethiopians captured 56 artillery pieces and 11,000 rifles.

Thousands of Eritreans who fought for Italy – which had colonized Eritrea– were also killed. Many of the captured 800 Eritreans were subjected to severe punishment: they had their right hand and left foot amputated. There were even some reports that some defeated Italian soldiers were castrated. Other accounts suggest that rumors of such punishment were enough to scare Italian soldiers into throwing down their weapons and fleeing.

As Italian prisoners entered Addis Ababa, Ethiopian women lining the streets jeered at them and spit on them for daring to invade their country to kill their sons, brothers, and husbands.

Some prisoners were forced to work like slaves, building Addis Ababa – yes, the tables were turned – for more than one year. Finally, they were released after Ethiopia and Italy signed the Treaty of Addis Ababa and Rome paid several millions of dollars as reparations.

As a result of the Adwa victory Ethiopia was never colonized.

This African victory over imperialism can inform any sequel to *Black Panther*. It's a story that all Africans including Diaspora must know.

.

Milton Allimadi publishes The Black Star News and teaches African History at John Jay College of Criminal Justice. He's revising the second edition of his book The Hearts of Darkness, How White Writers Created the Racist Image of Africa. He's also writing a graphic book (maybe call it "Real Wakanda–Ethiopia's and Africa's Triumph"?) about The Battle of Adwa and Empress Taytu's brilliant role.

8

WISHING FOR WAKANDA, MAROONED IN AMERICA:
Movies and Matters of Reflection and Resistance

Dr. Maulana Karenga

In the midst of the wide-spread euphoria about the debatable real and actually imagined qualities, achievements and benefits of the fantasy movie, "Black Panther," it is good to remember that no matter how long we stay in the theater and no matter how many times we return to cheer, clap and dance in the dark, sooner or later the lights will come on, and we will have to exit and confront the off-screen, cold-water reality of America. We must know in moments of clarity and calm consideration, that even if we wish it to be otherwise, this is only a movie, a comic book story on screen and we have every right and at least some reasons to enjoy it as we wish. But talking about it as if it is a pathway and push forward to liberation, resistance and racial pride runs recklessly into the face of reality and any concept of critical reasoning, and pretends for a movie what only a movement of hard work and long struggle can achieve.

And it is such an unbounded and unreflective embrace that leads to the need and tendency to deny the movie's flaws, overlook its stereotypes and explain away its misrepresentations of continental African and African American culture and African peoples themselves; its discrediting and misrepresenting revolutionary struggle and resistance; and its cultivating the idea of the oppressor as an ally and enabler for African people.

Thus, so influenced we can overlook racist stereotypes of continental Africans in spite of their advanced technology: still carrying spears, even though sonic ones; trapped in tribalism; engaging in blood ritual battles to determine who will rule instead of using elections; and requiring the White CIA agent to save the Black woman and Black people from the Black man, asking the CIA agent to pilot their attack ship as if no Black person is technologically capable, assuring the agent "We're counting on you." And this in spite of the CIA's brutal and bloody history and current activities in Africa and around the world. We can also explain away the reductive translation of relations of continental Africans and African Americans, using a dehumanized would-be liberation fighter that ends up being little more than a gangster from the ghetto, indicted from the beginning by his name "Killmonger," one who promotes and deals and participates in killing.

And we can explain away why a technologically superior country hides itself from Whites who obviously know it exists and whom it can easily protect itself from or defeat, does not defend the continent and its people, and spends its hours on screen fighting within itself. Also, we can accept, without thinking critically, the gratuitous and generalized indictment of the ancestors for a problem of failure to share which the imaginary country's leader could take responsibility for himself and easily solve and not just with a charity center in the USA. This, as other attacks on the past and tradition, is a disguised calling into question the value and usefulness of the past (and the enduring insights of the people who made it) in understanding and changing the present and moving forward to forge our future in the most ethical, effective and expansive ways. And finally, we can close our critical eyes to the imposed low material level of life of the people outside the miracle city who are used as human camouflage—a situation which in more thoughtful times would be deemed and condemned as irrational, immoral and unjustifiable.

The film's appeal is understandable, not simply because of its favorably and mistakenly interpreted content and technological skill and glitz, but also because of the favorable context in which it was produced and positioned. It comes at a time, as the audiences and on-liners explain, when the attacks on African people, Black people, on the continent and in the diaspora, have taken a wild and openly racist turn. And the film becomes an alternative narrative for many to the rampant racist reductive translation and claims of who we are.

Moreover, many said it took them away from the more serious side of Black life, gave them a chance to relax and enjoy themselves watching a predominantly Black cast portray Black people highly advanced, in control of their lives and triumphant. And it was positioned in February, Black History Month, in which we traditionally celebrate and sing ourselves, reference and revisit our roots, identify and raise up heroes and heroines, extract lessons and models, and wonder out loud or silently "how we got over", knowing deep down the struggle must and does continue.

But let's face it, it was the marketing that created much of the marvel of the film. What film with Blacks as the subject has been so massively and skillfully advertised? Was "Selma" or "Malcolm X" or any other Black subject film made a must-see all over the world, with funds being collected and offered to send thousands of Black children to see it? And when have we seen almost every major media source doing approving and praising articles and commentaries on a Black subject coming attraction?

Surely, after all the before-now talk about the predatory and profit-seeking character and conduct of a racist and capitalist society, we can't possibly not know that this marvel of marketing of make-believe and this apparent established order consensus of approval and praise of the film means that it is clearly profitable for them and problematic for us. Clearly, capitalism is in it for the money, but also for the message, a message which maintains dominance, cultivates loyalty to the system in spite of its White supremacist and capitalist character, and lowers the oppressed conception of what they deserve, what they think possible and what they should accept.

Indeed, it is a central Kawaida contention that one of the greatest powers of any society, class or race is the capacity to define reality and make others accept it even when it's to their disadvantage. It is the Hon. Marcus Garvey who teaches us that the propaganda of the oppressor is one of the key "organized methods used to control the world," that "propaganda has done more to defeat the good intentions of races and nations than even open warfare." It is, he says, a regularly used organized method employed "to convert others against their will," against their best views and values.

And Min. Malcolm taught us to reject and resist the power and manipulation of the media, a weapon used constantly in the war to win the hearts and minds of our people and other oppressed and turn them against themselves and others. The people in power, he says, are skilled at the science of image making and can "create a humanitarian image for a devil or a devil image for a humanitarian." And they "can make the victim of a crime look like the criminal and can make the criminal look like the victim." Indeed, Malcolm concludes, "If you aren't careful the (media) will have you hating the people who are oppressed and loving the people who are doing the oppressing."

Yes, it's good to see Black people celebrating themselves, wearing African clothes, understanding themselves as African people, doing a version of the greeting/salute of the women in the '60s, and discussing issues of right and wrong in the way we do politics, distribute wealth, share resources and honor our obligations of solidarity to our brothers and sisters at home and abroad. But can we move beyond movie inspiration and episodic engagement with ourselves and continuously engage each other and issues more extensive than the ones the movie provokes some of us to discuss? And can we do this, not to defend a movie and our liking it, but in defense and advancement of our peoples' lives and interests and the well-being of the world?

Our oppressors tell us we were abandoned or marooned in America by our people, but we are our people, the ones the enslaver enslaved. And taking seriously the other meaning of maroon, we are at our best, the maroons of our history, the maroons of America, the people who in the midst of the Holocaust of enslavement dared to reject the established order, free themselves, be themselves and build free communities. It is a lasting legacy and unfinished fight, and we owe it to ourselves to maintain its commitment to resistance and struggle, regardless of the movies we like or the real or fantasy lands in which we live.

Dr. Maulana Karenga is professor and chair of the Department of Africana Studies at California State University, Long Beach. An activist-scholar of national and international recognition, Dr. Karenga has had a major effect on Black intellectual and political culture since the 1960s. Through his organizational and intellectual work, and his philosophy, Kawaida, he has played a vanguard role in shaping the Black Arts Movement, Black Studies, the Black Power Movement, the Black Student

Union Movement, Afrocentri¬city, ancient Egyptian studies as an essential part of Black Studies, Ifa ethical studies, rites of passage programs, the Independent Black School Movement, African life-cycle ceremonies, the Simba Wachanga Youth Movement, Black theological and ethical discourse, Black united fronts and the Reparations Movement. Dr. Karenga is the executive director of the African American Cultural Center and the Kawaida Institute of Pan-African Studies, Los Angeles; national chairman of The Organization Us and the National Association of Kawaida Organizations (NAKO); and co-chair of the Black Community, Clergy and Labor Alliance, Los Angeles (BCCLA). He served on the executive council of the national organizing committee of the Million Man March/Day of Absence and authored its Mission Statement. Moreover, Dr. Karenga is internationally known as the creator of the pan-African cultural holiday, Kwanzaa and the Nguzo Saba and of Kawaida philosophy out of which both were conceived and created. He is also the author of the authoritative book on the subject titled: Kwanzaa: A Celebration of Family, Community and Culture. Moreover, Dr. Karenga is author of numerous scholarly articles and books, including: Introduction to Black Studies; Selections from the Husia: Sacred Wisdom of Ancient Egypt; Odu Ifa: The Ethical Teachings; Maat, The Moral Ideal in Ancient Egypt: A Study in Classical African Ethics and Essays on Struggle: Position and Analysis. He is currently writing a book on The Liberation Ethics of Malcolm X: Critical Consciousness, Moral Grounding and Transformative Practice. Finally, Dr. Karenga is the subject of a book titled Maulana Karenga: An Intellectual Portrait by Dr. Molefi Kete Asante, which is the definitive text on his intellectual and organizational work.

9
BLACK FEMINIST MEDITATIONS ON THE WOMEN OF WAKANDA
Robyn C. Spencer, Ph.D.

Like hundreds of thousands of people in the US, my week was defined by the opening of Ryan Coogler's long awaited Marvel film, "Black Panther." Coming on the heels of the American president dubbing African countries as "shitholes" and renewed national attention on the sexual harassment and discrimination women face in Hollywood, "Black Panther" offered a stunningly beautiful technologically advanced African country that had escaped the ravages of colonialism; and storylines where Black women were central. The main character T'Challa is surrounded by Ramonda, his mother; Shuri, his brilliant younger sister; Nakia, his political comrade and ex; and Okoye, his loyal protector, general and head of his intelligence structure which includes the Dora Milaje, a group of female elite fighters. Given the often-stereotypical depictions and thin roles often available for Black women actors, any two of these characters in a film would be notable. The presence of all of them was nothing short of path breaking. I knew I had to take my 12-year-old daughter.

I watched the film through my eyes and hers. In hushed tones, she marveled at the flawlessness of Nakia's skin in one of the many close-ups of the dark skinned Black women of Wakanda who effortlessly subverted Eurocentric standards of beauty. She buried her head and watched through her fingers as Black women led the charge in one explosive fight scene after the other. And she fell in love with Shuri, the millennial princess who demonstrated that technological mastery is where the real power lies and that elder brothers can be annoying, even in advanced societies.

After leaving the theater, I reflected on the portrayal of Wakandan women. I asked myself how could a Black feminist lens enrich the vibrant conversations about the political meaning and historical resonance of this film? What political messages could be distilled? What would I discuss with my daughter, the day after?

EMPIRE IS NOT LIBERATION
The rivalry between T'Challa (Chadwick Boseman) and Killmonger (Michael B. Jordan) is a key plot point of the movie. Given Black feminism's deep anti-imperialist roots it is important to start with a criticism of Killmonger's plan to arm the children of the Diaspora with

| 30 |

Wakanda's weapons and technology. While this plan was introduced as a means to achieve liberation from oppression, it was intertwined with the language of empire — specifically a Wakandan empire where the sun never sets. The use of this infamous phraseology, which is widely associated with the glorification of the British colonial project, is a jarring reminder of the slippery slope between domination and liberation that has historically vexed masculinist visions of Black liberation. Killmonger, as a figure associated with the CIA (an organization presented uncritically in the film despite its well documented role in political repression, surveillance and disruption of foreign governments and murder of leaders), represents a flawed vision of power.

He is the primary African American figure in the film and carries the burdens of the afterlife of slavery and the struggle for Black self-determination in the US. He greets his father's death with a world-weary resignation about violence that demonstrates the precarities of Black childhood. His solution is to share Wakanda's technical prowess and military might with oppressed people of African descent so they can invert white supremacist hierarchies of race and power (not be rid of these hierarchies). His vision held the promise of selective liberation, not revolution.

Killmonger is a monarch seeking a throne, a familiar figure in the history of Black protest. Despite his flawed ideas and violent actions as a CIA operative, he is presented as having a redeemable vision of Black futurity. The struggle between T'Challa's way and Killmonger's alternative have fueled some of the most provocative think pieces about the meaning of the movie to Black history and politics. However, it is the women of Wakanda who have offered the most justice centered view of what Wakanda can mean in the world.

WAKADAN WOMEN AS THINKERS

Nakia (Lupita Nyong'o) first appears in a scene where she is coming to the aid of African women and children, an unmistakable nod to Boko Haram kidnaping of women and girls and a comment on the reality of child soldiers. From the start, her character presents a challenge to the isolationist policies of Wakanda and suggests the potential of justice driven interventions into the outside world. This history follows her throughout the film as she hints at entanglements in North Korea and other places around the globe. It is this political commitment that is the wrench in the works in her love story with T'Challa. She is an ideologue hidden in plain sight, advocating a different path than T'Challa's isolation or Killmonger's expansionism with her praxis.

It is Nakia's way that seems to have the most radical potential. History is not fiction but the mechanisms that silence Black women's intellectual production even while seeming to herald their numerical presence is present in each realm. Scholars of Black women's intellectual history have pointed to the ways that racism and sexism combine to easily dismiss Black women as "doers," rather than thinkers. This allows commentators and pundits to herald Nakia as one of Wakanda's most visible and brave women, analyze her character's bold style politics and paradigm shifting beauty, while engaging with the male characters (rather than her) as thinkers.

| 31 |

HIDDEN *(LEADERSHIP)* FIGURES

Shuri (Letitia Wright), Wakanda's brilliant scientist and technological powerhouse, steals every scene she is in. She masterminds everything from T'Challa's fight strategy to the high speed train system that will frame T'Challa and Killmonger's battle to the death. Her centrality and power is evident in the scene where she coaches Everett Ross (Martin Freeman) through his mission to short circuit Killmonger's plan while simultaneously fighting for her country, family and life. However, her ability to create technology and master science is narrowed in the end when T'Challa imposes his vision of skill transfer between Wakanda and Oakland. She arrives to an impoverished Oakland confused about the location and her purpose there. Taking the role of teacher, she answers the preliminary questions curious urban youth in an ending which juxtaposes her tremendous knowledge with the contested notion that STEM education is a panacea for structural inequality.

In the end T'Challa, the king of the most advanced country in the world, has purchased a few buildings and committed to a plan of education in the inner city. This is as anti-climactic as it sounds. He has positioned his sister and comrade, his two closest allies and the two characters with the broadest and most intriguing vision of Wakanda in the world, at the helm of his first attempt at outreach. However their hand in the project is unclear and the result is a cooptation of their vision and a blunting of the radical edge of their politics.

MATRIARCHS AND GENERALS

While the film revolves around the loss of T'Challa's father T'Chaka, his mother Ramonda (Angela Bassett) is in a supporting role in the film. Bassett brings deep gravitas to her every line in her role as a royal elder but does not serve as a strong counterpoint to her son. Killmonger's mother, and entire upbringing, is also missing in the film. Viewers are left to surmise that it is men, through their presence or absence, who leave the strongest imprint on their boys. This is an inversion of the role that Black mothers have historically played in the lives of their children.

Okoye (Danai Gurira) is fierce as a loyal general but once Killmonger becomes king it is clear that her power is channeled through the throne, a symbol of maleness. She is trapped in a structure that leaves her with few choices until the very end when she boldly decides to help T'Challa regain power and fights for Wakanda. The notion that "we were kings and queens" (and generals) resonates deeply in an anti-Black world where Black history and culture is often presented as debased and nihilistic. But these are also deeply limiting tropes. Ryan Coogler has discussed how the film focuses on the interplay between the modern and traditional, a key reminder about the perils and possibilities of making the future out of the cloth of the past.

MOTHERING FUTURES

"Black Panther" reflects a deep, global and collective hunger for cultural products that represent people of African descent with dignity and power, but that doesn't mean that one has to swallow everything uncritically. There is potential in this moment. Activists have raised awareness about the 1960s Black Panther Party, rallied for support for political prisoners and held voter registration drives at movie screenings. Fewer have asked why the African future — as imagined in "Black Panther" — and the African past — as sold by ancestry.com — is so much more appealing to some Americans than the African present. There is no better time to launch critical conversations about what liberation could look like; connect new people to pre-existing organizations and political networks; re-center aesthetics in freedom making projects and have some frank transnational diasporic dialogue.

Perhaps the best thing about "Black Panther" is that it grounds these conversations in intergenerational soil. The day after the film, I will ask my daughter to use the tools of Black feminism to re-imagine Wakanda. How should it be organized, run and led? Could she think beyond monarchy and create an alternative system of governance based on values like egalitarianism and collectivity? How might she redistribute, rather than hoard, the wealth of Wakanda for the greater good? What would she do with Killmonger, who at the end finally grasps the splendor of Wakanda yet is incapable of imagining that it had evolved beyond imprisoning vanquished enemies? (A burning question in a country where 2.3 million people are incarcerated.) Most of all, I will ask her about her favorite thinkers and suggest that the women of Wakanda might be the leaders that we have been calling for.

Dr. Robyn C. Spencer *is a historian and author of* The Revolution Has Come: Black Power, Gender and the Black Panther Party *in Oakland, California, Duke University Press, 2016. She is an Assistant Professor of History at Lehman College (CUNY) in the Bronx, New York and has a B.A. from the State University of New York at Binghamton; and M.A., M.Phil., and Ph.D., from Columbia University.*

Professor Spencer taught African and African American studies and history at Penn State University from 2001-2007. Before that, she was a Visiting Predoctoral Fellow at Randolph College in Lynchburg, Virginia.

Her areas of interest include black social protest after World War II, urban and working-class radicalism, and gender. She is completing a book on the Black Panther Party and will teach courses at Lehman on twentieth-century African American history.

In 2016-17 she received a Mellon fellowship at Yale University to work on her second book project, To Build the World Anew: Black Liberation Politics and the Movement Against the Vietnam War. *This project examines how working class African Americans' anti-imperialist consciousness in the 1950s-1970s shaped their engagement with the movement against the Vietnam War. In 2020-2021 work on this project will be supported by an ACLS Frederick Burkhardt Residential Fellowship for Recently Tenured Scholars at the Institute for Advanced Study, School of Social Science. She is also working on a short biography of Angela Davis for Westview Press' Lives of American women series.*

10

IT'S ALL ABOUT THE MONEY
Fred Logan

I saw *Black Panther* at a Cinemark theater in Pittsburgh on Wednesday, March 14, 2018. On that same day thousands of American high school students walked out of school in protest against the endemic gun violence that is sweeping across the United States. "The Black Panther" is a Marvel Studios film rated PG-13. It's a direct appeal to Black youth.

A lot of Black adults have flocked to see it, and they argue it features positive Black heroes and heroines for Black youth. It is no surprise that Black teenagers would eat popcorn, drink soda pop, laugh, clap, and scream at the top of their voices at this comic book movie. They are out to have a good time. The same is more or less true for the Black adults who don't try to argue the film is anything more than a Sunday funny-paper cartoon on the silver screen. It is altogether different for full grown Black folks to try to defend it.

Most important, is there any empirical evidence that Black youth believe this film is anything more than just another hyper-action movie like *Spiderman*?

The Wayan Brothers' animated satire "Thugaboo: Sneaker Madness" has a far more important political and economic message for Black youth and adults than The Panther film. Thugaboo is also very humorous. But Donald Trump and the international sneaker industry must despise it.

"The Black Panther" is the 18th film in Marvel's Superheroes series. Captain America and Spiderman are in the series. The Panther is based squarely on the motion picture industry's staple consumer product. That product is glorifying mass violence for mass entertainment and profit. Factor out the violence and the Black Panther has nothing to attract its audience.

Hollywood's western, gangster, horror, and Sci-fi films have glorified every kind of violence imaginable. Rambo and Freddie Krueger are two well-known examples of the countless violence-mongers that White America loves.

White America is searching frantically in every nook and cranny for the roots of the gun violence that killed 56 people in Nevada, 17 people in Florida, and many others elsewhere. This everyday real world "White-on White violence" terrifies, and allegedly confounds White America. White America blames violent video games, the National Rifle Association and so on. White America is right. The blame lies everywhere.

Hollywood is a major culprit. Hollywood's "Cowboy and Indian" movies were made to justify and sanctify the genocide of the indigenous nations of the Americas. Mainstream America refuses to acknowledge that this genocide is directly related to the "White on White" gun violence that killed school students and staff members on February 14, 2018 at Parkland High School in Florida. But it is.

Black Panther opened to overwhelming receptions in Black enclaves as far apart as Kenya and Chicago. Gun violence is a major problem in both locales and in many others where the Panther film glorifying mass violence has been targeting Black youth. This critical aspect of The Black Panther craze is being ignored by many prominent Black spokeswomen and men.

The film is so juvenile that it is very difficult not to be sarcastic in reply to the full-grown Black folks who try to defend it. National Urban League CEO Marc Morial praised the film as "a significant milestone." He praised the image of Black women in the film. A lot of other Black people have also. The Panther's Black female warriors are nothing but slightly revised replicas of the comic book super heroine Wonder Woman (A.K.A Diana Prince), this time killing African people. If the Panther's Black cheering section argues on the one hand the film is just entertainment and should not be taken seriously, they have no grounds to argue, on the other, the Panther's image of Black women can be taken seriously. Marvel Comics cannot establish the image of Black women on the motion picture screen or anywhere.

Independent Black cinema is replete with images and portrayals of Black women that are light years ahead of the Marvel Comic Black women. The astounding captivating images of Black women in Julie Dash's 1991 groundbreaking film "Daughters of the Dust" set new cinematic standards for African American women. This epic cinema also recognizes and cherishes indispensable cultural links between continental Africans and African Americans that stand autonomous of the European American cultural hierarchy. For this reason, the motion picture establishment has never sought Julie Dash for a full length theater film.

And in all of world cinema, there is no more powerful image of African women than Princess Doir Yacine in Ousman Sembene's masterpiece "Ceddo." Doir Yacine stands bold, rooted in the image of Yaa Asantewaa of Ghana, Queen Nzinga of the Congo, and Africa's real-world warriors.

Marvel Studios' deep pockets purchased raves for the Panther in the mainstream US media. And it surely paid for some of the "unprecedented" high profile film-related parties that were widely reported in the media. This was to get-the-ball-rolling. It worked. Black folks who love to party, and will party at the drop of a hat, took the cue immediately. They dressed up in African-print outfits made in Hong Kong. They flocked in mass to the nearest screening of The Black Panther. They came eager to talk trash, drink Marvel's liquor, and pose for the local TV station to spotlight them on the next news broadcast. They raved about how "Black" the film is when even from the on-line trailer, it is, at its very best, just another episode in the Marvel Comic's Batman, and Spiderman fantasies.

In the final scene, the Black superhero T'Challa stands before, apparently, the United Nations and promises to work for world prosperity and peace. This is ballyhooed as the film's closing Black liberation moment. After 2 hours and 15 minutes of comic book flying saucers, robot rhinos running wild, cartoon cinematography, super-duper iPhones, and endless nonsense, it does not work. T'Challa comes across like Daffy Duck standing before the United Nations General Assembly reading from the works of Frantz Fanon. T'Challa is Black, they argue. Well, Daffy is too.

Be clear on this point, Marvel Studios not Black folks produced "The Black Panther." And Marvel not the Black community has raked in some $1 billion and is still making money.

Measured by that yardstick of capitalism, it's a resounding unprecedented success for a "Black movie." As one of my late friends loved to say, "Hey! It's all about the money!" That's the bottom line.

The media reports *Panther* has been a box office hit in Kenya, Brazil and across the African diaspora. Now, the American film industry is gearing up for the "globalization" of films based on the Panther's production and promotion template and it is ready to rake in billions from across the Black World. Marvel Studios heard Trump recently tell US capitalism to go and get rich by further exploiting Africa's material resources and its peoples, and Marvel aims to do that.

In the Tarzan tradition, the white former CIA agent, who saves the African kingdom appeals to many white people. This is another audience for Marvel Studio's box office receipts. So, get ready for "Black Panther II," the return of "Blacula" and "Blackenstein" and Blaxploitation films at large.

Fred Logan *is a member of the Sembene Film & Arts Festival based in Pittsburgh. This commentary does not reflect the views of this organization.*

11

BLACK PANTHER:
A Nuanced Film for a Nuanced People
C. Liegh McInnis

At the core of *Black Panther* is the notion that African people are not a monolith. One of the major elements and accomplishments of white supremacy is making African people appear as one-dimensional beings that come from a land that is just as one-dimensional. Yet, that myopic notion of Africa and African peoples could not be further from the truth. Africa is a continent not a country. More ethnic groups exist in Africa than any other landmass. And, more languages are spoken on Africa than on any other landmass. Even the colonizers realized and utilized the cultural diversity of Africa to their advantage to divide and conquer Nubian peoples. This is seen specifically in the method of chaining individual Africans to individuals from differing tribes so that they could not communicate to develop a strategy to escape while being transported from Africa across the globe.

Yet, this is what makes stories, such as the Amistad rebellion, so amazing that even these Africans, speaking different tongues, were able to communicate and develop a strategy of escape. As such, *Black Panther* offers a reminder of the diversity of African peoples and the type of determination and communication needed to create a force capable of freeing and restoring themselves. Combining W. E. B. Du Bois' notion of Africans relearning themselves with Marcus Garvey's notion that all Africans see themselves as part of the African Diaspora no matter where they are located will enable African peoples to do what Frantz Fanon recommended years ago, which is to slay the oppressor of the mind so that the body/ Diaspora can be free. Or, as the great poet/philosopher George Clinton reiterated a few years after Fanon, "Free yo' mind, and your behind will follow."

To this end, the freeing of the mind begins when more African people realize their connection to other Africans dislocated across the planet while also realizing that what it means to be African is neither a finite nor prescribed reality. Just as Du Bois, Garvey, Shaka kaSenzangakhona, Booker T. Washington, Martin Luther King, Jr., el-Hajj Malik el-Shabazz (Malcolm X), Nelson Mandela, Patrice Lumumba, Kwame Nkrumah, Haile Selassie, Jesse Jackson, Ella Baker, Fannie Lou Hamer, Medgar Evers, Kofi Atta Annan, Jomo Kenyatta, Obiageli Ezekwesili, Desmond Tutu, Louis Farrakhan, and Chokwe Lumumba embody the wide-ranging genius and beauty of what it means to be African, Black Panther shows viewers that the only way for humanity to fulfill its potential is to recognize and embrace African diversity, to recognize the value of women in the African liberation struggle, and to accept that white supremacy is an ill with which white people must do battle. In doing this, humanity will finally be able to build a world that Margaret Walker Alexander forecasts in "For My People," a world that will hold "all the Adams, and all of the Eves, and their countless generations" (7). Accepting this call to action will enable African people to reduce the societal ills created by the umbrella of white supremacy, such as the large rate of high school drop-outs, teen pregnancy, teen violence, discriminatory arrests and sentencing practices, and the general poverty and hopelessness that keeps African people from returning to the blueprint of the people who developed civilization.

First, the film presents well-developed and nuanced characters to the point that it is having a discourse regarding the definition of protagonist and antagonist. Historically and culturally African people have often been indoctrinated of having to choose between battling ideologies rather than embracing their full humanity and critical thinking prowess by synergizing various aspects of ideologies into a well-develop plan of liberation. This pressure to choose one ideology over another has forced African people to label one position as good or right, making the other position bad or wrong. Therefore, African people have, themselves, been historically guilty of labeling their own people as protagonists and antagonists based on what ideology the majority of people have chosen as the most effective. Whether it was Du Bois and Booker T. Washington disagreeing over the type of education—academic or trade—that would best service African Americas or whether it was Du Bois and Garvey debating which of their organizations—the National Association for the Advancement of Colored People (NAACP) or the Universal Negro Improvement Association (UNIA)—would best allow African people to develop as first-class citizens, in each case public bickering forced the mass of African peoples to choose one over the other, stopping each great man and organization from fulfilling the mission of liberating African peoples from white supremacy.

All three men would attack each other publically, in speeches and in print, with Du Bois calling Garvey the "most dangerous enemy of the Negro race in America and the world" (Lewis 465). In contrast, Carter G. Woodson's The Miseducation of the Negro is great because it refuses to choose between Washingtonian and Du Boisian ideologies, opting to merge them into a more holistic plan of intellectual liberation. Similarly, one leaves Black Panther not discussing good versus evil or the right and wrong way to respond to white supremacy but making sure to engage in discourse that includes the complexity of what it means to be African and African American in a world smothered by white supremacy and how that unique and complex understanding colors or impacts one's choice of how best to respond to inhumanity and injustice. During the film's climax when Wakanda has been plunged into civil warfare, what saves Wakanda is not the super powers of the Black Panther but the realization by its citizens that maintaining Wakanda is more important than revenge or the desire to be right for the sake of being right.

After W'Kabi, head of the Border Tribe security, asks his love, O'Koye, head of the Dora

Milaje, the all-female Special Forces, "Would you kill me, my love?" he scans the field of battle to see the chaos and destruction that his myopic anger has created and realizes that the existence of Wakanda is more important than his desire for revenge. At that moment, he drops his sword, causing his soldiers to drop their swords. The civil battle for Wakanda is a commentary of the ongoing warfare that continues to exist throughout Africa, which is excellently shown in *Hotel Rwanda* as well as the black-on-black intellectual assaults that continue between leading Black scholars, such as Cornel West, Henry Louis Gates, Ta-Nehisi Coates, and others, who, like Washington, Du Bois, and Garvey in the past, seem to spend as much time fighting each other as they spend fighting white supremacy while the mass of African peoples languishes in poorly funded educational facilities that perpetuate their poverty.

Often, individuals and groups have been unable to realize that the liberation of African people is more important than a particular ideology that one embraces to obtain that liberation. This aspect is exasperated by the heavily promoted theme of American individualism that co-opts community leaders, such as Frederick Douglass, Martin Luther King, Jr., and Malcolm X, and organizations, such as NAACP, the National of Islam, or the Student Nonviolent Coordinating Committee (SNCC), and retells their stories as examples of individualistic endeavors rather than as stories of communal endeavors. This is often manifested when music companies co-opt Black talent from Black communities through the process of identifying what they view as the shining star of excellence and removing that star from its community by taking members of a group, such as Diana Ross from the Supremes, Lionel Richie from the Commodores, Michael Jackson from the Jackson Five, Beyoncé from Destiny Child, and many others, and converting them into solo acts because that is less expensive and easier to control than managing several members of a group.

Moreover, separating the individual from the group makes it easier to make an example of one person as in the NFL's current exiling of Colin Kaepernick to send a message to the reminder of the players in the league. As such, W'Kabi's dropping of his sword for the good of Wakanda is a refutation of American individualism, showing the extent to which it is detrimental to the community when the desires of the individual are placed before the needs of the community. W'Kabi's submission for the good of Wakanda should cause scholars to teach moments of history, such as the development of the Congress of Federated Organizations (COFO) to enable multiple Civil Rights organizations to cooperate in the success of Freedom Summer or even the brief but powerful moment, like the Million Man March, as an example of the success that can be obtained when African people are able to remember that the goal of a liberation movement is to create and sustain a sovereign people rather than the success of one or a few Africans. As former NAACP President Ben Jealous stated when asked if the election of Barack Obama meant the NAACP was no longer needed, "We must remember that the acronym is NAACP and not NAAACP. That is—we are the National Association for the Advancement of Colored People and not the National Advancement of A Colored Person, which means our struggle is not complete until all people are free."

Further, Killmonger's ability to divide and conquer Wakanda, even briefly, is due to the discontent that already exists there. This is a replaying, if not a reminder, of Chinua Achebe's Things Fall Apart, which shows that Christian missionaries were able to exploit the division that existed within tribes and between neighboring tribes, enabling the European merchants and military to launch a full attack against African people who were unable to develop a unity that would have enabled Africa to remain under the control of people who had the best interest of the land and the indigenous peoples. The issue is not that Killmonger creates chaos and destruction in Wakanda; the issue is that the seeds for this chaos and destruction had already been sown before Killmonger arrives. First and foremost, T'Chaka plants the largest seed of discontent by failing to embrace and bring home N'Jobu's son, especially since T'Chaka is partly responsible for making him an orphan in the same manner that Africans are partly responsible for the enslavement of their own people. Next, Nakia, T'Challa's former lover and one of Wakanda's global spies, already thinks that Wakanda should be doing more to help Africans dislocated and oppressed all over the planet.

Finally, W'Kabi is not pleased with the failure of T'Challa's father to capture and kill Ulysses Klaue. These three elements symbolize the manner in which current issues of differing ideologies and years of mistrust make it difficult for various organizations within the African community, such as Black Lives Matter, the Black Church, NAACP, the Urban League, My Brother's Keeper, National Action Network, and others, to combine their efforts in their struggle for local and global first-class citizenship. Each of these organizations have the necessary resources, manpower, and agenda to move African people forward, but the slightest difference in gender or class politics as well as strategic methodology makes it almost impossible for them to work jointly with any effort. Yet, T'Challa is able to recognize his father's failure and not repeat it in contrast to the many African and African-American leaders who have been unable to recognize the failings of Achebe's Okonkwo or the failings of current leaders and avoid the missteps of alienating the very people that they are trying to help, such as impoverished single mothers and young people who have sought solace in gangs.

T'Challa and Killmonger's clash should force African people to ask one simple question. How can African people either synergize their differing ideologies or learn to work separately in peace toward a common goal? Again, one of the best examples of this was the establishment of the COFO to manage the logistics of Freedom Summer and the Mississippi Freedom Democratic Party (MFDP), both of which eventually led to the passage of the 1965 Voting Rights Act. Yet, according to Boston Review critic Christopher Lebron, "Ryan Coogler makes viewers choose" one ideology over another:

> "...viewers have two radical imaginings in front of them: an immensely rich and flourishing advanced African nation that is sealed off from white colonialism and supremacy and a few black Wakandans with a vision of global black solidarity who are determined to use Wakanda's privilege to emancipate all black people. These imaginings could be

made to reconcile, but the movie's director and writer (with Joe Cole), Ryan Coogler, makes viewers choose...In the end, all comes down to a contest between T'Challa and Killmonger that can only be read one way: in a world marked by racism, a man of African nobility must fight his own blood relative whose goal is the global liberation of Blacks."

Similarly, Achebe's "Marriage Is a Private Affair" raises the question of Africans being able to draw well-defined lines in the sand that separate themselves from Blacks as well as whites. Achebe's short story asks for whom is marriage a private affair?—the bride and groom?—the family of the bride and groom?—the tribe of the bride and groom? Achebe explains that the law against marrying outside the tribe is created to prevent outsiders/colonizers from ever causing havoc again. When explaining the tribe elder Okeke battling to retain his way of life, he writes "It was a reenactment of that other struggle" (333). Like Okonkwo and T'Challa, Okeke is forced to realize that his decision to exclude certain African people for the good of his tribe may be something that he and his tribe might later regret. "Okeke was trying hard not to think of his two grandsons...How could he shut his door against them? By a curious mental process he imagined them standing, sad and forsaken, under the harsh angry weather—shut out from his house. That night he hardly slept, from remorse—and a vague fear that he might die without making it up to them" (333).

T'Challa is in the same position as Okeke and Okonkwo. But, unlike his father, T'Challa does not make the same mistakes as Okeke and Okonkwo. By the end of the film, T'Challa realizes the error of the binary notion of us versus them, which causes him to merge the traditional notions of Wakanda for Wakandans with the evolving notion of Wakanda being a blueprint and helpmate for rest of the African Diaspora. The man who states "I'm not King of all people; I'm King of Wakanda" evolves into the global leader who realizes that no one is free if anyone is enslaved. What Washington said about the union between whites and Blacks must be applied to the union of African peoples with differing liberation ideologies. "In all things that are purely social, we can be as separate as the fingers, yet one as the hand in all things essential to mutual progress" (151).

The point is not that African people clash over the best way to obtain liberation and first-class citizenship but that far too many African people do not accept that these types of clashes/disagreements are normal and that they do not mean that one person or organization must cease to exist for the other person or organization to achieve its ultimate goal. A differing ideology does not automatically make one an adversary or antagonist. Through T'Challa's evolution, viewers learn that duality and diversity in people and ideology is not a bad thing and can often be a productive development. This is often seen in that the Black Lives Matter Movement is generally a movement of various local and regional groups organizing under the banner of BLM to impact specific legal change. "A coalition of more than 60 organizations affiliated with the Black Lives Matter movement called for policing and criminal justice reforms in a list of demands released ahead of the second anniversary of the fatal shooting of Michael Brown in Ferguson, Missouri" (Whack).

Furthermore, one of the most powerful aspects of the film is that through the female characters it shows that beauty, intelligence, and power come in all forms and that only those who realize and respect this fact are able to help humanity evolve to its highest form. As Adam Serwer asserts, "it is Wakanda's women—Lupita Nyong'o's Nakia, Danai Gurira's General Okoye, Letitia Wright's Princess Shuri, Angela Bassett's Queen-Mother Ramonda—who sustain Wakanda through its darkest moments. Where T'Challa cannot survive or triumph without Okoye, Shuri, or Ramonda, Killmonger is alone. His African-American mother is absent from the story; Killmonger kills his own lover the moment her body stands between him and his ideological ambitions." If diversity is the calling card of humanity, then the women of *Black Panther* are the clearest example of what it means to be human. Being the most nuanced characters of the film, the women of Wakanda are not just examples of female diversity but of human diversity. Queen Ramonda is every bit the presence, power, and wisdom of the elder as her husband, T'Chaka. As a queen-mother figure, she is everything her people and her children need her to be. She can be the doting and encouraging mother when her son needs it, "Your father and I talked about this day [the day that T'Challa becomes king] often," as a way to comfort and refocus her son on the task at hand. She can be the disciplinarian who commands respect from her people and children with a glace or word, allowing "Shuri" to roll, lovingly yet firmly, off her tongue to remind her daughter to be respectful at all times. And, in the moment of battle, when all seems lost, she can be the spirit of the warrior as she yells to T'Challa, "Show him who you are!" which gives him the strength to overcome the challenge of M'Baku.

At the other end of the spectrum is Shuri who represents the wonder/curiosity, fearlessness, and hope for the future that youth provides. She is the opposite of the adage that youth is wasted on the young. Like her parents and brother, she is a whole being, both nerd and warrior—an intellectual warrior who can slay evil mentally or physically. Thus, she is often T'Challa's intellectual superior having constantly to remind him what progress truly is. "How many times, brother, must I teach you that just because something works well does not mean that it cannot be improved?" Yet, she is also allowed to be a child with a flippant mouth and a brash cockiness that has not been tempered by age. Who else but one's sister is able to mock and love her brother, the king, simultaneously? For all of her strengths, viewers love Shuri because she is a child whose dreams and confidence to achieve those dreams have not been crushed, limited, or perverted by the proverbial glass ceiling of white supremacy. Despite her intellectual prowess and her physical courage, her joy is her strength. When she smiles, laughs, and jokes, she is the sun emanating a ray of hope that "we gon' be alright." When she playfully gives the finger to her brother or mockingly calls CIA Agent Everett Ross "colonizer," viewers realize that she is metaphorically giving the finger to and mocking anyone who does not recognize the genius that she is.

Then, there is Nakia, the War Dog and spy who is the epitome of womanism. She outfights and outthinks any man, is defined by her own sensibilities, and is a highly successful professional woman who loves on her terms rather than by the terms of her male lover. When T'Challa attempts to rescue her, she holds her own and keeps him from mistakenly killing a captive that he thinks is a villain. And, she does this without super powers. In various aspects, the women of Wakanda share leadership roles because they are eminently more qualified for those positions, such as director of technology. In fact, with both Nakia and Okoye having male love interests and being, often, physically, emotionally, and intellectually stronger than their male counterparts, Black Panther is reintroducing womanism in a manner that presents African women, such as Kandake Amanirenas, Nandi (Mother of Shaka), She-Dong-Hong-Be, Amina of Zazzau, Nzinga Mbande, Harriet Tubman, Sojourner Truth, Ella Baker, Diane Nash, Fannie Lou Hamer, and many others, as the forerunners of the female liberation struggle while showing that demanding one's place as an equal is not tantamount to waging war on one's male counterpart. Therefore, viewers learn that the natural state of male and female energy is not to be at war with each other but to supplement and complement each other so that duality becomes holistic human existence, which can function to reduce domestic violence and sexist hiring and promotion practices while also adding even more brainpower to reduce ills, such as global warming, the growing amount of food deserts across the United States, and the absence of economic infrastructure in inner cities.

Finally, whiteness or, more specifically, white supremacy, is more of an umbrella than a driving factor of the film's plot. This does not mean that the film presents white supremacy as a non- or minimal factor in the lives of African people. Quite the contrary, the film simply posits that the best defense against white supremacy is a great offence or that being proactive is always more effective than being reactionary to white supremacy. Wakanda presents viewers with peoples who have developed such a positive sense of self because, of course, they have never been colonized. The weight of double consciousness or self-hatred does not impact, limit, or pervert their notion of who they are and what they can be. Because of this, they believe they have the ability and eventually arrive at the decision to help other African people liberate themselves from their psychological and physical oppressors and achieve the same level of full humanity. Even though, when presented with the notion of allowing non-Wakandans into Wakanda, W'Kabi warns that "You let in the refugees, you let in their problems," he still believes that Wakandans have the mental and physical ability to aid in the liberation of their global relatives from white supremacy. And, he is willing to travel across the globe to do so if his King will "just say the word." Later, W'Kabi declares, "The world is changing. Soon, there will only be the conquerors and the conquered. I'd rather be the former," asserting the need for Wakanda to be proactive in engaging white supremacy. Yet, the ultimate power and beauty of *Black Panther* is that it is a nuanced film. Not only does the film clearly show that might does not make right; it refuses to be sweeping or fatalistic in its engagement of white supremacy, providing the notion that even the colonizer can be redeemed. While "Ross's heroism in the film, even in a fantasy, [can feel] like a kind of [Americana] propaganda," as Serwer asserts, it also shows that for the planet to survive whites must find a way to overcome their own white supremacy by realizing that there is no way that they can remain safe from evil as they, themselves, perpetuate evil to colonize other lands. When Ross requests "put me back in" to the machine to complete his mission of not allowing Wakanda's weapons to leave the country, he, at that moment, is transcending his indoctrination and training of being an American [read white supremacist] operative and is becoming an example of Du Bois' global or cosmopolitan citizen. Yet, sadly, even after the most recent mass shootings in Florida and Nevada, a vast majority of white Americans still do not understand exactly what Elder Malcolm was stating when asserting that Kennedy's death was merely the "chickens coming home to roost." And, fifty years later, those chickens are still "coming home to roost" as the evil that white supremacy perpetuates unto people of color across the globe constantly returns to claim the lives of their own in mass shooting after mass shooting. For every unarmed black person killed by a police officer or every nation of color colonized by white invaders, thousands of white children and adults continue to die by the same weapons used against black bodies. But, the blinders of white supremacy cause many whites not to be able to act as Ross acts because they fail to realize that no citizen of the planet is safe as long as weapons of mass destruction are disseminated locally or globally merely for the purpose of continued colonization.

Ultimately, Black Panther is a story about what it means to be an evolved and complex human. The Black Panther, himself, is not a savior but a symbol for the manner in which people use their resources to become better beings. The Heart-Shaped Herb, then, is a metaphor for the manner in which people cultivate their minds, bodies, and spirits into tools that enable them to reach their potential. In this manner, N'Jobu and his son (N'Jadaka) are correct, as N'Jobu pleads with T'Chaka, "With vibranium weapons they can overthrow all countries, and Wakanda can rule them all, the right way!" After realizing the error of his father, T'Challa is able finally to hear Nakia, N'Jobu, and N'Jadaka with his heart and not merely with his head, synergizing his mind and heart to cultivate a plan of action that destroys a corrupt system to rebuild a just system. T'Challa's final actions show the difference between a revolutionary and a thug. Both the revolutionary and the thug destroy. However, a revolutionary destroys a corrupt system to rebuild a just system whereas a thug destroys merely for the sake of destruction with no plan of rebuilding anything constructive. After viewing the film, noted scholar Dr. Eddie Glaude posted on Facebook, "Just saw Black Panther. Really enjoyed the movie. Beautiful and powerful in so many ways. But there is a representation of the Black radical imagination in the film that I find disturbing. It is irrational and bitter (even if it is understandable)—a politics that can only lead to destruction. So, we're left with a vision of liberal humanism (the UN after all) shorn of white arrogance." While I completely understand Professor Glaude's assertion of how "Black radical imagination" is often portrayed, I would slightly differ on two points. One, the imaging of the black women in the film along with T'Challa's concession of his father's failure to embrace all African people must also be read as part of the "Black radical imagination." What is more radical than African people in 2018 embracing some form of Pan Africanism, even in baby steps? Additionally, I would ask Professor Glaude to have faith that the Black folks who see the film will be able to do as T'Challa eventually does—see and understand the essence of N'Jobu and his son's assertion of the need for Black folks to unify around a proactive plan even as they reject the aspect of violence being a necessity. After all, nuance is the core that defines African people. Even in this time of reality television and news production doing all that it can to distort the image of African peoples, the hope is that African peoples will see the nuances of the film and recognize those nuances within themselves to know that they have all that they need to be all that they desire to be.

WORKS CITED

Achebe, Chinua. Things Fall Apart. Anchor Press, 1994.

Achebe, Chinua. "Marriage Is a Private Affair." World Literature: An Anthology of Great Short Stories, Poetry, and Drama. Donna Rosenberg, ed. McGraw Hill Glencoe, 2004.

Alexander, Margaret Walker. This Is my Century: New and Collected Poems. University of Georgia Press, 1989.

Du Bois, W. E. B. The Souls of Black Folk. Bantam Books, 1989.

Fanon, Frantz. Wretched of the Earth. Grove Press, 1963.

Fanon, Frantz. Black Skin, White Masks. Grove Press, 2008.

Garvey, Marcus. "African for the Africans." The Norton Anthology of African American Literature. Gates and McKay, eds. W. W. Norton Company, 1997.

Glaude, Eddie S. "Just Saw Black Panther..." Facebook, 18 Feb 2018, 4:38 p.m., https://www.Facebook.com/eddie.s.glaude

Jealous, Ben. "Opening Comments at the NAACP Poetry Celebration of the Election of Barack Obama." Landsburg Theatre. Washington DC. January 18, 2009.

Lamar, Kendrick. "Alright." To Pimp a Butterfly. Top Dawn, 2015.

LeBron, Christopher. "Black Panther Is not the Movie We Deserve." Boston Review. net. February 17, 2018. http://bostonreview.net/race/christopher-lebron-black-panther. Accessed March 22, 2018.

Lewis, David Levering. W. E. B. Du Bois: The Fight for Equality and the American Century 1919–1963, Owl Books, 2001.

C. Liegh McInnis is an English instructor at Jackson State University, the former editor/ publisher of Black Magnolias Literary Journal, the author of eight books, including four collections of poetry, one collection of short fiction (Scripts: Sketches and Tales of Urban Mississippi), one work of literary criticism (*The Lyrics of Prince: A Literary Look at a Creative, Musical Poet, Philosopher, and Storyteller*), one co-authored work, *Brother Hollis: The Sankofa of a Movement Man*, which discusses the life of a legendary Mississippi Civil Rights icon, and the former First Runner-Up of the Amiri Baraka/Sonia Sanchez Poetry Award. His work has appeared in *The Southern Quarterly*, *Konch Magazine*, *Bum Rush the Page*, *Down to the Dark River: Anthology of Poems about the Mississippi River*, *Black Hollywood Unchained: Essays about Hollywood's Portrayal of African Americans*, *Black Gold: Anthology of Black Poetry*, *Sable*, *New Delta Review*, *Black World Today*, *In Motion Magazine*, *MultiCultural Review*, *A Deeper Shade*, *New Laurel Review*, *ChickenBones*, *Oxford American*, *Journal of Ethnic American Literature*, and *Red Ochre Lit*.

12

BLACK PANTHER:
REFLECTIONS ABOUT THE MOVIE
A Historical and Mystical Symbolism Phenomena
Aminifu R. Harvey, MSW, DSW
Harmony is the Union of Opposites

BLACK PANTHER PARTY FOR SELF-DEFENSE

I am not a Marvel comic book person nor a sci-fi person. In fact, I have never watched an entire episode of Star Wars or I think ever read a Marvel comic book—and I mean even as a child. But when I was aware of this movie with the title *Black Panther*, I became excited—mostly because of the title Black Panther, knowing that in 2016 the 50th year celebration of the Black Panther Party for Self-Defense founded by Huey P. Newton and Bobby G. Seale was celebrated. The Black Panther Party was founded in Oakland, California, and as I discovered once seeing the movie, there are a number of scenes that take place in Oakland. In particular, in the beginning of the movie when we see the young Eric Killmonger playing basketball on a court in Oakland. Then in one of the last scenes when T'Challa is in Oakland on the same basketball court telling his sister Shuri that he has purchased a number of buildings (including the one that his father King T'Chaka actually killed Killmonger's father in) to house various social programs.

Even though I was not a member of the Panther Party, I had some relationship with the Party and respected it for standing up for the rights of all people, especially Brothers and Sisters of African descent. I also respected them for being the forerunners of many social programs (is this not a reference to the Party in the movie) that the federal government adopted, such as the free breakfast program, legal assistance programs for the poor, and many programs for the elderly.

Even though there were differences between the ethnic groups in the movie, M'Baku (the leader of the Jabari who gets defeated by T'Challa in his bid to be King) comes to the aid of Wakanda when it came down to fighting Killmonger's forces, which included W'Kabi, T'Challa's friend. This is just like how the Panther Party had relationships with the Students for a Democratic Society (SDS), a predominately Caucasian organization, to rise up against the oppression by the government of poor and disenfranchised people.

WAKANDAN WOMEN

The Wakandan respected women and wanted them to play an important role in their culture. Examples are Okoye, General of the Dora Milaje, the all-female military, and Shuri, the STEM person and technological inventor. The color issue is interesting as all the women are of a darker shade, except for the Queen Mother—even the men are of a darker hue. The Mother in many African societies is known as the Queen Mother who has a final say in most tribal decisions, but always is highly respected by the society. Just as Queen Ramonda was in the movie.

The movie had some fine women of African descent, highlighting the darker shades of African women. In the past, mostly lighter skinned sisters got the parts. But even before this movie, we witnessed a change in movies, TV shows, etc. showing Black women of all shades of Blackness and sizes. All the women in the movie had their natural hair styles, from bald to crown rolls—so much symbolism. In the movie there is a scene in the hotel where Okoye is dressed in European clothing and wearing a wig. When the conflict starts she throws off the wig and clothes to prepare for the fight—transition and such symbolism, as African descent women should throw off their European-isms and be their natural African self.

African and African American cultures have a history of warrior women—whether physical fighters like Queen Yaa Asantewaa of the Ashanti people who lead her country's army to fight the British in the War of the Golden Stool, Queen Nzingha in Angola, the Dahomey female warriors, Queen Sarraounia of the Housa people who successfully fought the French in what is present day Niger, or Harriett Tubman who lead many kidnapped Africans out of slavery with firearms in her possession. Then we have the social activists like Ida B. Wells, Fannie Lou Hammer, and Judy Richardson of SNCC (read: Hands on the Freedom Plow) who risked their lives for liberation and freedom. The Black Panther Party had many women who were on the front line as fierce revolutionaries and in some key administrative positions. For example, Elaine Brown took the leadership position when Huey was sentenced to prison. Remember, at this time in the '60s modern-day feminist and womenist's rights are just emerging. The Black Panthers are setting the tone for the involvement of women in society, just as the UNIA (did you appreciate all the red, black, and green) did when Amy Garvey devoted an entire section of Black World to Black Women in the '20s, '30s, and '40s.

AFROCENTRISM – AFRO-FUTURISM

Key features in the movie is the respect for the Ancestors, Ancestor veneration, and the ability to communicate with the Ancestors, as T'Challa did when he actually goes into the Ancestral realm to speak with his father. What does this remind me of? It reminds me of the concept of transition. We see this concept it the Judeo-Christian world and in Ancient Kemet. In the Judeo-Christian belief system Jesus Christ is crucified and the two Marys—one being his mother and the other Mary Magdalene, a follower of Jesus—prepare Christ's body for "burial." They later find him gone as he has gone into the heavenly realm to speak with his Father. He then returns to earth and is greeted by the two women. In the Kemetian version—25,000 to 5,000 years before the Christ story—there is Osiris the King, Isis the Queen, and Horus the son. Set is the brother of Osiris who kills him (Eric is the 1st cousin who wants to be King and "kills" T'Challa). Set cuts Osiris' body up into 16 parts and it is Isis the Queen Mother who gathers up all his parts for him to live again.

In the movie it is the women, Shuri the sister, Queen Mother, Ramonda, and T'Challa's girlfriend Nakia, who is a spy in the unit called War Dog, that find him being preserved in ice with M'Baku of the Jabari tribe. It is at this point that T'Challa goes into the underworld to meet with his Father T'Chaka, who then tells him how he killed Eric's father (T'Chaka's brother and T'Challa's uncle) and then abandoned Killmonger (he is family we never abandon our own). A key African philosophical principle is inclusiveness and compassion, demonstrated when T'Challa fights with Killmonger again. He then understands why Killmonger is acting like he is and forgives him. Killmonger refuses the compassion and makes a historical statement: saying he would rather die like his ancestors, who jumped overboard from the kidnapped African ships, than live in prison.

Another Africanism is the use of African masks—one wears the masks in fighting to take on the energy of the animal the masks represents and to impart to the fighter its strengthens, skills, strategies, and tactics. I am watching the movie and hear T'Chaka, oh, Shaka Zulu the military genius. Okay, now we know where all the military alignments in the movie come from. Remember in Kemet the Pharaohs were laid to rest with folded crossed arms just like the Wakandan salute. Thanks to producer Ryan Coogler for bringing African philosophy and cultural history to the screen. This is a true Afrocentric movie, ostensibly and in its esoteric and mystical aspects.

Let me put some parameters around this concept of Afrocentrism. I am suggesting there are four critical frameworks of Afrocentrism: the comparison of Euro-centric and Afrocentric World Views, by Vernon Dixon; the Nguzo Saba, by Maulana Karenga; the Seven Virtues of MA'AT (see Hunter Adams III); and The 42 Confessions Coming Forth by Light (there are many names, all begin with 42 Confessions) from traditional African culture, 2,500 to 5,000 years before Christ. I will take a principle of each one and provide an example from the movie.

- Afrocentric worldview, axiology (the focus on human relationships): Okoye and W'Kabi have a romantic relationship but take different sides during the war, yet they choose to keep the relationship rather than fight each other.
- Nguzo Saba – Kujichagulia (Self-Determination): The entire movie concerns itself with the Wakandans deciding for themselves how they will or will not interact with the world.
- Seven Virtues – Justice: This is demonstrated when T'Challa decides to fight to return Wakanda back to its original society before Killmonger makes it a dictatorship and oppressive society.
- 42 Confessions – I have not caused terror: When Killmonger becomes king he rules through terror which causes T'Challa to rise up and fight Killmonger.
- As an exercise you might do the latter for each principle of each framework.

LAST REFLECTION

I hope that after all the African clothes are worn for the first time and all the djembe drums are played and all the dances are danced that all people no matter their ethnicity, race, creed or color will explore the world of Africa, its rich history, rituals, customs, and philosophy and its influence on the history of Africans in the Americas.

Olodumare, Olorun, the Orishas, and the Ancestors Bless Us

P.S.

I know I did not mention colonialism. My friend said that Wakanda was fantasy and of course movies are fantasy but Wakanda having never been colonized is based on a historical fact, as Ethiopia is the only country in Africa to never have been colonized.

Special Thanks to Mama Makini and Steve Fountain for their input and other persons whom I spoke with in regards to the movie. Thanks also to Assata Lee for her editing assistance.

Dr. Aminifu Richard Harvey is a retired tenured Professor of Social Work from Fayetteville State University. Dr. Harvey was an associate and assistant professor at the School of Social Work, University of Maryland Baltimore and also a tenured Associate Professor of Social Work at Chico State. From June of 1986 until July of 1997, Dr. Harvey served as the Executive Director of the MAAT Center for Human and Organizational Enhancement, Inc. Dr. Harvey founded the MAAT Center to provide culturally competent services to African American families and youth. Dr Harvey was a practicing clinician for over 25 years; he is the key pioneer in developing and implementing an Afrocentric approach to psychotherapy and social service delivery systems. He has been a licensed independent clinical social worker; a member of The Academy of Certified Social Workers, and was listed in the National Association of Social Workers' Register of Clinical Social Workers, a Diplomat of Clinical Social Work, a certified hypnotherapist, a practitioner of neurolinguistic programming and has served as a consulting editor to the journal: Social Work.

Dr. Harvey has authored numerous professional articles. He most recently authored an article for the publication: Not Our President: New Directions from the Pushed Out, the Others and the Clear Majority in Trump's Stolen America. Dr. Aminifu R. Harvey's Reader of Afri-Centric Theory and Practice: Philosophical and Humanistic Writings of Aminifu R. Harvey was published in April of 2018.

Dr. Harvey was one of 14 professors chosen by the University of North Carolina Higher Education System to be a member of the Board's UNC Tomorrow Commission. The commission's role was to assist in determining the role of the University System for the next 20 years in funding the universities and colleges in its system. He also served as a member of the Disproportionate Minority Contract Subcommittee of the North Carolina Department of Crime and Public Safety. He is the recipient of numerous awards, such as the First Howard University School of Social Work Alumni Association's Outstanding Social Worker and Maryland Chapter of the National Association of Social Workers' Educator of the Year (2004).

13
BLACK PANTHER: VIEW FROM THE COMICBOOK GEEK DEN
Todd Steven Burroughs

"The Black Panther is loose!" Imhotep Gary Byrd proclaimed live in February 2018 on 107.5 WBLS-FM/1190 WLIB-AM. For the uninitiated, he is a Black radio legend who broadcasts simultaneously on two legendary (and, unfortunately, now formerly Black-owned) New York City radio institutions. This writer had the honor of being on Express Yourself, the latest incarnation of his Gary Byrd/Global Black Experience radio program that will celebrate its 50th anniversary next year. The other guest discussing Black Panther was a former DC comicbook staffer.

Loose indeed. Somehow, a comicbook character created by two white Jewish men during the beginning of the African independence movement and the height of the Civil Rights Movement and re-created and screened by Disney in the Trump era, had done something improbable: it hijacked Black History/African Heritage Month, for decades a sacred space for real Black heroes and real African connections. Somehow, the *Roots* phenomenon from my television-obsessed childhood had returned, but this time, it was designed for, and by, the San Diego Comic-Con crowd. In rapid response mode to the release of Black Panther, Hoteps around the country began to immediately jump on the bandwagon, quickly brushing up online on T'Challa, Shuri and Wakanda.

This geek writer—one on Marvel's bandwagon for at least 35 years, waaayyy before it was cool in the Black community—turned out to be tuned into the right place on the world pop-culture dial at the right time. This writer's book tour was in full force for Marvel's *Black Panther: A Comic Book Biography, From Stan Lee to Ta-Nehisi Coates* (Diasporic Africa Press), a collection of chronological thoughts about the 52 years this character has existed.

The first in-depth textual study of the first Black superhero to appear in American mainstream comics, the book is a group of chronological essays—a critical "biography" of a comicbook character—exploring what this writer thinks about how this Black/African hero character has been shaped: first by white liberal American men—Stan Lee, Jack Kirby, Roy Thomas and Don McGregor—then by a Black American liberal man, Christopher J. Priest, and even later by American neo-Black-nationalists Reginald Hudlin and Ta-Nehisi Coates.

Marvel's *Black Panther* is about race, mainstream superhero comics and the Black American imagination within the backdrop of American history and world history. It's about the limitations of white liberalism and the power of Black-centered but white-controlled American popular culture; ultimately, it's how 20th century white liberalism had to yield to the 21st century multicultural reality.

A new addition to the growing scholarly literature on the growing literature on Black American comic books, it shows how Black writers helped the African world get to the place where Byrd, a cultural hero himself in communications, would discuss this fictional film hero on New York Black-oriented AM/FM radio. It shows the character's growth under Priest, Hudlin and Coates, writers who understood what the entire world knows now, with more than $1 billion in movie tickets spent: that The *Black Panther* was at least as cool as *Batman*.

This triumph of Black comicbook cool was not always so. When Marvel's (white) writers took over Panther after he first appeared in Lee/Kirby's The *Fantastic Four* in 1966, he became significantly watered-down: he went from being Lee/Kirby's super-powered Patrice Lumumba to Roy Thomas' circa 1967 Sidney Poitier-type to McGregor's universal commentary on human endurance in a paradise filled with metaphorical and literal serpents. After 32 years of this (1966 to 1998), Black writers took over the character. Both Priest and Hudlin turned Panther, a character known primarily for leaping around, into a literal Dark Knight; thanks to them, Marvel finally had a character that imitated and matched Batman's powerful, brawn-meets-tech aura. Priest brought him back to his first, dangerous Lee-Kirby Fantastic Four appearance, and Hudlin then followed up by bringing him out of the comicbook store into the larger 21st century Black popular-culture world on unapologetic Black, hiphop/James Bond-swagger-flavored terms. (Hudlin's Black Panther animated miniseries in 2010, based on his first Marvel storyarc, Who Is The Black Panther, is required online viewing, particularly for those who consider themselves Pan-Africanists and cultivators of decolonized minds.) The character now properly established, Coates put T'Challa in the complex world of 21st century African domestic politics. By letting the Black writers control T'Challa, Marvel now had the Batman-like character it had long wanted, and Black comicbook readers, Afrofuturists and Black fantasy-lovers had essentially a brand-new, culturally-relevant version of an established Marvel superhero.

Thanks to Priest, Hudlin and Coates, one of Marvel's greatest Hollywood blockbuster film superheroes in 2016, 2018 and beyond is an unapologetic Black Cat. But how much of their Panther made it into the 2018 *Black Panther* film?

Comicbook superhero movies are, for the most part, not direct adaptations as much as they are original stories that use freely the voluminous source material. The goal of a great superhero comicbook movie is to encapsulate the best of the character and his or her environment and mythos in one complete, accessible story at a time.

Black Panther was far from the exception. The Bond-flavored plot (which Hudlin had to like), starring Chadwick Boseman (sounding reminiscent of a young Nelson Mandela), combined several decades of story ideas, items and dialogue from the comics, from Panther's vibranium-weave suit and foot soles (Priest), to the Wakandan Tribal Council (Priest and

Hudlin), to the open tribal challenge for the Panther religious rank and leadership of the kingdom of Wakanda (mostly Hudlin), to T'Chaka's line of "it's hard for a good man to be king (Coates)." Some/what organized thoughts:

Erik Killmonger (McGregor): Pan-Africanism's newest symbolic hero was created in 1973 by a young white man, Donald McGregor. In the comics, he and Priest portrayed the film's "villain" as a more calculating, sophisticated character who would never have burned the garden of the heart-shaped herb and physically threatened the tribeswoman who pleaded for him to reconsider. One of my favorite Priest plots had Killmonger attempt to defeat T'Challa using national economics.

Nakia (Priest): A complete revision. She went from being a rebellious, teenage Dora Milaje to a grown-up, much-centered spy. Her one-on-one conversations with T'Challa remind longtime Panther comicbook readers of T'Challa's intimacies with Monica Lynne, an African-American woman created by Thomas and shaped by McGregor into the love of T'Challa's life.

Dora Milaje: Priest and Hudlin should take equal credit on this one. Under Priest, there were only two: Nakia and Okoye, two young women chosen from different Wakanda tribes as T'Challa's wives-in-training to keep tribal peace. Under Hudlin, the Dora became the royal guard in Black Panther.

Ulysses Klaue (Klaw): a Lee/Kirby character, it was actually Hudlin's version Marvel Films used—the South African mercenary with the transforming hand. Klaw is notoriously hard to kill in the comics, so seeing Killmonger kill him outright and drag his body onto Wakandan soil was deeply satisfying.

Shuri: Created by Hudlin to be T'Challa's jealous little sister, the complete makeover Marvel did—turning her into Wakanda's equivalent of James Bond's "Q"—was a masterstroke. This writer would not be surprised if Hudlin is reminding Marvel Studios that, down the road a ways, Shuri becomes The Black Panther! Marvel, who just re-released the trade paperback of that story as this is being written, definitely remembers.

W'Kabi: Created by Thomas, the relationship the two had in the flick's beginning, particularly that first personal conversation about T'Challa's relationship with Nakia, is pure McGregor. Interestingly enough, the film takes T'Challa's Panther origin and gives it to W'Kabi: in the comics, Klaw invades Wakanda and kills T'Chaka.

M'Baku: The character fanboys and fangirls call Man-Ape, created by Thomas, arguably got the greatest makeover here. Turning a comicbook character who hates T'Challa into the film's unofficial hero was genius.

Everett K. Ross: The most unpopular character for Panther's Black filmgoers was created by Priest in order to make sure white comicbook fans would buy the book. Placing him on film in the same type of role as Lando Calrissian in the classic *Star Wars: Return of the Jedi* doesn't seem like too bad an idea, until it is realized that Ross is much more important to Panther's plot than Calrissian was to Jedis'! In the film, Ross seems to also take over the role of Taku (McGregor), T'Challa's communications officer created for/in the comics by McGregor. It's a crime Taku was not in the film: how could such an advanced society and its rulers depend on the CIA (!) for critical intel? It was difficult for the Black filmmakers, led by director and co-writer Ryan Coogler, to justify the existence of Ross, and they clearly did the best they could.

This film happened because Marvel Studios understood it had a largely untapped world film audience to convert to geekdom, and that, during/after the election of a U.S. president of direct African descent followed by the election of a white nationalist president, The Lion King was no longer sufficient for the African imagination. Marvel understood it had a character that its Black writers showed could rival any superhero's charisma and presence if done right (the way the Priest, Hudlin and Coates had done, literally, on paper). So, *Captain America: Civil War* in 2016, and *Black Panther* and *Avengers: Infinity War* in 2018: three major-studio, blockbuster films featuring The Panther in as many years. This phenomenon happened because Disney, the unrivaled master of children's imagination around the globe, had a clear understanding of the human psychology of oppressed people.

So *Black Panther* has become, if Byrd can forgive this writer, a Global Black Experience. Regardless of the anti-Pan Africanist politics of this film, *Tarzan* has been killed (permanently?) by vibranium weapons, African women are—at last—publicly seen and acknowledged as the superheroes they always were and still are, running into danger to save African men from themselves, and Wakanda is now undeniably Forever.

Todd Steven Burroughs, Ph.D., is the author of Marvel's Black Panther: A Comic Book Biography, From Stan Lee to Ta-Nehisi Coates, and Warrior Princess: A People's Biography of Ida B. Wells, both published by Diasporic Africa Press. Greg Carr wrote the Afterword to Marvel's Black Panther. Burroughs is an independent researcher and writer based in Newark, N.J. He has taught at Howard University, the nation's top historically Black university, in Washington, D.C., and Morgan State University, Maryland's top historically Black college, in Baltimore, Maryland. A professional journalist since 1985, he has written for The Source, ColorLines, Black Issues Book Review and The Crisis magazines, websites such as BlackAmericaWeb.com and TheRoot.com and newspapers such as The New York Amsterdam News, the New Jersey edition of The Afro-American newspaper chain and The (Newark, N.J.) Star-Ledger, New Jersey's largest newspaper. He served as an editor, contributing columnist and national correspondent for the NNPA News Service (nnpa.org; BlackPressUSA.com), the nation's only newswire for Black newspapers. Burroughs, a Ph.D. in Communication from the University of Maryland's Philip Merrill College of Journalism, is a lifelong student of the history of Black media. His audiobook, Son-Shine On Cracked Sidewalks, deals with the 2014 mayoral election of Ras Baraka, the son of the late activist and writer Amiri Baraka, in Newark, N.J. The co-author with Herb Boyd of Civil Rights: Yesterday and Today and co-editor, with Jared A. Ball, full professor and faculty member of the Institute of Urban Research at Morgan State University, of A Lie of Reinvention: Correcting Manning Marable's Malcolm X, he is currently co-writing a book, with Wayne J. Dawkins, an associate professor of Morgan State's School of Journalism and Communication, on Freedomways magazine.

14

AN ECONOMIC ANALYSIS OF BLACK PANTHER:
Separating Myth from Reality
Patrick Delices

INTRODUCTION

There is nothing new about mythologizing and lionizing a big cat as an influential political and cultural symbol of beauty, grace, agility, valor, power and protection. As a matter of fact, regarding these majestically powerful and sacred big cats, the ancient Egyptians are known for such veneration, mythmaking, and symbolism. In ancient Egypt (Kmt), the black panther was frequently presented to gods as a valuable political and cultural offering where ancient Egyptian priests would also be draped with the skin of the black panther. In the Egyptian Book of the Dead (the *Book of Coming Forth by Day*), to enter heaven, Pharaoh Pepi wears the skin of the black panther. Even prior to Pharaoh Pepi, during the First Dynasty of Egypt, Mafdet (Maftet), the first big cat goddess, was often depicted as a leopard/panther and was revered as the protector of the Egyptian sun-god Ra along with sacred places, such as the pharaoh's chambers and ultimately, Wakanda and the world in the form of Black Panther.

As the protector of the universe, the big cats known as black panthers are highly melaninated leopards in Africa known as Panthera pardus. Indistinguishably however, today like ancient times, many of us continue to mythologize and view the black panther as a puissant political and cultural symbol as illustrated in the military (the Black Panthers of the 761st Tank Battalion of the United Sates Army), professional sports team (Carolina Panthers), political parties (the Black Party Panther), insignias, coats of arms, books (C.F. Lascelles Wraxal's 1864 novel *The Black Panther: A Boy's Adventures Among the Redskins*), comic books (*Fantastic Four* #52, the first appearance of Marvel's *Black Panther*, July 1966) and movies (*Captain America Civil War* and The *Black Panther*).

Similar to ancient African deities, many comic book heroes, such as the *Black Panther*, can find their mythical and symbolic origins in Africa. As a matter of fact, the term hero is said to be derived from the ancient Egyptian mythical savior god Heru (Horus). However, an overreliance on myths and symbols, can impair our ability to seek and accept the truth, deal with reality, and analyze and solve problems. According to preeminent scholar Cheikh Anta

Diop's protégé, the public intellectual Edgar J. Ridley:

A thoroughgoing, careful reading of history tells us that it is only when we are not able to face the realities of life that we tend to mythologize and distort anything and everything that we do not want to be true. Symbols produce myths, superstition, and ritual, and these elements cannot be allowed to stand if we are to progress as a people. Nothing makes sense when it is carried out from a mythological point of view and when it is acted out symbolically. This is the dividing line between civilization and barbarism. We have to make the choice to live either symbolically (which is to live a mythical existence) or to live symptomatically (which means to live in a state of ultimate reality). We must face issues as they really are in their ultimate state. We must stop mythologizing to avoid dealing with reality and truth in any given situation. Quite to the contrary of many psychologists and psychiatrists, mythologizing events and things is tantamount to the most severe cases of mental illness. If we lived in a society in which we tackled problems honestly, without the excess baggage of our phobias and neuroses, the mythologizing of events could be prevented.

The hero/movie *Black Panther* is a fictional, mythological albeit influential political and cultural symbolic phenomenon, but a critical analysis of the economics of Black Panther separates key facts from fiction. Black Panther is not only a fictional Marvel Comic "superhero," (one can also argue that his cousin and adversary, Erik Killmonger is the true superhero), but as a realist, the movie *Black Panther* represents a veridical enduring and elastic economic system known as capitalism which must be analyzed despite its political and cultural symbolisms. Hence, economics is the primary matter that determines the infrastructure of a sovereign people and nation; whereas, politics and culture determines the superstructure of a sovereign people and nation. Without economics, there is no politics (the governance, management, structure, and development of humankind based on rules, regulations, and laws regarding our land, labor, and resources) and culture (the collective manifestations of human identity that governs our intellectual and emotional activities). Yet, the collective human manifestations that govern our intellectual and emotional activities seem to be mythology (idealism) and symbolism not realism nor symptomatic or critical analysis of economics.

Therefore, in lieu of advancing political and cultural mythmaking and symbolism, the aim of this essay is to provide an analysis of the movie *Black Panther* by surveying it critically in terms of the first and foremost infrastructure of any human system: economics, which is directly linked with land, labor and resources. However, given the broadness and depth of economics as an academic discipline, this essay will be notable for its brevity and incisiveness as it will mainly discuss the economics of land, labor, and resources in relation to Marvel/ Disney's *Black Panther*.

AN ECONOMIC ANALYSIS OF BLACK PANTHER

At its core, economics deals with the systematic and scientific production, distribution, and consumption of raw materials, agricultural products, and useful, valuable, and inanimate resources, such as time, water, air, and information (knowledge). Economics is therefore associated with land, labor, and resources, not necessary money; even though this "Marvel/ Disney film earned an astounding $652.5 million at the U.S. box office and more than $1.2 billion worldwide." Thus, making it "the fourth highest grossing domestic film of all time" behind "Avatar, Titanic, and Star Wars: The Force Awakens" as it earns the title of "the top grossing superhero film of all time."

In terms of global measurement, it must be noted disturbingly that the earnings for the movie Black Panther amazingly surpass the Gross Domestic Product (GDP), which is basically a nation's economic health and size based on the total dollar value, of four African countries:

1. Guinea-Bissau at $1,126 billion;
2. The Gambia at $964.6 billion;
3. Comoros at $616.7 billion;
4. São Tomé and Príncipe at $ 351.1 billion.

Unfortunately, at a global level, the money spent patronizing this Marvel/Disney film could have jumpstarted the economies of the above-mentioned African nations by way of foreign capital investment, but Wakanda forever and Africa never seems to be the clarion call and reality of our financial economic constitution and apportion. In addition, the money spent watching *Black Panther* could have created schools, hospitals, banks, businesses, and employment opportunities for Black America given our high unemployment, low income earnings, and poverty level.

According to Claud Anderson of the Harvest Institute, "the poverty level for Blacks is three times that of whites and Hispanics. Nearly one-third of Blacks are classified as poor. And 50 percent of all single, Black female heads of household are poverty stricken." Furthermore, "as far back as 1790, the richest 10 percent of white households has held half of the nation's wealth. By the eve of the Civil War, one percent of the wealthiest whites owned 24 percent of the nation's wealth. One hundred years later, in 1969, they owned 24.9 percent." Hence, journalist Tracy Jan of the *Washington Post* reports that "white families have nearly 10 times the net worth of Black families. And the gap is growing."

In patronizing the movie *Black Panther*, we support and enrich the multinational corporation known as Disney, which was exposed in 2011 to be involved in sweatshops and child labor, especially in Haiti. Haiti is recognized as the first and only successful slave revolution in the world and the first Black republic in the Western Hemisphere, but it is also recognized as the poorest country in the Americas due to western exploitation and oppression. In regard to Disney's exploitation of Haitian labor, the Institute for Global Labour and Human Rights asserts the following:

For their labor, the workers are in many cases paid as little as 15 gourdes per day, or 12 cents per hour. This is well below the legal minimum wage of 30 cents per hour based on the daily rate of 36 gourdes (US $2.40). The workers are paid on a piece-rate system, and production quotas are raised to the point where the majority of workers have no hope of meeting them. One experienced worker we spoke to, for instance, is supposed to sew seams on 204 pairs of Mickey Mouse pajamas in a day, for which she would be paid 40 gourdes (US $2.67); in 8 hours, however, she is only able to complete 144 pairs, for which she is paid 28 gourdes (US $1.87). In Creole, this system is referred to as "sa ou fè, se li ou we," or, roughly translated, "what you do is what you get."

Moreover, in Haiti, "the Gross National Income per capita (at Purchase Power Parity) is $1730," where "59% of the population lives on less than US$2 per day." Yet, with all the capital being generated by Disney as illustrated in the total gross earnings of the movie *Black Panther*, Disney has yet to repair the financial damages done to Haiti and its workers. Equal as important, Black America along with the rest of the world has yet to demand for Disney to payback Haiti and its workers because we want to see a mythical Black superhero on the big screen at all cost even if it hurts us financially in the long run. Thus, financially, don't be euchred by Mickey Mouse or Black Panther - let us not finance our own oppression by enriching a multinational corporation that exploits our land, labor, and resources, while oppressing our people.

In 2009, the Walt Disney Company paid cash and stocks to purchase Marvel Entertainment for $4.24 billion with its comic book publisher and movie studio along with its 5,000 characters. By 2017, Disney as a multinational media conglomerate netted assets worth $95.79 billion. The CEO of Disney, Robert A. Iger, who earns a $30 million annual salary is worth $100 million, while the co-founder, president, and chairman of Marvel Comics, Stan Lee is worth $50 million. This is the same Stan Lee in co-creating the *Black Panther* with Jack Kirby, found it fitting to feature *Black Panther* in its first series of Marvel's *Jungle Action*, which is the offspring of Atlas Comics' *Jungle Tales* that featured Prince Waku of the Bantu as Marvel's first African superhero. Nonetheless, regarding the African jungle myth, prominent Guyanese scholar Ivan Van Sertima states the following:

> The United States reports Africa has less jungle than any other continent comparable with its land space. By that has meant Africa has less jungle than South America. Africa has less jungle in terms of land space, comparable land space, than two Europes which would be the comparable land space of Africa. But we get all this fascination about 'the African is related to the jungle, he is a man of nature.' There are no men of nature. Man jumps out of nature. Man takes nature and shapes it. Man makes things. He has always, from the beginning that is the beginning of science.

In terms of land, the main setting for the movie *Black Panther* is the continent of Africa in a place designated as Wakanda which is located somewhere in East Africa girthing the nations of Ethiopia, Kenya, Sudan (South Sudan to be exact), and Uganda. According to Van Sertima, the word Africa, actually Afruika, is an African word meaning beginnings. However, given the vastness and diversity of the continent of Africa in terms of landmass, people, and languages, Van Sertima does not pinpoint exactly where in Africa or from whom or in what language does the word Afruika and its meaning derived. Despite Africa's vastness and diversity, for Van Sertima and his intellectual mentor, the great scholar Cheikh Anta Diop, there is a cultural unity of African people and languages.

Interestingly, the fictitious nation/country known as Wakanda is located in East Africa, where humanity had its beginnings in the areas designated as the Great Lakes Region or the Great Rift Valley (Ethiopia, Kenya, Tanzania, and Uganda). Still, others have proclaimed that South Africa is where humanity commenced. The term Wakanda(s) is described as a mythical African group in 1915 by Edgar Rice Burroughs in his book of fiction, *The Man-Eater;* even though, in reality the Wakamba (Akamba or Kamba) group are a Bantu people from Kenya – the same Bantu people of the fictional Waku, Prince of the Bantu who predated Marvel's *Black Panther* by over a decade. However, the word Wakamba (kanda meaning family in the Bantu language of Kikongo) is a people/word not only found on the African continent, but it is also found in the Americas.

For the Native peoples known as the Kansa, Omaha, Osage, and Ponka, the word Wakanda (Wah'Kon'Tah and/or Wak-an-da) is a term meaning God and/or place for the Gods or the country of god/life (beginnings). Even in Paraguay within the African-Paraguayan community, there is the Kamba people who are descendants of the Wakamba group from Kenya. They arrived in Paraguay by 1820 with the exile revolutionary leader General Jose Gervasio Arigas of Uruguay as a regiment of 250 spearmen/women.

The massive, majestic landmass known as Africa is not only the birthplace of humanity and the cradle of civilization, it is also the wealthiest continent in terms of its abundant natural resources (sugar, salt, cocoa, coffee, etc.), valuable minerals (gold, silver, iron, cooper, uranium, bauxite, coltan, cobalt, etc.) and commodities (natural gas, oil, petroleum, timber, etc.). Thus, given its massive wealth in terms of land, labor, and resources, Africa and Africans became the victims of European and U.S. American encroachment via slavery, colonialism, imperialism, and trade liberalization (free trade).

In his canonical, highbrow text, *Capitalism and Slavery*, illustrious lawyer and scholar Eric Williams, the first Prime Minister of Trinidad and Tobago argues that it was African land, labor, and resources (economics) not politics and culture that industrialized Europe, particularly Great Britain as seen in the Industrial Revolution via slavery, colonialism, and capitalism. In concert with the reasoning of Williams, the distinguished Guyanese scholar Walter Rodney advances Williams' thesis by stressing the fact that the land, labor and resources of Africa not only developed the European-American world and underdeveloped Africa, but it also moved Europe and the United States from the Industrial Age to the Nuclear Age. In his classic scholarly text, How Europe Underdeveloped Africa, Rodney propounds the following point:

African minerals played a decisive role both with regard to conventional weapons and with regard to the breakthrough to atomic and nuclear weapons. It was from the Belgian Congo during the Second World War that the U.S.A began getting uranium that was a prerequisite to the making of the first atomic bomb. In any case, by the end of the colonial period, industry and the war machine in the colonizing nations had become so intertwined and inseparable that any contribution to one was a contribution to the other. Therefore, Africa's massive contribution to what initially appears as peaceful pursuits such as making of copper wire and steel alloys ultimately took the shape of explosive devices, aircraft carriers, and so on.

The above economic realities not myths as voiced by Williams and Rodney are the factors that urged Erik Killmonger's quest to utilize the resources in Wakanda, particularly vibranium to end global exploitation and oppression and to enrich and empower Africans at home and abroad. Despite the non-isolationist policy of Prince N'Jobu (Killmonger's father/ T'Challa's uncle), Killmonger and Nakia (King T'Challa's inamorata) along with Wakanda's indestructible vibranium, Wakanda remained isolationist as it practiced non-interventionism and isolationism while fighting other African groups and remaining silent as other people of African descendant suffer the wrath of global white supremacy.

In terms of economics, Wakanda's non-intervention and isolationist stance is actually a form of protectionism. However, protectionism is only used by young (newly, formed or developing) nations to protect and develop its infant industries. Once that nation is fully developed and its infant industries are now fully matured, that country not only adopts trade liberalization, but it also encourages (forces) other weaker nations that are trying to develop their infant industries. More than often these countries, under pressure, forego protectionism for free trade as seen with western economic hitmen and displayed by United States trade relations with Latin America, the Caribbean, and Africa. Therefore, for Latin America, the Caribbean, and Africa to really take-off (develop), foreign aid and free trade liberalism must be avoided in favor of protectionism and institutional building.

For economic growth in Latin America, the Caribbean, and Africa and against the backdrop of "good governance," prominent South Korean economist Ha-Joon Chang of Cambridge University proposes "quick-footed policies," activist/interventionist industrial, trade, and technology (ITT), and the promotional and protection of higher value-added activities to promote infant industries like the United States and other European countries did during their early stages of their development. However, in most countries in Latin America, the Caribbean, and Africa, given the political climate, institutional building is challenging and "quick-footed policy" is difficult to implement.

Ultimately, to take off, these countries must adopt an economic policy that taps into remittances; unlocks laden resources; adopts a market based economic policy; manages their commodity prices; exports more than imports; encourages domestic savings by way of financial investments, micro-finance lending, and allocating their credit; rejects harmful long-term conditional foreign aid and loans; pays their debts or requests a debt/loan forgiveness; demands reparations; fosters good governance and accountability; invests in human capital and infrastructure development; and seeks and develops strong relationship with other foreign investors, especially with stronger nations in Africa, Asia, Latin America, and the Caribbean. Most importantly though, is that these nations cannot take off unless the de-colonization of power, knowledge, and being are preconditions for that take-off.

Globally, regarding international trade, the fictional nation of Wakanda does not need to practice protectionism because it has a comparative advantage given its wealth, development, superior technology, formable military, monopoly on the valuable resource vibranium, and the maturity of its infant industries. In reality, most of Africa, Latin America, and the Caribbean cannot yet properly manage all of its resources and expected revenues from international trade due to the unequal balance of trade (trade imbalance) and other constraints as the economic prosperity of Europe, the United States, and China depend heavily on Africa's natural resources, valuable minerals, and commodities. As such, the cobalt, coltan, and tantalum from the DRC in addition to the cobalt in South Africa fueled the Digital Revolution which enriched and empowered other nations and people; while, for the most part, African nations and people worldwide remain impoverished and disempowered.

The gold from Ghana, Ethiopia, Zimbabwe, and the Democratic Republic of the Congo (DRC) in addition to the gold and diamonds in South Africa feeds the economy of the world and the luxury market at a global scale. South Africa's petroleum and uranium in addition to the oil from Nigeria, Angola, and the Sudan feed the world's energy market. Ethiopia's natural gas and platinum in addition to coal from Malawi serve as the world's appetite for energy. The copper from Ethiopia, South Africa, and Zambia, along with the DRC and South Africa's iron ore contribute immensely to the world's transportation, railway (electronic) technology, and modern-day skyscrapers networks of supertall and megatall buildings. Without Africa's land, labor, and resources, China would not have the most skyscrapers in the world with 943 and the United States, second to China, would not have 668 skyscrapers. The entire continent of Africa has only three modern-day skyscrapers which are all located in South Africa. At least, we still have our pyramids in Egypt and other parts of Africa, which by the way, were conceived and constructed by Africans not aliens or any other people.

In the movie *Black Panther*, Wakanda's splendor is attributed to a key resource, vibranium which is not of African origin, but of alien radix. Hence, giving agency to an alien force not African initiative and ingenuity similarly to the building of the pyramids. In the *African Origin of African Civilization: Myth or Reality*, Diop identifies this mythmaking political and cultural phenomenon as the "Modern Falsification of History." Eminent psychologist Amos N. Wilson, in his must-read text, *The Falsification of African Consciousness: Eurocentric History, Psychiatry and the Politics of White Supremacy*, associates this type of belief and acceptance of historical mythmaking with disorder, hallucination, oppression, and psychological slavery. In economics, mythmaking could be equivalent to information asymmetry.

Information (knowledge) is an inanimate, but valuable resource. Similarly, to mythmaking, information asymmetry allows a buyer who knows that the product that he or she is selling is defective. The seller nonetheless markets that defective product as adequate to the buyer. The buyer has no knowledge (information) that the product that he or she is about to buy is defective because the seller misrepresented the truth about the defective product. The seller simply created a myth about the product by exaggerating and idealizing its utility to the buyer. The great Black leader (hero), Malcolm X would identify this economic process known as information asymmetry as being hoodwinked and bamboozled.

Information asymmetry creates not only an unequal economic exchange or transaction, it also creates market failures (inefficiency, social welfare indebtedness/dependency, and an unequal distribution of goods and services), moral hazards (bearing all the cost of a risk), adverse selection (belief in the mythmaking which leads to irrational/poor decision making), and an imbalance of information, knowledge, and power. This monopoly of information (knowledge) as illustrated in information asymmetry is seen in the movie *Black Panther* when the white male Central Intelligent Agency (CIA) agent is portrayed as a hero and friend to Wakanda. The fact is that the CIA is not a friend of Africa and African people at home and abroad given its history of assassinating Black leaders (heroes/heroines), creating/financing coups, and overthrowing governments in Latin America, the Caribbean, and Africa, while supplying crack-cocaine in Black neighborhoods throughout the United States.

The crack-cocaine epidemic devastated the Black community and destroyed Black families – so, why would Marvel/Disney's *Black Panther* portray the CIA as a friend to Africans and people of African descent? The answer could be found in the fact that the CIA has an enduring legacy with Hollywood. In regard to the liaison between the CIA and Hollywood, investigative journalist and author, Nicolas Schou states the following:

The agency has established a very active spin machine in the heart of the entertainment capital, which works strenuously to make sure the cloak-and-dagger world is presented in heroic terms. Since the mid-1990s, but especially after 9/11, American screenwriters, directors, and producers have traded positive portrayal of the spy profession in film or television projects for special access and favors at CIA headquarters.

Ever since its inception in 1947, the CIA has been covertly working with Hollywood. But it wasn't until the mid-1990s that the agency formally hired an entertainment industry liaison and began openly courting favorable treatment in films and television. During the Clinton presidency, the CIA took its Hollywood strategy to a new level—trying to take more control of its own mythmaking. In 1996, the CIA hired one of its veteran clandestine officers, Chase Brandon, to work directly with Hollywood studios and production companies to upgrade its image.

An image that has facilitated on the continent of Africa the following:

- The overthrown and assassination of the first Prime Minister of the Democratic Republic of the Congo Patrice Lumumba in 1961;
- The 1962 arrest of Nelson Mandela in South Africa;
- A military coup to overthrow Ghana's first President Kwame Nkrumah in 1966;
- Military support and funding for the FNLA and Unita to depose the MPLA under the leadership of Angola's Agostino Neto during the 1970s;
- Support for the brutal rule of Hissene Habre in Chad by deposing President Goukouni Oueddei in 1982 who sought an alliance with Colonel Muammar Gaddafi of Libya before his deposal;
- Providing military weapons and support to Libyan rebels under the leadership of President Barack Obama to overthrow and assassinate Libya's leader Colonel Muammar Gaddafi in 2011.

Malcolm X was concerned (and warned us) about the CIA and the image it conjured up during his overseas travel to various parts of Africa, Europe, and what is referred to as the

"Middle East." Moreover, the late journalist and author Gary Webb broke the story that "a San Francisco Bay Area drug ring sold tons of cocaine to the Crips and Bloods street gangs of Los Angeles, and funneled millions in drug profits to a Latin American guerrilla army run by the U.S. Central Intelligence Agency." Despite these facts, many of us still believe in the symbolic power of Marvel/Disney's *Black Panther*.

CONCLUSION

Since ancient times, human beings have engaged in mythmaking and the creation of symbols and giving those symbols meaning, while giving the myths power over them and their sense of reality. In ancient Egypt, the Egyptians along with other people engaged in zoolatry where animals, such as panthers were deified, glorified, and sacrificed. Given the advancement of human society due to information, knowledge, science, technology, etc., people still idealized, worship, praised, and hold on tightly to mythologies and symbols as illustrated in Marvel/Disney's *Black Panther*.

Marvel/Disney's *Black Panther* was indeed a blockbuster success, but for whom and at what cost? The economic success of Marvel/Disney's *Black Panther* has not and will not empower and enrich the global African community. It was made specifically to enrich and empower others at our expense. The tendency to be overjoyed with a fictional Black superhero along with his nation that befriends and saves a white CIA agent, but rejects and kills his own kin and blood is problematic politically and culturally given the reality of how the CIA truly operates globally and nationally concerning Africans and Africa.

Equally as disturbing is the fact that despite our impecunious state or perhaps because of it, mythmaking and symbolism as exemplified in the movie *Black Panther* make us feel good - it is a short-term high with long-term economic lows. Once reality sets in, we will be in the same economic state or perhaps worse when the CIA/Disney's *Black Panther* is no longer a hallucinogen. After spending our money to watch Black Panther, enrich Disney, and view the CIA and its actions as palatable, our land, labor, and resources in Africa will continue to be exploited, while our people worldwide will continue to be oppressed. Therefore, unlike Back Panther, we as a people do not need a drug dosage to make us strong and give us valor; a fictional hero to idealized; a fictional landmass with an alien resource to hope for; or a white CIA agent to befriend and save us. All we need is each other and a strong dose of economic, political, and cultural reality about our land, labor, and resources with a second dosage of who our true heroes, heroines, and friends are. Mythmaking and symbols alone will not make us powerful given the reality that the true and ultimate power resides not only in our land, labor, and resources, but most importantly in our minds and hearts.

Zawadee, "The Majestic African Black Panther," May 18, 2016, http://www.zawadee.com/blog/ca/the-majestic-african-black-panther

Ibid.

Anthony Browder, From the Browder File: 22 Essays on the African American Experience, (Washington, DC: The Institute of Karmic Guidance, 2000), 27-32.

Edgar J. Ridley, Symbolism Revisited: Notes on the Symptomatic Thought Process, (Trenton: Africa World Press, 2001), 6-7.

Jay Scott Smith, "Black Panther Now the Fourth Highest Grossing Domestic Film of All Time," TheGrio, April 3, 2018, https://thegrio.com/2018/04/03/black-panther-domestic-gross-record/.

Ibid.

Ibid.

TheGrio, "Black Panther is Now the Top-Grossing Superhero Film of All Time," TheGrio, March 25, 2018, https://thegrio.com/2018/03/25/black-panther-is-now-the-top-grossing-superhero-film-of-all-time/.

The World Bank Group, "World Bank National Accounts Data, and OECD National Accounts Data Files, The World Bank Group, 2018, https://data.worldbank.org/indicator/NY.GDP.MKTP.CD

Claud Anderson, Black Labor, White Wealth: The Search for Power and Economic Justice, (Bethesda: PowerNomics, 1994), 32-33

Ibid, 32.

Tracy Jan "White Families Have Nearly 10 Times the Net Worth of Black Families. And the Gap is Growing", Washington Post, September 28, 2017, https://www.washingtonpost.com/news/wonk/wp/2017/09/28/black-and-hispanic-families-are-making-more-money-but-they-still-lag-far-behind-whites/?utm_term=.8354f77319f8

Dana DA Silva, "South Africa: The Exploitation of Children Taints Many Consumer Products," allAfrica, June 10, 2016, http://allafrica.com/stories/201606110205.html

The Institute for Global Labour and Human Rights, "The U.S. in Haiti," The Institute for Global Labour and Human Rights, April 1, 1996, http://www.globallabourrights.org/reports/the-u-s-in-haiti

Haiti Partners, "Haiti's Statistics: Haiti by the Numbers," Haiti Partners, November 18, 2015,

https://haitipartners.org/haiti-statistics/

Ibid.

Brooks Barnes and Michael Cieply, "Disney Swoops into Action, Buying Marvel for $4 Billion," The New York Times, August 31, 2009, https://www.nytimes.com/2009/09/01/business/media/01disney.html

Statista, "Total Assets of the Walt Disney Company in the Fiscal Years 2006 to 2017 in Billion U.S. Dollars,"

The Statistics Portal, 2018, https://www.statista.com/statistics/193136/total-assets-of-the-walt-disney-company-since-2006/

Celebrity Net Worth, "Robert Iger New Worth," accessed April8, 2018, https://www.celebritynetworth.com/richest-businessmen/ceos/robert-iger-net-worth/

Maya Deleon, "Stan Lee's Net Worth is $50 Million," Celebrity Money, May 12, 2017, https://www.bankrate.com/lifestyle/celebrity-money/stan-lee-net-worth/

Ivan Van Sertima, "Future Directions for African and African-American Content in the School Curriculum," in Infusion of African and African American Content in the School Curriculum: Proceedings of the First National Conference, eds., Asa G., Hillard, III, Lucretia Payton-Stewart, & Larry O. Williams, (Morristown: Aaron Press, 1990), 99 -100.

Ibid, 97.

Ibid, 87 – 109. See also, Cheikh Anta Diop, The Cultural Unity of Black Africa: The Domains of Patriarchy and of Matriarchy in Classical Antiquity, (Chicago: Third World Press, 1990).

Evan Hadingham, "Where Is the Birthplace of Humankind? South Africa and East Africa Both Lay Claims," National Geographic, September 11, 2015, https://news.nationalgeographic.com/2015/09/150911-hominin-hominid-berger-homo-naledi-fossils-ancestor-rising-star-human-origins/

Peter Manseau, "The Surprising Religious Backstory of 'Black Panther's' Wakanda," The Washington Post, March 7, 2018, https://www.washingtonpost.com/news/acts-of-faith/wp/2018/03/07/the-surprising-religious-backstory-of-black-panthers-wakanda/?utm_term=.a6e5f2bdf4bf

Investment News, "Appreciating the Akamba of Paraguay in South America, Investment News, October 15, 2016, http://investmentnews.co.ke/travel-and-culture/appreciating-akamba-paraguay-south-america/

Walter Rodney, How Europe Underdeveloped Africa, (Washington, DC: Howard University Press, 1982), 179.

Ha-Joon Chang, Kicking Away the Ladder: Development Strategy in Historical Perspective,

(London: Anthem Press, 2002), 125 -127.

Nicolas Schou, "How the CIA Hoodwinked Hollywood," The Atlantic, July 14, 2016, https://www.theatlantic.com/entertainment/archive/2016/07/operation-tinseltown-how-the-cia-manipulates-hollywood/491138/

BBC, "Four More Ways the CIA has Meddled in Africa," BBC News, May 17, 2016. http://www.bbc.com/news/world-africa-36303327

Erin C.J. Robertson, "Here are Five More Recent Examples of the CIA's Operations in Africa,"

Okay Africa, May 17, 2016, http://www.okayafrica.com/five-recent-examples-cias-operations-africa/

Alex Hannaford, "The CIA, the drug dealers, and the tragedy of Gary Webb," The Telegraph, March 21, 2015, https://www.telegraph.co.uk/culture/film/11485819/kill-messenger-gary-webb-true-story.html

SELECTED BIBLIOGRAPHY:
Anderson, Claud. Black Labor, White Wealth: The Search for Power and Economic Justice.
Bethesda: PowerNomics Corporation of America Publishers, 1994.

Barnes, Brooks and Michael Cieply. "Disney Swoops into Action, Buying Marvel for $4 Billion." The New York Times, August 31, 2009. https://www.nytimes.com/2009/09/01/business/media/01disney.html

BBC. "Four More Ways the CIA has Meddled in Africa." BBC News. May 17, 2016. http://www.bbc.com/news/world-africa-36303327
Browder, Anthony. From the Browder File: 22 Essays on the African American Experience. Washington, DC: The Institute of Karmic Guidance, 2000.
Celebrity Net Worth."Robert Iger New Worth." Accessed April 8, 2018. https://www.celebritynetworth.com/richest-businessmen/ceos/robert-iger-net-worth/

Chang, Ha-Joon. Kicking Away the Ladder: Development Strategy in Historical Perspective
London: Anthem Press, 2002.

Clarke, John H. and Yosef Ben-Jochannan. New Dimensions in African History. Trenton: African World Press, 1991.

DA Silva, Dana. "South Africa: The Exploitation of Children Taints Many Consumer Products." allAfrica. June 10, 2016. http://allafrica.com/stories/201606110205.html

Delices, Patrick. "Africa Lags Behind as its Resources Power China's Growth." The Black Star
News. May, 4, 2013. http://www.blackstarnews.com/global-politics/africa/africa-lags-behind-as-its-resources-power-chinas-growth.html
Deleon, Maya. "Stan Lee's Net Worth is $50 Million." Celebrity Money. May 12, 2017. https://www.bankrate.com/lifestyle/celebrity-money/stan-lee-net-worth/
Diop, Cheikh. Anta. Black Africa: The Economic and Cultural Basis for a Federated State.
Chicago: Chicago Review Press, 1987.

Diop, Cheikh. Anta. The African Origin of Civilization: Myth or Reality. Chicago: Lawrence Hill Books, 1974.

Diop, Cheikh Anta. The Cultural Unity of Black Africa: The Domains of Patriarchy and of Matriarchy in Classical Antiquity. Chicago: Third World Press, 1990.

| 67 |

Du Bois, W.E.B. (1979). The World and Africa. New York: International Publishers.

Hadingham, Evan. "Where Is the Birthplace of Humankind? South Africa and East Africa Both Lay Claims." National Geographic. September 11, 2015. https://news.nationalgeographic.com/2015/09/150911-hominin-hominid-berger-homo-naledi-fossils-ancestor-rising-star-human-origins/

Haiti Partner. "Haiti's Statistics: Haiti by the Numbers." Haiti Partners. November 18, 2015.
      https://haitipartners.org/haiti-statistics/

Hannaford, Alex. "The CIA, the Drug Dealers, and the Tragedy of Gary Webb." The Telegraph. March 21, 2015. https://www.telegraph.co.uk/culture/film/11485819/kill-messenger-gary-webb-true-story.html

Investment News." Appreciating the Akamba of Paraguay in South America. Investment News. October 15, 2016. http://investmentnews.co.ke/travel-and-culture/appreciating-akamba-paraguay-south-america/

Jan, Tracy. "White Families Have Nearly 10 Times the Net Worth of Black Families. And the Gap is Growing." Washington Post. September 28, 2017. https://www.washingtonpost.com/news/wonk/wp/2017/09/28/black-and-hispanic-families-are-making-more-money-but-they-still-lag-far-behind-whites/?utm_term=.8354f77319f8

Jeffries, Leonard. Educational Power Packages. Unpublished. Accessed April 8, 2018.

Kunjufu, Jawanza.   Black Economics: Solutions for Economic and Community Empowerment.

Chicago: African American Images, 1991.

Manseau, Peter. "The Surprising Religious Backstory of 'Black Panther's' Wakanda." The Washington Post. March 7, 2018. https://www.washingtonpost.com/news/acts-of-faith/wp/2018/03/07/the-surprising-religious-backstory-of-black-panthers-wakanda/?utm_term=.a6e5f2bdf4bf

Ridley, Edgar J. Symbolism Revisited: Notes on the Symptomatic Thought Process. Trenton: Africa World Press. 2001.

Robertson, Erin C.J. "Here are Five More Recent Examples of the CIA's Operations in Africa."

Okay Africa. May 17, 2016. http://www.okayafrica.com/five-recent-examples-cias-operations-africa/

Robinson, Randall. An Unbroken Agony: Haiti, From Revolution to the Kidnapping of a President. New York: Basic Civitas Books, 2007.

Rodney, Walter.   How Europe Underdeveloped Africa.   Washington DC: Howard University Press, 1981.

Schou, Nicolas. "How the CIA Hoodwinked Hollywood." The Atlantic. July 14, 2016. https://www.theatlantic.com/entertainment/archive/2016/07/operation-tinseltown-how-the-cia-manipulates-hollywood/491138/

Smith, Jay Scott. "Black Panther Now the Fourth Highest Grossing Domestic Film of All Time." TheGrio. April 3, 2018. https://thegrio.com/2018/04/03/black-panther-domestic-gross-record/.

Statista. "Total Assets of the Walt Disney Company in the Fiscal Years 2006 to 2017 in Billion U.S. Dollars." The Statistics Portal. 2018. https://www.statista.com/statistics/193136/total-assets-of-the-walt-disney-company-since-2006/

TheGrio. "Black Panther is Now the Top-Grossing Superhero Film of All Time." TheGrio. March 25, 2018. https://thegrio.com/2018/03/25/black-panther-is-now-the-top-grossing-superhero-film-of-all-time/.

The Institute for Global Labour and Human Rights. "The U.S. in Haiti." The Institute for Global Labour and Human Rights. April 1, 1996. http://www.globallabourrights.org/reports/the-u-s-in-haiti

The World Bank Group. "World Bank National Accounts Data, and OECD National Accounts Data Files, The World Bank Group. 2018. https://data.worldbank.org/indicator/NY.GDP.MKTP.CD

Van Sertima, Ivan. "Future Directions for African and African-American Content in the School Curriculum." In Infusion of African and African American Content in the School Curriculum: Proceedings of the First National Conference, edited Asa G., Hilliard, III, Lucretia Payton-Stewart, & Larry O. Williams, 87 -109. Morristown: Aaron Press, 1990.

Williams, Eric. Capitalism and Slavery. Chapel Hill: The University of North Carolina Press, 1994.

Wilson, Amos. The Falsification of Afrikan Consciousness: Eurocentric History, Psychiatry and the Politics of White Supremacy. New York: Afrikan World Infosystems, 1993.

Zawadee. "The Majestic African Black Panther." May 18, 2016. http://www.zawadee.com/blog/ca/the-majestic-african-black-panther

Patrick Delices *is a Haitian scholar and public intellectual who taught the History of Haiti, Caribbean Politics, Black Politics, and African-Caribbean International Relations at Hunter College, Department of Africana and Puerto Rican/Latino Studies. Patrick Delices served as a research fellow at Columbia University for the late, Pulitzer Prize historian Manning Marable and as a research assistant for Dr. Leonard Jeffries Jr., the former chairperson of the Department of Black Studies at the City College of New York. During the winter of 2014, as part of the first African-American delegation to Western Sahara and as a valuable member of the Institute of the Black World, Pan-African Unity Dialogue, Patrick Delices visited Algeria and various Western Sahara refugee camps on a fact finding mission. Furthermore, Patrick Delices engaged in a research project and conference in Haiti during the fall of 2014 with Professor James Small and Mambo Asogwe Bayyinah Bello in honor of Emperor Jean Jacques Dessalines and the Haitian Revolution. Patrick Delices has also visited and conducted research in the Dominican Republic, Cuba, Brazil, Chile, China, South Korea, Spain, Kenya, Tanzania, Zanzibar, and Egypt. Currently, Patrick Delices is working on two research projects: a book about his father, Georges Chardin Delices, who is considered the greatest soccer legend in Haiti and another book regarding the global impact of the Haitian Revolution. Patrick Delices also published "The Digital Economy" in the Journal of International Affairs; "Cementing Scholarship with Service: Dr. Ben at the Foothills of the Mountains of the Moon Where the God Hapi Dwells" in the Journal of Pan-African Studies; "The African Origin of Haitian Vodou: From the Nile Valley to the Haitian Valleys" in the text Vodou in the Haitian Experience; "Oath to the Ancestors: The Haitian Flag is Rooted in Vodou" in the text Vodou in Haitian Memory, and "To Decolonize the World: Thomas Sankara and the 'Last Colony' in Africa" in the text A Certain Amount of Madness: The Life, Politics, and Legacies of Thomas Sankara. Patrick Delices earned a BA in International Relations and Black Studies along with an MS in Educational Administration and Supervision from the City College of New York. Patrick Delices also earned an Ed.M in Higher Education Administration from Teachers College, Columbia University; an MBA in Quantitative Finance, Business Law, and Global Business from New York University, Stern School of Business; and an MPA in International Economics Policy and Management from Columbia University, School of International and Public Affairs. Moreover, Patrick Delices holds a certificate in Performance Measurement and Management from Harvard University, Kennedy School of Government; a certificate in Decolonial Studies from the Universitat Autonoma de Barcelona in Spain; and a certificate in Critical Islamic Theology and Muslim Liberation Studies from the Universidad de Granada in Spain.*

15
IMAGE MAKERS REVISITED:
Quest For A Noble Black Super Hero
Useni Perkins

During the sixties, I wrote a play entitled IMAGE MAKERS which satirized how the predominantly white movie industry capitalized on the obsession of Black people to see Super Black Heroes on the big screen. The play was produced by the Kuumba Theater, founded by Val Gray Ward, and performed throughout the Midwest and at the FESTAC World Festival of the Arts in Lagos, Nigeria in 1977. From this genre of Blaxploitation films came Shaft, Superfly, Sweet Sweetback and a plethora of other "Black Super Dudes" outwitting and beating up on white people as though white supremacy was a fabrication of Black history. Despite the fact these films were a dramatic departure from many earlier films, like Birth of a Nation, Gone With The Wind, Hearts in Dixie and Way Down South, which portrayed Black people as being submissive, child-like, corrupt and hardened criminals, these images were only replaced with new cinematic Black stereotypes. It didn't matter if some of these "Black Super Dudes" were flawed with transgressions, the fact that they performed heroic feats against white people compensated for any lack of moral attributes they may have had. More importantly, these films filled a void in the emotional psyche of many Black people to see Black heroes on the big screen, regardless of how disingenuous they may have been.

Although after the sixties the proliferation of these films slightly diminished, the movie industry failed to produce films which provided us with a Noble Black Super Hero until the arrival of the Black Panther. In an earlier Marvel Enterprise film, Black Panther did appear in Captain America: Civil War, but only in a supporting role. (It should be noted, too, that in 1997 Robert Townsend, a multi-talented actor, writer and director, produced the Meteor Man which featured a Black Super Hero but did not receive the recognition I felt it deserved.) But when Black Panther arrived on the big screen in 2017, Black people had a "super hero", like Superman, Batman and Spiderman, who was not only noble in character but personified the greatness in our traditional African cultures. Now as the charismatic King of the fable African nation of Wakanda, his character becomes monumental in statue. Black Panther was destined to be a cinematic success due to its unprecedented promotional campaign, financial resources, ensemble of outstanding actors, staff of excellent writers and the extraordinary talent of its young director, Ryan Coogler.

Black Panther has already exceeded the expectations of the Marvel Cinematic Enterprise and is being acclaimed an epic milestone that has lifted the consciousness of many Black people to appreciate their African heritage and celebrate their African culture. To its credit *Black Panther* also depicted Black women whose complexion was free of colonial miscegenation and dispelled many of the misconceptions we have of African women. Granted this mythical version of a Utopian African nation, with the moral principles and technological advancements to humanize the planet, has its moments of Black pride and archival images of great African civilizations, we must be cautious not to elevate it to a height that is immune from constructive criticism. I say this not to discredit or to minimize the extraordinary achievement of Black Panther but to acknowledge that art of any genre can best be assessed when it is exposed to a wide range of diverse views. In this regard, I would like to state several concerns I have before Black Panther becomes indelibly etched in the pantheon of classic Black films.

1. It is highly improbable that the white creator of the *Black Panther* intended it to become a paragon to symbolize the superior ethos of African people and the achievements of African civilizations, past present or in the future. While this may appear to be a petty concern, I'm an ardent believer that our Black heroes and Black leaders should be created, identified and sanctioned by Black people. History has shown us that when Black people have abrogated this responsibility, white people are eagerly waiting to do this in our behalf. In fact, even when we do assume authorship of our Black heroes, and Black leaders, white America makes every effort to discredit those who not conform to its stereotypic criteria of being subservient, obedient and reconciliatory.

2. Although Erik Killmonger, the embittered cousin of King T'Challa, is portrayed as the antagonist in Black Panther, I felt that his character is more complex than the villainous role prescribed to him. On the contrary, I felt that the ultimate antagonist should be the white ruthless arms dealer, Klaw, who wants to market the vibranium to rogue nations around the world to create an international catastrophe. Killmonger's motive to control vibranium is to give it to African nations to avenge the years of oppression they have suffered from colonialism and imperialism. While some may argue that one is malicious as the other, Killmonger is also a victim of white oppression but Klaw epitomizes the zenith of white supremacy, the perpetrator of Black oppression.

3. Despite the fact that King T'Challa is clearly the hero of *Black Panther*, in the end the white CIA agent also achieves heroic status when he pilots the aircraft that aborts the planes loaded with vibranium to arm those African countries who are determined to destroy the imperial white nations that have afflicted oppression and chaos over their people for centuries. Although this scenario may have been included to appease white audiences, to use a white agent who represents one of the most clandestine and destructive agencies (CIA) with a history of destabilizing Africa e.g. assassination

of Patrice Lumumba in the Congo, assisting in the coup of Ghana which led to the exile of its president Kwame Nkrumah and its nefarious role in the maintenance of apartheid in South Africa is a travesty and insult to all African nations which have been victimized by colonialism and imperialism.

4.   How seriously should we use the *Black Panther* as an African centered pedagogy to enlighten and educate Black people about the achievements and humanity of African people? *Black Panther* has already been presented in various educational curriculums designed to educate Black people. While these curriculums may have some merit, let us not be mistaken, movies are to entertain no matter how uplifting and informative some may be. They can never be substituted for reading authentic narratives like Chancellor Williams *The Destruction Of Black Civilizations*, John G. Jackson, *Introduction To African Civilization*, Yosef ben Jochannan, *Africa: Mother Of Western Civilization* or Cheikh Anta Diop, *Civilization Or Barbarism*, to name a few.

5.   Black people need to be very cautious about placing the panacea to our protracted struggle to achieve liberation on the shoulders of any one person, fiction or non-fiction.

While Black Super Heroes may provide us with inspiring images of fortitude, courage and resiliency they are not infallible and when they do expire we cannot always be assured that their legacies and deeds will be replicated by future generations.

Finally, since the durability of a cinematic super hero depends on how well it does at the box office, judging from early gross earnings of Black Panther, this leads me to believe we will be watching extended versions of it for some time. If my prediction is accurate, I hope the concerns I have articulated will be addressed without comprising its noble intentions.

Useni Eugene Perkins has been truly blessed to have had two successful careers. As a human service practitioner, he has been the president of the Better Boys Foundation in Chicago, president of the Portland Urban League and director of the Chicago State University Family Life Center. As a poet, playwright and author, he has served as president of the DuSable Museum of African American History, president of the African American Arts Alliance and was the chairman for the Artists for Harold Washington, a city wide coalition of artists that campaigned on behalf of Chicago's first black mayor. He also is the presiding elder for the National Rites of Passage, a history maker and was inducted into the Gwendolyn Brooks National Literary Hall of Fame for writers of African Descent in 1999.

16

WILL THE REAL WAKANDA WAKE UP?

Molefi Kete Asante

I went to see the popular movie *Black Panther* and was amused at its faux Afrocentric overlay and the stunning beauty of its actors. These two initial responses are probably what make the movie so exciting for thousands of viewers especially since the Afrofuturist nature of the idea is right in front of one's eyes. In the first place the director Ryan Coogler (of Fruitvale fame) creates a film that caters to various memes, symbols, traditions, customs, and aesthetic styles that are derived from real African culture, especially from Swahili, Zulu, ancient Kemet, and various other African societies; in an authentic sense the film gives us a Pan African stylistic perspective. Coogler meshes genuine African memes with the elasticity of stereotypical racist ideologies that provide comfortable entry points for people who cannot stand to see real African heroic examples. As Jennifer Williams questions in her satire "Wakanda Shakes the World," published in *Foreign Policy* on April Fool's Day 2018, "What if the most progressive countries in the world were not former or current imperialist nations? How would the world be different if an African country were the model of ideal nationhood? What if we constructed the future with Africa in mind?" I ask, "What if we take historical figures like Sojourner Truth and Harriet Tubman and infuse them with vibranium? Of course, the truth is that we can do that in a fictional way and this movie might very well give other creative writers and filmmakers something to think about. Secondly, the director gives us exceptionally perfect black bodies with just enough sensuality to heighten the imagination and to demonstrate what range of blackness is possible. Choosing the basic black body for production and reproduction and then overlaying it with the endless varieties and shades of blackness to capture the physical space aligned to the cultural projections of the characters heighten the delectable qualities of style and spirit. There is something to be admired in the courage of this movie despite the imperfections we are sure to discover as we analyze it; however, it is not to be murdered simply because it does not do all it could do to bring consciousness to the viewer. I say this although I am shocked, in the old school way, that it has in fact changed the algorithms of cultural competency. Family members I know who would not have given a dime to "learn" about Africa have now come out with their Wakanda fashions.

POINT OF VIEW

To be clear this movie does not entertain us with a Tyler Perry storyline with its simplistic and non-attempt at Afrocentric invention or reinvention. This film does not play to the lowest common denominator in order to jerk laughter; it is an attempt at serious moviemaking in the creation of myths that carry with them nuggets of golden wisdom. No, *Black Panther* means to make a point that advances serious conversation about relationships, power, and the role of women, science, economics, art, and intra-African dynamics. It does this on many levels and with various audiences.

At a dynamic gathering at the Molefi Kete Asante Institute in Philadelphia right after the movie came out one young woman exclaimed in discussion, "After seeing the film I now want to go to Africa and will definitely practice Kwanzaa this year!" Another lady handed out a two-page statement that lauded the film for its emphasis on fashions derived from African culture. There were many statements in this line of thinking and with this strong emotional attachment to the latest artistic vehicle to deliver to African people some gilded baggage that could be used to avoid real Africa. Yet I am convinced that the director, and the producers, may have unintentionally utilized the Marvel super-white template to once again lull to sleep those who "looked upon the Nile and raised the pyramids above it" without ever thinking how to advance African consciousness toward cultural, political, and economic liberation. There is a Cambridge Analytical storyline somewhere in this movie that has allowed the moviemakers to use our psychological profiles to capture our emotions. They have discovered through audience analysis what the Afrocentrists and systematic nationalists have been saying for generations: the central challenge to our conscious creativity is that we fear Africa and Africans and until we overcome this fear we will not be able to advance. What Coogler captures is that we also wish to see Africa displayed in glory, bathed in the historical truths that we know exist somewhere in our memory. It is in this artistic and projective juncture that I praise the movie and cast my vote for some really serious discussions around what a genuine African future would look like.

I loved the visual dynamism of Blackness arrayed and displayed so expertly on the screen and I could not resist the natural talent of the actors who all seemed to have been born for the celluloid platform. However, I asked myself, "What could you have done with this explosive combination of impressive talents and inspirational images?" As the father of someone who makes films, MK Asante, I am convinced that you have to understand that a film cannot and does not do everything everyone wants it to do. In the end, the judgment belongs to the filmmaker. Nevertheless, I also know that in a racialized society the pitfalls of filmmaking are great and treacherous both for the creators and for the audiences. You can give us corn flakes to eat and entertain us by throwing cotton balls at racism that make no impact on our lives or you could try as Spike Lee and others have tried to maximize African American truths. I would never minimize the work of Coogler like I would never deny the genius of Spike Lee, but I can as an Afrocentric historian evaluate and judge productions on the quality of their seriousness about the themes and memes they purport to assert in the face of the doctrine of racial dominance. It is truly the duty of the intellectual activist to raise the most uncomfortable questions in all sectors of society.

SUBLIMINAL DANGERS?

Here is where I first sensed the dangers of filmmaking when you do not have the freedom or historical information to create from your own agency. This is not to say that those who have "freedom" from the constraints of Hollywood have done any better. Nigeria, for example, is the third or fourth largest producer of films in the world and yet there are few truly great Nigerian films that raise the moral and economic consciousness of African people beyond local Perry-esque social, sexual or religious propaganda; often they feed us our own worst examples of negative religious, social, and personal behaviors as if those represent our best interests or something more than trivial. In these Nollywood productions there are the themes of fear of the unknown, petty jealousies, fake hair crises, and screaming. Rarely do such films inspire us to greatness or use our ancestors in a positive way for elevation on a spiritual plane. The richness of Nigerian literature and history alone are enough to bring that industry to greatness, but alas, back to Hollywood. So, the question that I asked after viewing the movie is, "What are we supposed to believe, accept, identify with, after seeing the movie?" That may even be an irrelevant question for any movie, but we are often starved for proof of our appearance in the future.

THE STORYLINE PROBLEM

Black Panther uses double entendre, nuance, and pop culture to deliver its complex message that must be deciphered by a critical decoding of the film. The story begins in an American city, Oakland, California, with children playing basketball on an urban court in a partly dilapidated neighborhood.

Five centuries ago, just as Europe is getting ready to war on Africa and bring millions of Africans into slavery, five African nations (the film uses the pejorative "tribes") wage war to determine who should control the meteorite filled with vibranium that has struck the earth. One of the fighters, T'Chaka, swallows an herb in the shape of a heart and is declared the first *Black Panther*. Because of his superhuman powers he is able to unite four of the nations but no matter how hard he tries he cannot bring the Jabari nation under his power. Nevertheless, the united nations are called Wakanda. Using their access and control of vibranium the Wakandans create a super scientific society, isolate themselves, and present themselves as a relatively poor country until necessary to reveal their power.

King T'Chaka, with the name of the Zulu general Chaka, visits his brother in Oakland. He finds that his brother N'Jobu is working undercover but is helping a black-market arms dealer Ulysses Klaue to steal vibranium from Wakanda. N'Jobu's partner Zuri is also an undercover Wakandan. T'Chaka does not trust them. However, T'Chaka soon dies and his son, T'Challa goes to Wakanda to assume the throne of his father.

At his coronation T'Challa has his friend Okoye, general of a militia, and Nakia, his ex-lover, and his mother Ramonda in attendance. Other dignitaries attend the powerful event. However, M'baku the leader of the Jabari nation challenges him for the throne. In this ritual combat T'Challa defeats M'Baku and in exchange for his life he decides to support T'Challa. Now he must deal with the criminal activity of Klaue and Erik Stevens who steal a vibranium artifact from a London exhibition. A group of Wakandans travel to South Korea to disrupt the sale of the artifact. The artifact was to be sold to a CIA agent posing as a buyer. When Klaue is captured he is turned over to the CIA agent, Everett K. Ross. When the criminal escapes T'Challa catches him and when Ross is injured he is taken back to Wakanda where their technology can save him.

It was revealed that T'Chaka had been forced to kill N'Jobu. He then ordered Zuri to lie that N'Jobu had disappeared. However, his American son, Erik, became an American special operations soldier with the name Kill-Monger. He kills Klaue and takes the body to Wakanda where he challenges T'Challa for the throne. He reveals his identity and is brought before the elders who sanctioned a ritual battle where Killmonger apparently defeats T'Challa hurling him over a cliff. Kill-Monger ingests the herb of power and orders the rest to be burned but Nakia takes one first before burning it. Kill-Monger prepares to distribute power around the world so that Wakanda could help Blacks overcome oppressors. The royal family flees to the Jabari nation for help. Eventually, T'Challa returns and leads his army against the forces of Killmonger. Fighting in the vibranium mine T'Challa kills Killmonger. An outreach center built in Oakland to memorialize the death of N'Jobu serves to cover a multitude of critical relationship issues between African people of the world.

THIS IS THE STORY–THE BEAUTY OF THE BEAST

I am the first to admit that I like the amusement and am a part of that audience looking for a positive African hero, but the Marvel character *Black Panther* and the storyline create several issues for me and, I believe, ultimately for Black people.

The movie made nearly a billion dollars in the first three weeks after its release; it is a financial success. This is good and this is bad. It is good because it shows that people will go out to see movies attempting to demonstrate that Africans have the same interests, desires, and competitions as all humans. It is bad because it can create an exploitative regime in the movies that is nothing more than an update of the Blaxploitation Era in the 1970s. There will be more movies but less substance. So, although the movie costs 200 million to make it is really one of the biggest moneymakers in movie history.

I do not forget that *Black Panther* is a movie and movies are meant for entertainment and amusement. But this movie sows the seeds of inter-African conflict in a subliminal manner. The urbanized African from the Diaspora is made to lack an attachment to African realities although in some ways he expresses a more potent example of nationalism. A key component of this film is the difference between the cousins, although related they have been brought up in different circumstances, and hence cannot recognize each other. Kill-Monger, an isolated individual, appears to have a chip on his shoulder, to have anger management problems, and to dwell on violent responses to situations while the *Black Panther*, living in Wakanda, has the assistance of elders and advisers, and is calmer, cooler, and wiser.

While I have heard several Black people say that *Black Panther* is the best movie they have ever seen; I think that the sentiment comes from a feeling that they have rarely seen powerful Black heroes of any kind in the movies. I can think of Haile Gerima's *Sankofa* and Spike Lee's *Malcolm X* as far more significant to me from historical, inspirational, and creative dimensions. A lot of people of this generation have not seen these movies. There may be others that have grabbed attention for their special relationship to African life. But movies are still fantasies with all of the unreality of speculative imagination. Perhaps the response to the movie is an indication that our bars are too low for what is a great movie. I think for an Afrocentric feature film there are several attributes that should exist.

1. THE PLOT SHOULD DEMONSTRATE THE AGENCY OF BLACK PEOPLE IN CHARGE OF THEIR OWN AFFAIRS.
2. THE THEME SHOULD ALWAYS ENCOURAGE A POSITIVE OUTCOME FOR THE MAIN CHARACTER REGARDLESS OF THE CHALLENGES.
3. THE FILM MUST LEAVE THE AUDIENCE INSPIRED THAT GOOD WILL CONQUER EVIL,
4. THE FILM MUST USE AFRICAN SYMBOLS AND MEMES FROM THE CONTINENT OR THE DIASPORA,
5. THE FILM MUST NOT HAVE ANY GRATUITOUS USE OF AFRICAN PEOPLE OR CULTURES IN ORDER TO PLAY TO EXOTICISM.

SOME THINKING THROUGH ISSUES

Some of the writing in *Black Panther* disturbs me for several reasons. Of course, the writer did not pay attention to the use of words like tribe. There are no people in Africa who speak a language that includes the word tribe in the language. It is a pejorative for African people and for forty years Afrocentric scholars have written against the use of the term because whites reserve it or Africans or First Nation peoples. We do not speak of European tribes but of European people, nations, and ethnic groups. The Zulu, Xhosa, Yoruba, Hausa, Ibo, and Baluba are nations and many African nations are more populous than European nations,

This was too much to take right off the bat when I saw the film. The fact that the African –born actors did not object does not mean that it is correct; they are often educated in the same system of white racist understanding as we are with the memes of whiteness running through their education and cultural responses.

The use of the word tribe to describe African nations or peoples is antiquated and has been roundly condemned by Afrocentric scholars. The movie could have used some expert guidance from Afrocentric consultants for cultural and historical accuracy.

Wakanda is supposed to be technologically superior as a civilization and yet it does not come to the rescue of other Black people in bondage, colonial situations, or the oppressed in other societies. Why did not Wakanda become a liberating power with all of its technological superiority? It is mentioned in connection with the power of vibranium but one would have suspected that Wakanda could have acted out of its own national interest to save more African nations.

Wakanda is technologically amazing and yet there is no culture of science, only one brilliant female scientist responsible for the entire civilization! I am sure that the filmmakers have left this to be developed in a sequel.

The black female scientist is closest to a white male CIA agent who eventually assists Wakanda in defeating its Black enemies. He is depicted flying around in space vehicles killing the empire's enemies. Isn't Wakanda supposed to be so superior that it does not need help? You know, there are Black male or female CIA agents. What do we make of the smart white man's entry? Perhaps Marvel will do something else with him later, like make him a bad guy?

Speculation is never better than reality when it comes to creating a "best" film of any kind. Feet on the ground and imagination based on historical reality would really inspire the youth and toggle the imagination. Black Panther is an OK hero but where is Nat Turner, Zumbi, Thutmoses III, Ramses II, Opoku Ware I, Sundiata, Nehanda, Mansa Musa, Abubakari II, Yenenga, Hatshepsut, Frederick Douglass, Marcus Garvey, Antenor Firmin, or Steve Biko? There are literally thousands of heroic stories that could be told from a historical reality point of view, but that is not what this film is about, and that is all right except now we need to see Okomfo Anokye's Golden Stool descend in thunder and lightning and land on the knees of Osei Tutu I. We need to see Nat Turner flying in the night through the forest like High John de Conqueror to discover those who oppressed Black people and to rip the evil from their bodies. Abubakari's 1000 fishing boats crossing the Atlantic in 1311-12 must have faced and defeated natural and physical enemies. Harriet Tubman was a superhero and will remain an ancestor in the forever future!

Perhaps the most worrying aspect of *Black Panther* is the confusion around the idea of Black self-determination, self-definition, and aspiration based on the value of the ancestors. Killmonger, the character with some of the most positive lines for liberation, is the character who is considered the spoiler. Why? What is the true meaning of this character? Why must positive thoughts be delivered in a vessel that is broken? Like millions of other people, I saw the movie and was awed and wooed by the technics. When I see it for the second time I will listen more closely to dialogue to see why it is that Hollywood fears to do a truly Afrocentric movie. Nevertheless, I send a shout out to Ryan Coogler for once again affirming the genius of Black filmmakers. May he never forget those upon whose shoulders he stands! And may those of us who seek to be wise bind the light and dark, the sky and earth, the hope and despair of our people and live in the manner of the kings and queens from whom we did descend.

Molefi Kete Asante is author of The History of Africa.

17

AFRICA AND WHAT WE KNOW:
The Visceral Response of Black People to Black Panther the Movie

Michael Simanga

We descendants of Africa, people who have been embattled for centuries in the fight to restore our place as free people in the human family, we know some things. We pause occasionally and sometimes frequently to listen casually or with great intensity to the pulsing, chanting sound of the black river flowing around the skeletal structures, through the organs and muscle of our black body. We know that in our blood is the black river that is the spirit of Africa bringing oxygen and nutrients and the codes we ingested to pass on for every generation to unlock the secrets to our humanity. We pause and hear those rivers and streams humming to us with the consistency of sunsets and the steadiness of sunrises seen by our relatives on the entire planet.

We pause to listen because sometimes we need to be reminded. The signs are everywhere loud and silent, kinetic and still. We breathe them in through our skin. They are song and rhythm, the smell of our food or the color of our clothes, the freedom of our beauty and the poetry in our talk. We paint those markers on the inside, reminding us that we were first, we began the journey of humanity, our gifts have benefited the world, but the crime and atrocity of slavery and colonialism and the lies that accompanied it have tried to deny us even our own selves. But we know. Even under the mountainous collection of textbooks and church sermons and in the dusty stacks of countless legal archives that justify the atrocity, and under the tutelage of those who teach the culturally defining distortions, we still know. We are not always conscious of our knowing, but down in the seemingly unreachable depths of our memory we know. Black Panther the movie is the most recent proof.

Our family was able to get opening day tickets, but only in the early afternoon because every other showing was sold out. Our expectation was that the cultural norms of Black movie watching would enhance the collective experience of seeing the highly anticipated film. In a theater packed with Black people, many in African or African inspired clothing, and in complete defiance of our tradition of call and response, not one word was uttered during the film. When it ended the silence was attacked with a volcanic eruption of emotion, clapping and cheering, some tears and laughter, and a long standing ovation as the credits rolled. It was clear to me that we had heard the black river of Africa flowing through our veins, and through our history and through our pain and through our lives. We know something about the Africa in us even when it is obscured by our wounds. The Black Panther was a telling of what we know. It came when we needed it the most, like all the other times we needed to rejuvenate our collective spirit and revel in our collective beauty.

Ryan Coogler, Lupita Nyong'o, Chadwick Boseman, Michael B. Jordan, Danai Gurira and the other film makers, most of them the children of the Civil Rights/Black Power/ African Independence Movement era, took the responsibility of a mythological film about Africa's people seriously. They entered the Marvel Universe determined to disrupt the racist narrative about Africa's people in American and world culture with superheroes and sheroes and legend as history draped in the real and imagined past and future of Africa's descendants. They entered the project with implicit instruction from their families and their communities and the long list of ancestors who fought for us. They were determined to honor Africa and her people and created the film from the sweep of the African continent and the African world. The language, garments, spirituality, courage, contradictions and immense ancient, contemporary and visionary knowledge and wisdom can be found on every continent that they gathered into the film. They knew and we know, like Aime Cesaire knew, "there is no place on this earth without our fingerprints/ and our heels in the skeletons of skyscrapers/ and our sweat in the brilliance of diamonds."

They centered African women as the foundation and leadership of the Black nation, in Wakanda and everywhere else we are. We know and they knew, like Anna Julia Cooper knew, "Only the BLACK WOMAN can say when and where I enter, in the quiet, undisputed dignity of my womanhood, without violence and without suing or special patronage, then and there the whole Negro race enters with me."

They photographed the beauty of the Black world because they knew for too long we have stared at the cosmic geometry of our faces and the earth tones of our skin and swallowed the bitterness of the distorted reflection in the mirror of white empires that scarred us from our head to our feet and from our minds to our hearts. They knew that our girls and boys need to see themselves and their genius thinking through the problems of the world and standing up for the people who need them.

They cast a character cloaked in an African American sorrow song so we could mourn those who are lost and remember they are still ours and we have to search for them, find them. We know and they knew to let us hear the wail of those who had been abandoned singing, "Sometimes I feel like a motherless child. A long way from home."

They reminded us of all of our ancestors, those lost in the ocean between continents and those whose lives and labor was stolen to build the nations of the Americas and the modern empires of the US and Europe. The film makers understood that ours is a fight for power, to live as full human beings, to defend against those who attack us, to build a new world. Even in mythology, Black people's human right to self-defense and self-determination are rarely presented. The film makers understood that depicting the totality of our struggle for human rights was absolutely necessary. They knew and we know that only we have the power to be who we've been and are destined to be. We know like Malcolm X knew, "We declare our right to be a human being."

Black Panther the Movie – lifted us because we know, we know that inside us is that black river flowing and that river is the spirit of Africa. We know it and we feel it. We know what was lost because we've searched furiously for it. Black people celebrate *Black Panther*, because it gives us joy, strength, inspiration and imagination, not because it is a perfect rendering of what was or what we need. Our people are thankful for a film that gave us a moment to rest in ourselves away from the death grips of the oppressive places where we became Africa's diaspora.

The vast majority of Black people who saw the film understand what *Black Panther* means to their spirit and why this moment is important for their children. If we listen to that collective response, it will teach us something we need in our struggle for a new world.

We know because we hear Angela Davis chanting, "Freedom is a constant struggle" and Curtis Mayfield singing, "…while you stand in your glory/I know you won't mind if I tell the whole story/…I know we've come a long way/ But let us not be satisfied/ for tomorrow can be an even brighter day" and in the chorus of spirituals the voice of our ancestors reminding us, "We ain't no ways tired." No, "We ain't no ways tired," and from the vision of the next generation claiming the future we march forward to Kendrick Lamar singing, "do you hear me, do you feel me, we gon' be alright."

Michael Simanga *is an activist writer scholar, educator. He is the author of* No One Can Be at Peace Unless They Have Freedom; Amiri Baraka and the Congress of African People; *and* In the Shadow of the Son. *He is also co-editor of* Brilliant Flame! Amiri Baraka; *and* 44 on 44: forty four Black writers on the election of Barack Obama the 44th president.

He grew up in the Black Power and Black Arts Movement in Detroit and lives in Atlanta with his wife, the poet Lita Hooper, and their children and grandchildren.

18
WHAT IS AFRICA TO ME NOW?
Greg Tate

Met a grown ass sister yesterday who joyfully admitted she'd seen *Black Panther* 8 times. And counting. Another BFF in Cali has announced to friends she's pretty much up to going again with any of her crew who haven't Panthered yet. Michelle Obama Herself and Beyonce's Visual Album are the last media phenomenon we've seen which engendered this degree of enamored spectatorship and addictive representational pleasure amongst our drylongso Warrior-Queens and Monarchs. Wakanda Forever, the new Black Field of Dreams. Yawl built it, yawl keep showing up at the box office and invoking your Palestinian-akin Right of Return privileges. Some more religiously than others apparently, but hey, we can dig it. Like the man said, Its Nation Time and Black Utopic Visual Imagineering matters. Now more than ever as Babylon steady be a-falling seen, Rasta?

Eritrean sister at San Francisco State recently asked this reporter, "What did you think of Killmonger being the only Black American representation in Black Panther?" Replied that the entire film is a Black American fantasia of an uptopic-superhoic dream-Africa. A PTSD- and genocidal imperialist-free Africa that we can readily embrace from the safety of our multiplexes. An Africa where the nightmare of colonial and slave history never happened and the super-civilizations of medieval Africa evolved into high-tech global superpowers.

Meaning the Panther phenom also subtly resurrects the Pan African dream-states of Garvey, Du Bois, Sun Ra, Rasta Fari and others-- Africa re-purposed as a Zion fantasia that will embrace US. Or To echo Countee Cullen, What is Africa to me NOW? Ha--Wakanda Forever, baby!

But the dream has never seemed more necessary as Black communities across the country are disappearing quicker than hen's teeth as majority-Black populated land-based propositions.

The Black Music and Radical Prophetic Activism of previous generations was full of Black Utopians dream-weaver and change-agents hot (and haute) in pursuit of Black Free States. States prolific with wildly insurgent acts of Black imagination and maroon fugitivity if nothing else.

Today our most current, coherent shared collective vision of ourselves as a Community --or the mythic stand-in for one-- are provided by trap rap pipedreams, The Church, HBCUs and the prison-industrial complex.

So the imperative for taking the Utopic-invoking capacity of The Kulcha and Movement into the Virtual --especially for the babies-- has never seemed more acute.

But The Panther also wisely and surreptitiously speaks to the topical, zeitgeist reality of Black Lives Matter as a Black woman intellectual led Movement and the super macho pushback against that in certain throwback quarters. And in its Mandingo-beefcake Battle Royale moments it feeds a nostalgic throwback desire for balls-out hyper-masculine Black militant dick-slinging once again unleashed on the masses in the peanut gallery.

But folk been jumping on Team T'Challa and Team Killmonger without considering how cunningly the tandem were conceived to represent our classic stag conundrum--that of internecine Black Siamese twins not so artfully going at The Art of War. Repping a hoary Black male leadership binary equation driven by the pairs Daddy-issues and raging Inner Hamlets.

End of the day, the patriarchal blood-soaked tandem complete (and nearly exterminate) each other but they don't complete US. Lacking the equipment to reproduce the Chi of gender balance--and the spiritual/cognitive/strategic genius thereof-- how could those two nut-sacs not?

Like Obama's election, The *Panther's* success --in the narrative and at the box office--is obviously dependent on how empoweringly and superheroically weaponizes and 'Visibilizes' the Stealth Authority and Action-Figuration of our endangered body politics Warrior-Sistren: How smartly it seizes the time to say I Really Truly See You to They Who Bind, Protect and harmonize all the Other parts of The Kulcha during Wartime/ Nation Time.

All the dangling particulars most necessary for our Total Survival. All that which cannot can't be simplemindedly settled by two testosterone fueled super-nickas beating each other's brains out over--per Richard Pryors's Mudbone-- How Cold our situation be and How Deep.

Greg Tate *is a writer, musician, and cultural provocateur who lives and thrives atop Harlem's Sugar Hill. His most recent book is* Flyboy 2 The Greg Tate Reader.

19
YOU'RE PRETTY (AWESOME) FOR A DARK GIRL: Beauty, Power and Strength in the Movie Black Panther

Marita Golden

Images are precious and potent. They ignite and produce emotions that can sweep those viewing them into unchartered, renewing territory, or reinforce misperceptions. The images of womanhood in Black Panther are familiar and new, and resonated deeply with how I live, want to live and dream of living, as an African-descended, Black woman in America.

Like many viewers I was astonished and reassured by what I witnessed unfolding on the screen. Astonished because I had never seen a celebration of black power in the world of politics and global power and in our personal lives, intertwined and dramatized so vividly. Reassured because Black Panther affirmed what I know and what poet Sonia Sanchez said, "We a BaddDD people."

In much of African American fiction and creative representation of Black life, we suffer from a "hero deficit." Black audiences are famished for images of Black life and possibilities that are more about life than death, more about joy than pain, and that present us with Black people as heroic. This, even though we witness in our daily lives the heroic woven into the tapestry of our families and friendships. Black Panther gave us Black people to envy, root for, cheer on, and mostly, want to be.

UNDENIABLY WARRIORS

From the first moments of the film, it is clear that Black female intelligence and strength is a powerful engine driving the narrative. Nakia, the daring spy and former lover of King T'Challa is the first person to urge the King to "share what we have" with the Black world beyond Wakanda. General Okoye saves T'Challa's life when he literally freezes at the sight of Nakia during the rescue operation that sets the film in motion. And Nakia stays in Wakanda only because she can fulfill her larger mission of global outreach, not only because she clearly loves T'Challa.

The women of Wakanda felt like my sisters because, as an African American woman I am a warrior. On guard, reflexively trying to protect myself, my family and my community from the daily macro and micro assaults of racism, "outright" and disguised. The women of the Dora Milaje, the Wakandan king's security detail were fiercely intelligent, focused on a clear knowledge of their mission, brave and strong. Strong physically and mentally. As I sat in the packed theater, one literally enthralled into respectful silence, I thought of "the strong Black woman" stereotype and how *Black Panther* rewrites the meaning of that label which too often in African American culture manages to be simultaneously a curse, an admonition, and an only half- hearted compliment. There were no apologies in *Black Panther*, not even one, for the physical power, and charisma of the Dora Milaje and their leader, Okoye.

In *Black Panther* a warrior is observant and thoughtful, and willing to speak truth to power, even when that power is the person she is charged with protecting. A warrior can, and, actually needs to love, as it is clear that for much of the film Okoye's marriage to W'Kabi is as central to her life as is protecting her nation, even if in the end the nation comes first. Still, the crucial scene in the film in which W'Kabi and Okoye confront each other from opposing sides on the battlefield, and Okoye answers W'Kabi's taunt that she surely would not kill the man she loves, with the answer that she would, reveals that for Okoye the love they share, the marriage they have made, can only exist legitimately within the framework of the Wakanda that she fights to preserve. Their marriage is an expression of the values of Wakanda, not a footnote.

Black Panther allows Black women viewers to both exult in the necessary emotional and intellectual strength we have honed to lead families and movements. Here we witness a nearly joyful celebration of the many often unexplored dimensions of personal and political leadership.

In African American history, ask Harriet Tubman, Fannie Lou Hamer, Ida B. Wells, ask Rosa Parks, whose actual lives beyond mythology were dimensional, complex and conflicted. Women who changed diapers and history. If we are warriors now, it is in part because they were warriors then.

It is important to remember that the warrior women of Wakanda are not fantasy. They were inspired by the women soldiers of Dahomey. By the end of the 19th century an estimated 4,000 women, many of whom began their training as teens, were among the Dahomey military ranks. And the King's reliance on his female advisors in the film replicates a historical system where men and women had joint control of political institutions.

UNDENIABLY BLACK

Black Panther reveals and revels in the actual physical beauty of blackness. Dark flawless skin. The unapologetically broad nose, the full lips. The tightly coiled or braided hair. The shaved head that thrusts the dark black face into full view. Blackness is the norm, the standard. The film has become nearly a form of initiation for some Black families because of the ways in which the Black African phenotype is on celebratory display. And yet the world outside the theater is one in which Black women in the Caribbean spread lye on their skin, wrap their bodies in plastic and sit in the sun to peel off the top dark layers of melanin. They have seen how power and influence and wealth in their countries goes to those who are "light and bright," and endanger their health and their lives for a tiny slice of what they feel they can get no other way. In the world outside the theater in 2018, skin lighteners are used by men and women throughout Africa and Asia, and dark-skinned Black girls in America still wrestle silently, and often alone with the impact of a culture within and outside their communities that deems them second best.

And yet images are precious and potent. No dark-skinned Black girl in America who sees Black Panther can ever say that she has never seen her skin color portrayed in a context where it was accepted, normalized, and irrelevant to what makes a woman a person of value. The inclusion of dark-skinned women in advertising and film (which plays a dangerous and inordinate role in creating young people's self-image) is usually limited to women who are poor, marginalized, angry, and sexually undesirable. Even the presence of Gabrielle Union, Issa Rae, Viola Davis, Lupita Nyong'o and Danai Gurira as acclaimed, popular actresses has not yet "normalized" the brown to black woman as a symbol associated with wealth, love, the good life, progress, all those things an audience wants or wants to be.

The conversation begun by Black Panther needs to be woven into family conversation. A film can inspire re-evaluation, but it cannot do the heavy day-to-day lifting of altering attitudes. That is where we have to turn away from the film and look into the faces of brown and black Black girls and tell them they are valuable, they are beautiful and they are loved.

UNDENIABLY BEAUTIFUL.

One of the most satisfying aspects of the film was the way in which it allows us to expand the definitions of female beauty. The film equates intelligence, innovation, daring, courage, thoughtfulness with beauty. As much as Black Panther glorifies physical Black beauty, it offers women viewers a vision of a world, a space, where they are adored and desired for non-physical attributes.

These are not women masquerading as men. These are women whose "feminine" and "masculine" qualities defy that kind of antiquated description. The film liberates viewers from the need to pick a box for Okoye, Nakia, and Shuri. The truly revolutionary dimension of the film is that it makes such a riveting argument not for "women's equality," in the political sense, but an equality that already exists and is simply awaiting expression. The kind of "equality" that at its core cannot be granted by laws or voted into office, or hired or fired, but is an intrinsic power source that is more human, than male or female.

Black viewers see the women of Wakanda as beautiful because they are confident and at peace with their gifts. Surely Shuri, the young sister of T'Challa, and who is the technological wiz is so appealing and irresistible because the joy she finds in creating and thinking and imaging gives her a radiance that is powerfully seductive. Nakia's quiet elegant reflectiveness only magnifies her physical beauty. And the knowledge that Okoye is deeply principled makes her a dazzling sight to see. These women are lit by a powerful internal fire that they fan and that flames and lights the world they inhabit.

We need to teach our daughters and our sons that beauty and power is rooted in our souls and shines outward to bless those who look upon us. One of the most damaging effects of racism is the amnesia it imposes on its victims, how it lulls them into forgetfulness that erases knowledge and memory of who and what they truly are and can be. *Black Panther* reminds us of our brilliance and heroism.

Now let's start living and thinking every day from that mental and spiritual space.

*Co-founder and President Emeritus of the Zora Neale Hurston/ Richard Wright Foundation, **Marita Golden** is a veteran teacher of writing and an acclaimed award-winning author of sixteen works of fiction and nonfiction. As a teacher of writing she has served as a member of the faculties of the MFA Graduate Creative Writing Programs at George Mason University and Virginia Commonwealth University and in the MA Creative Writing Program at John Hopkins University. She has taught writing workshops nationally and internationally to a variety of constituencies.*

Her new novel is The Wide Circumference of Love. Her other books include the novels After and The Edge of Heaven and the memoirs Migrations of the Heart, Saving Our Sons and Don't Play in the Sun One Woman's Journey Through the Color Complex. She is the recipient of many awards including the Writers for Writers Award presented by Barnes & Noble and Poets and Writers and the Fiction Award for her novel After awarded by the Black Caucus of the American Library Association.

20

THE BLACK PANTHER FILM HAS MERITS AND DEMERITS

Norman Richmond

It was great to see so many melanin rich sisters and brothers on the silver screen in the film *Black Panther*.

The African patriot in me makes me as Duke Ellington would say, "accentuate the positive". At the same time I unite with Black Agenda Report's Editor and Senior Columnist Margaret Kimberly. Says Kimberly: "The desire to see a black face in a high place is a legacy of slavery and the century of Jim Crow segregation that followed. The psychological impact of America's apartheid is enduring, and unlikely to end without true revolutionary change."

The new *Black Panther* film has raked in record breaking revue for Marvel Studios and Walt Disney Studios Motion Pictures and has African people from Cape Town, South Africa to Nova Scotia debating its merits and demerits. The Oscar Award winning film maker Charles Burnett gave me his take on the film. Says Burnett, "I can only say that, it has made history and will in the end serve to dispel the notion that Black films don't have a worldwide market. Sure the film is not perfect but there are a lot of films that to poke holes into."

Black Panther has made one billion dollars at the box office. It is officially the third highest grossing movie of all time in the U.S. Many of these dollars like Burnett says are coming from international sources. Thanks to a strong debut in China, where it opened with $20 million in its first day. It has moved past *Titanic* and is now the No. 3 highest-grossing film of all-time in the U.S.

If you compare what Marvel and Disney have made and will continue to make our great actors and actresses were paid sharecropping wages for their splendid work. Robert Downey Jr. pocketed $50 million for his role in *Iron Man*. This is ten times what the Pan African cast of *Black Panther* made. Chadwick Boseman who played T'Challa/Black Panther received the biggest check earning three million dollars; Lupita Nyong'o who played Nakia received one million; Michael B. Jordan who played Erik Killmonger received one million; Dania Gurira who played Okoye received one million; Daniel Kaluuya who played (W'Kabi) received $800,000; Forest Whitaker (Zuri) received $600,000; Letitia Wright who played Shuri received $500,000 and Angela Bassett $400,000.

The 2018 film made me reflect on a 1995 movie directed by Mario Van Peebles. *Panther* is from a screenplay adapted by his father, Melvin Van Peebles, from his novel of the same name. The film's budget was a mere nine million dollars. The *Black Panther* film had a $200 million budget.

The younger Van Peebles' 1991 film *New Jack City* which featured Wesley Snipes, Ice-T, Chris Rock and others made $47, 624,253 in the United States. Despite these numbers Hollywood wanted *Panther* to star Tom Cruise or Brad Pitt as white student radicals leading Africans in Oakland and even suggested Bridget Fonda could be put on the silver screen leading the Black revolution.

Since 1915 Africans in the United States have been cooned and baffooned by Hollywood. W.D. Griffith's silent film Birth of a Nation got the racist ball rolling. The film's release is also credited as being one of the events that inspired the formation of the "second era" Ku Klux Klan at Stone Mountain, Georgia, This film was the first American made film to be screened in the Caucasian Crib aka White House. It was viewed there by President Woodrow Wilson. (He claimed he was unaware of its content.)

The Trinidad and Tobago- born Cyril Lionel Robert James told Farruker Dhondy one of his biographers a story about how James told a youth who ask him about the racism in the film: James remarked : "I would recommend you go see it in the morning and picket in the afternoon." This was no joke James told me the same story when I spent a day interviewing him in Washington D. C. in the 1970s.

Mr. Ellington also said, "Being vicious is delicious." In an interview with Lawrence Hamm, the Chair of the People's Organization for Progress (POP) on Diasporic Music on https://blackpower96.org/ We both agreed that the role of the CIA in the *Black Panther* film is problematic – to say the least. *Black Panther* is a glorification of the Central Intelligence Agency (CIA). Wakanda is a fantasy. Africa is a real place on this small planet called earth. The CIA is a reality and has a real history. This history is far from being glorious when it comes to Africa, Africans and progressive humanity.

I can vividly recall January 17, 1961. I had just begun attending John C. Fremont High School in Los Angeles. Patrice Emery Lumumba, the democratically elected Prime Minister of the Democratic Republic of the Congo; Joseph Okito who served as First Vice-President of the Senate of the Congo; and Maurice Mpolo who served as Minister of Youth and Sports were killed that day. History revealed the CIA played a major role in these murders. This event sent me to Muhammad Temple 27 in Los Angeles. For many of my generation the Nation of Islam was our boot camp in the struggle for world African Liberation.

Once again I point to Comrade/Sister Kimberly. Says Kimberly: "There are very few Americans of any race who know that Patrice Lumumba was assassinated with the help of the CIA. There are few Americans who know his name at all and therein lies the biggest problem."

Another example of the CIA's meddling in African affairs took place five years later. Kwame Nkrumah, who was the founder of the Convention Peoples Party (CPP) in 1949, which led the former British colony of the Gold Coast to national independence in 1957.

The Gold Coast became Ghana on March 6, 1956. Kwame, Lumumba, Sekou Toure of Guinea-Conakry, Modibo Keita of Mali and Ahmed Ben Bella of Algeria were heroes in my neighborhood. On February 24, 1966 Kwame Nkrumah was attempting to stop the war in Vietnam but received heart breaking news.

Nkrumah was traveling with the Richmond, Virginia-born Vicki Garvin ((December 18, 1915 – June 11, 2007). Garvin was a Pan-Africanist, and self-described "working class internationalist" before traveling to Nigeria, Ghana, and China. In Ghana, (Garvin was a member of a committee who received Malcolm X and created his itinerary, since Garvin had previously met him in Harlem.) and others were on a state visit to the Democratic Republic of Vietnam aka North Vietnam and China. He was informed by Chinese Premier Zhou Enlai the president had stopped over. In Beijing, Peoples Republic of China, for consultations with Premier Zhou Enlai and had planned to continue on to Hanoi.

Political activist and scholar Dr. Gerald Horne feels that too much time has been spent talking about what is on the screen. Dr. Horne feels we should be more concerned about what's happening behind the screen. Says Dr. Horne, "I would have to put it in a political and economic context. That is to say, recall some years ago when there was a profit downturn in the US film industry and that lead to the so-called Blaxploitation era with "Superfly", "Shaft", "Coffy" the rise of Pam Grier, and Fred Williamson.

"Once the industry trended to stabilize those kinds of productions went out of the window. Right now, the US film industry like most other US industries are faced with a stiff challenge from China. Indeed, many of the people who saw Panther might have seen it in an AMC theater which is owned by the (Dalian Wanda Group) which is a major Chinese conglomerate. China is also challenging Hollywood at the box office."

Dr. Horne has written several volumes on film. Africans and progressive humanity should study Dr. Horne's, Class Struggle in Hollywood, *1930-1950: Moguls, Mobsters, Stars, Reds,* and Trade Unionists and The Final Victim of the Blacklist: John Howard Lawson, Dean of the Hollywood Ten.

They are no longer King of the Hill. Hollywood is being challenged by Bollywood, and Nollywood as well as China. Dr. Horne continues discussing China and the film industry: "With the rise of China you see that Hollywood is going to have to adjust to a new market practically when you recognize that a lot of the money with regard to film are being made aboard that is to say the profits are being made aboard. This is the kind of competition that Hollywood has to contend with."

Since interviewing Dr. Horne China has overtaken Hollywood at the box office. According to an April 2nd article by Patrick Frater Asia Bureau Chief of Variety magazine China has accomplished this mission. The headline reads: "China Box Office Overtakes North America in First Quarter of 2018".

Why is Hollywood promoting the 2018 *Black Panther* film? Dr. Horne's continues: "Disney the company that invested tens of millions of dollars into this production *Panther* the CEO Rob Iger could fairly be considered to be part of the anti-Trump faction of the US ruling class. That is to say, that he resigned from Trump's climate change advisory council when Mr. Trump backed out of the Paris climate accord or said he would back off this accord."

"The problem with the anti-Trump faction of the US ruling elite is that they are far from having a majority in the all-important Euro American community. And they are not very adept and adroit in building a rainbow coalition but at the same time it seems to me factious to talk about why Hollywood would invest all this money in this black- themed film when that has not been their pattern and practice without taking into account some of these political and economy factors.

"Now you noticed that I've spoken quite a bit without even mentioning what's on the silver screen. And I do that because I think that to talk about what's on the silver screen without talking about the political and economic context is really sort of a non- analyze. That's one of the problems we have with hip-hop right now. People talk about the lyrics the personalities of the rappers but whose making the money and why are they investing in this particular form at this particular moment time?"

Charles Burnett has always maintained that distribution is the key to the success of Black film be they are made in North America, the Caribbean or Africa. We should look to the African Union for funding. Africa, China and India are fertile markets for our productions. The success of *Black Panther* in China proves Burnett's point. The world is ready for coon and buffoon movies about the Black experience at home and aboard.

Norman (Otis) Richmond, *aka Jalali, produces Diasporic Music a radio show for https://* *blackpower96.org/ and writes a column, Diasporic Music for the Burning Spear Newspaper monthly.*

Jalali won the Jackie Robinson Fortitude Award this year. Jalali was born on March 6th the same day as Ghana's independence. He grew up in Los Angeles. He left Los Angles after refusing to fight in Vietnam because he felt that, like the Vietnamese, Africans in the United States were colonial subjects.

After leaving Los Angeles in the 1960s Richmond moved to Toronto, where he co-founded the Afro American Progressive Association, one of the first Black Power organizations in that part of the world. Before moving to Toronto permanently, Richmond worked with the Detroit-based League of Revolutionary Black Workers. He was the youngest member of the central staff. When the League split he joined the African People's Party.

In 1992, Richmond received the Toronto Arts Award. In front of an audience that included the mayor of Toronto, Richmond dedicated his award to Mumia Abu-Jamal, Assata Shakur, Geronimo Pratt, the African National Congress of South Africa, and Fidel Castro and the people of Cuba.

In 1984 he co-founded the Toronto Chapter of the Black Music Association with Milton Blake. Richmond began his career in journalism at the African Canadian weekly Contrast. He went on to be published in the Toronto Star, the Toronto Globe & Mail, the National Post, the Jackson Advocate, Share, the Islander, the Black American, Pan African News Wire, and Black Agenda Report. San Francisco Bay View.

Internationally he has written for the United Nations, the Jamaican Gleaner, the Nation (Barbados), the Nation (Sri Lanka) and Pambazuka News. Currently, he produces Diasporic Music a radio show for Uhuru Radio and writes a column, Diasporic Music for the Burning Spear Newspaper. For more information: https://normanotisrichmond.wordpress.com/

21

BLACK PANTHER:
Race and Representation
Diane D. Turner, Ph.D.

INTRODUCTION

The blockbuster film *Black Panther* has surpassed the expectations of Marvel Studios and Walt Disney Studios Motion Pictures by earning over a billion dollars. Prior to its opening debut, a large marketing campaign was used to attract the widest audience possible. This science fiction film has entertained moviegoers both nationally and internationally and joined the ranks of other blockbuster film entertainment such as *Iron Man, X-Men, Thor* and *The Avengers*. To gain some understanding of the film and its impact, one might ask: What are the origins of superhero Black Panther? What is it about the film that compels Black viewers and others to view the film more than once? Why is the film so intriguing to moviegoers? What does this film mean for the future of Black filmmaker, screenwriters, comic writers, comic educators and comic artists and illustrators? This essay will provide some historical background about the superhero Black Panther and offer an African-centered critique of the film.

MARVEL COMICS BLACK PANTHER

The black superhero Black Panther, created by writer-editor Stan Lee and artist Jack Kirby, first appeared in Marvel Comics' *Fantastic Four*, number 52 during July 1966, which was a historically significant year in Black history and culture, the civil rights movement and the Black Power/Black Arts movement. The Lowndes County Freedom Organization, founded in April 1966, adopted the image of a black panther as their visual symbol against white supremacy in Alabama. That same year, The Black Panther Party for Self-Defense was organized by Huey Newton and Bobby Seale in October 1966. Adilifli Nama in his book entitled *Super Black: American Pop Culture and Black Superheroes* notes:

Although the Black Panther Party and the Lowndes County Freedom Organization's black panther emblem are not inspired by the *Black Panther* comic book figure, all three manifestations of a black panther are a consequence, of the politics of the period, during which "black" became a defining adjective to express the political and cultural shift in the civil rights movement.

A black panther becomes a symbol for courage, determination and freedom. Nama's assessment is important. When critiquing popular culture, it is crucial to place an analysis within the context of the times, especially the Black experience because Black people, have been assaulted with grotesque stereotypical images of themselves in popular culture and mass media for centuries. Their struggles have included gaining the power to define who they are.

The creation of *Black Panther* during a period where there was a call for Black Power which placed an emphasis on Black Pride and Black self-determination resulting in the establishment of Black institutions, an emphasis on a Black aesthetic and the promotion of the slogan "Black is Beautiful," gave birth to black superheroes like Luke Cage and Black Panther. Nama argues that:

INDEED, "BLACK" NOT ONLY BECAME THE APPROPRIATE TERM FOR A NEW TYPE OF POLITICAL CONSCIOUSNESS BUT ALSO A SYNCHRONOUS TEMPLATE FOR THE CREATION OF T'CHALLA, THE REGAL AFRICAN PRINCE WHO IS ALSO THE BLACK PANTHER, A SUPERINTELLIGENT AND HIGHLY SKILLED HUNTER-FIGHTER SUPERHERO FROM THE FICTIONAL AFRICAN NATION OF WAKANDA.

When Black Panther appears in *Fantastic Four*, T'Challa invites the superheroes to Wakanda where he sets up a series of traps to provoke them to fight him. His ulterior motive was to test his own strength to find out whether he had the strength and skill to fight his archenemy Klaw, a savage mercenary, who killed T'Challa's father to appropriate vibranium, a miraculous mineral. Found only in Wakanda, the abundant deposits of vibranium stimulate technological innovation and advancements unknown to the outside world.

Black Panther resurfaces as a thirteen issue series entitled *Jungle Action* from 1972 through 1976. During this period, William Henderson "Billy" Graham (1935-1997), an African American comic artist, worked with Marvel Comics on *Jungle Action*. In 1976, the final *Jungle Action* series was "Panther vs. the Klan." In 1998, Black comics writer/editor Christopher Priest transformed Black Panther in the series *The Client*. He became known for giving Black Panther an "edgy, dark and neorealistic flair." In award-winning author Dr. Sheena C. Howard's book entitled *Encyclopedia of Black Comics*, she writes:

"Blending humor, politics, and economics with the conventions of superhero genre, Priest laid the foundation for the kinds of cinematic narratives that have shaped recent Marvel films and television shows. Moreover, Priest's writing attracted a dedicated audience of writers, artists and scholars engaged with Afrofuturism."

Broadly defined, Afrofuturism is a movement in literature, music, art, etc. featuring futuristic or science fiction themes which incorporate elements of Black history and culture. Sam Fulwood II articulates that, "It's a way of seeing us move through the world that doesn't have anything to do with Wester impulses." Ytasha Womack, a Chicago-based author and filmmaker, writes in her book *Afrofuturism: The World of Black Sci-Fi and Fantasy Culture*:

WHETHER THROUGH LITERATURE, VISUAL ARTS, MUSIC, OR GRASSROOTS ORGANIZING, AFROFUTURISTS REDEFINE CULTURE AND NOTIONS OF BLACKNESS FOR TODAY AND THE FUTURE. BOTH AN ARTISTIC AESTHETIC AND A FRAMEWORK FOR CRITICAL THEORY, AFROFUTURISM COMBINES ELEMENTS OF SCIENCE FICTION, HISTORICAL FICTION, SPECULATIVE FICTION, FANTASY, AFROCENTRICITY, AND MAGIC REALISM WITH NON-WESTERN BELIEFS. IN SOME CASES, IT'S A TOTAL REENVISIONING OF THE PAST AND SPECULATION ABOUT THE FUTURE RIFE WITH CULTURAL CRITIQUES.

The *Black Panther* series was relaunched under the direction of Reginald Hudlin in 2006. Themes included as "Panther: Bad Mutha," teaming up with other black superheroes such as Luke Cage, Blade and Brother Voodoo and the use of New Orleans in the aftermath of Katrina as a battle ground. In 2016, Ta-Nehisi Coates became the writer for the new Black Panther series, followed by afrofuturist writer Nnedi Okorafor in 2017, entitled "Black Panther: Long Live the King."

MARVEL CINEMA'S BLACK PANTHER

Black Panther is directed by Ryan Coogler and co-written by Coogler and Joe Robert Cole. It stars a Black cast that includes Chadwick Boseman as T'Challa/Black Panther, Michael B. Jordan as N'Jadaka/Erik Stevens/Erik Killmonger, Lupita Nyong'o as Nakia, Danai Gurira as Okoye, Angela Bassett as Ramonda, Forest Whitaker as Zuri, Letitia Wright as Shuri, Winston Duke as M'Baku, Daniel Kaluuya as W'Kabi, John Kani as T'Chaka, Martin Freeman as Everett Ross and Andy Serkis as Ulysses Klaue. The director, writers and the majority cast are Black, representing a first in the Marvel action films. The making of the film cost $200 million. The cinematography in the film is strikingly beautiful and bold. The film was shot in Atlanta, Georgia; Busan, South Korea and Iguazu, Argentina. Aerial footage shots included South Africa, Zambia, Uganda and South Korea.

Black Panther introduces viewers to the Marvel Comics universe of T'Challa and the African nation of Wakanda an alternative world. It is an African nation that is economically and politically independent which choices to isolate itself from the rest of the world to protect the country's resources and citizens' interest. African traditions co-exist with high tech made possible because of vibranium.

The film begins in the year 1992, T'Challa's father, King T'Chaka visits his brother N'Jobu in a black ghetto in the United States to confront him about his involvement with Ulysses Klaue, a white mercenary and black-market arms dealer, who plans to steal Wakana's precious mineral vibranium. Zuri who is with N'Jobu but undercover confirms his plot. N'Jobu, who has a Black American son, is motivated to assist Klaue in order to help Blacks in the United States because of the degradation they experience as a result of racism. King T'Chaka ends up killing his brother, leaving behind his brother's son Erik Stevens known as Erik Killmonger.

When King T'Chaka is murdered, T'Challa returns to Wakanda to assume the throne. He is a noble, righteous warrior and prince. He always strives to do what is right and must prepare for his new responsibilities. In Wakanda, the viewer is introduced to high tech flying machines and scenic landscape. There are a number of Africanism in the film. In the African tradition, T'Challa, his family and citizens call upon the ancestors for guidance. African women have central roles. Viewers are introduced to African women warriors like General Okoye, who leads T'Challa's personal guard. She is a military leader in the tradition of other African women warriors like Yaa Asantewaa, Queen Nzinga Mbundu and Amanirenas. The women are fearless and beautiful like Nakia, who is a human rights activist that T'Challa is in love with. The men and the women dress in brilliant colored African attire and display intricate facial paint designs on their faces. Oral traditions and storytelling are incorporated. The use of drums is important for ritual and communication. African terms like Baba, a word for father in various African languages, is a part of the dialogue. Queen Mother is another word used. In the African tradition, Queen Mothers held great power and often co-ruled. The large scenes during the transfer of the kingship to T'Challa are similar to those in the film Quilombo, a maroon society set in Brazil.

T'Challa's sister Shuri is a young woman who has a prominent role in Wakanda. She is in charge of the country's technology and creates all types of inventions for her brother to utilize as Black Panther the protector of Wakanda. His country has a long tradition as a monarchy which is maintained. T'Challa finds himself in ritual combat for the throne with M'Baku, head of the Jabari Tribe, who are mountain dwellers. After an action-packed battle, T'Challa spares M'Baku life and becomes King. Later he will engage in another battle with his Black American cousin, Erik Stevens who was left in Oakland projects after the death of his father. T'Challa is disillusioned and hurt when he learns that his father killed his brother and left behind his son. Erik Stevens who is called "Killmonger" is made in America. Left alone to deal with being Black in America, he is full of anger and resentment. T'Challa refers to him, "As a monster of our own making." The film leaves no room for reconciliation between T'Challa and Erik also named N'Jadaka: he is the villain. There are several questions that come to mind: Does hate come from America? Why does T'Challa risk the security of Wakanda to save CIA agent Everett Ross? Could villain N'Jadaka, T'Challa's own flesh and blood, who starts out as an innocent young boy and becomes a monster/villain, have been healed of his resentment, anger and hate because of abandonment and the micro and macro aggressions he faced every day in an America where institutional racism was alive and pathological? I am sure many viewers like myself wanted to see N'Jadaka reunite with his African family. This is one of the criticisms of the film. That the gulf that exists among some Africans on the continent and Blacks in the United States, as a result of slavery, imperialism and lies, is irreconcilable: divide and conquer. Whereas, the Wakandans end of embracing Everett Ross. Ultimately, N'Jadaka dies. His last request makes reference to the Middle Passage when he asks to be buried in the ocean with his ancestors. In the end viewers are left with a sense of optimism, T'Challa haunted by the words of his cousin decides to take up residency in Oakland to help Blacks there by building a Wakanda International Outreach Center, enlisting his sister's aid and viewers are left wondering what is going to happen next. Hopefully, there is more to come.

Kenyan political cartoonist Patrick Gathara has a different view of *Black Panther*. He surmises that:

AT HEART, IT IS A MOVIE ABOUT A DIVIDED, TRIBALIZED CONTINENT, DISCOVERED BY A WHITE
MAN WHO WANTS NOTHING MORE THAN TO TAKE ITS MINERAL RESOURCES, A CONTINENT RUN
BY A WEALTHY, POWER-HUNGRY, FEUDING AND FEUDALIST ELITE, WHERE A NATION WITH THE
MOST ADVANCED TECH AND WEAPONS IN THE WORLD NONETHELESS HAS NO THINKERS TO
DEVELOP SYSTEMS OF TRANSITIONING RULERSHIP THAT DO NOT INVOLVE LETHAL COMBAT OR
COUP D'ETAT.

In response to his criticism, *Black Panther* is Marvel's first black superhero movie. It is entertainment not a documentary. Marvel films are known for creating scenes of "lethal combat." That's what their superheroes do! In the case of black superheroes, most were unrepresented in Hollywood films. *Black Panther's* extraordinary success at the box office might assure the long fight by Blacks for inclusion will bring more opportunities and the writing of more diverse stories that address some of Gathara's legitimate criticisms and concerns.

CONCLUSION

Overall, *Black Panther* is an excellent film. It offers a view of Africa very different from the stereotypical images in the television series and film *Tarzan* and other negative views of Africa as the "dark continent." The Africans in *Black Panther* are not child-like and inferior or animal-like. They are highly intelligent human beings that represent all that is good in the world. There is nothing primitive about them. *Black Panther* is a vehicle that create dialogue about race and representation in American popular culture but also the history of Black comics. Hopefully, *Black Panther* provides greater opportunities to the talented and creative Black filmmakers, screenwriters, actors, comic writers, comic educators and comic artists and illustrators, who have been underrepresented in comics and film. Last but not least, I am hopeful that Afrofuturism and its directions will be seriously examined in the academy in addition to race and representation in comics and film. There are capable Black scholars, artists, writers and illustrators like Dr. Sheena C. Howard, Christopher Priest, Deborah Whaley, Aaron McGruder, Tim Jackson, John Jennings, Ytaska L. Womack, Walter Greason, Ray Billingsley, Eric Battle, Stanford Carpenter, Julie Anderson, Dawud Anyabwile, Barbara Brandon-Croft, Adilifli Nama, Ta-Nehisi Coates, Vita Ayala, Yumy Odom, Kia Tamike Barbee, Reginald Hudlin, Jamie Broadnax, Akinseye Brown, E. Simms Campbell, Bertram Fitzgerald, William H. Foster, Mat Johnson, Denys Cowan, Keith Knight, Alitha Martinez, Jerry Craft, Kevin Grevioux, Jennifer Crute, Shawn Martinbrough and many others as well as comic book store owners like Ariell Johnson of Amalgam Comics & Coffeehouse in Philadelphia, PA. Black Panther is a first in what will probably become a series. It may have flaws but the film is meant to inspire audiences and it has, especially Blacks. One could imagine an African savior coming to America to help his Black brothers and sisters make it as far too many Africans who come to the United States do not understand the correlation between the privileges and benefits available to them are because of the intense long and perilous struggles and sacrifices of Blacks for civil and human rights and Black Power (economic, cultural and social) as well as justice and inequality for all that continues. Many viewers and comic book fans leave theaters after watching 135 minute film feeling good and afterwards many recite with genuine smiles, "Wakanda forever!"

With the current *Black Panther* film craze, the comic book is now a collectable item ranging in sale from $245 to $9,999 on ebay.

Adilfli Nama, *Super Black: American Pop Culture and Black Superheroes* (Auxtin,Texas: University of Texas Press, 2011), p. 42.

Ibid.

He also worked on the *Luke Cage, Hero for Hire*, Marvel Comic series (1972) for 16 series as well as the first retitle Luke Cage, Power Man (February 1974).

See Adilfli Nama, p 51.

Sheena C. Howard, Encyclopedia of Black Comics (Golden, CO: Fulcrum Publishing, 2017), p. 173.

https://thinkprogress.org/afrofuturism-imagining-a-black-planet,

Ibid. See Ytasha L. Womack, *Afrofuturism: The World of Black Sci-Fi and Fantasy Culture,* (Chicago, IL: Lawrence Hill Books, 2013). Octavia Butler's works, the film *Space is the Place* and the album cover of George Clinton and Parliament Funkadelic could be defined as Afrofuturism.

Black Panther first appears in the 2016 film *Captain America: Civil War.*

Yaa Asantewaa was the queen mother of the Edweso tribe of the Asante, who, in March 1900, raised and led an army of thousands against the British colonial forces in Ghana. Queen Nzinga Mbande was a highly intelligent and powerful 17th-century ruler of the Ndongo and Matamba Kingdoms, who fought against the Portuguese. Amanirenas was another one of the great queen mothers, who ruled over the Meroitic Kingdom of Kush in northeast Africa and led an army against the Romans in Egypt.

See Howard's *Encyclopedia of Black Comics*. Also see, Tim Jackson, *Pioneering Cartoonists of Color* (Jackson, MS: University Press of Mississippi, 2016) for a history of pioneering Black cartoonist from 1800 to 1970 and beyond. See Professor Frances Gateward and John Jennings, *The Black the Ink: Constructions of Black Identity in Comics and Sequential Art* (New Brunswick, NJ: Rutgers University Press, 2015) and Damian Duffy and John Jennings, *Black Comix: African American Independent Comics, Art and Culture* (New York: Mark Batty Publishing, 2010) and *Black Comix Returns* (St. Louis: Lion Forge Comics, 2018).

Dr. Diane D. Turner is Curator of the Charles L. Blockson Afro-American Collection, Temple University Libraries. Dr. Turner holds three Temple University degrees. Her areas of specialization and research include Pennsylvania and Philadelphia History, African American Labor, Cultural and Social History, Black Music, Jazz History in Philadelphia, Pennsylvania, Images of Blacks in Film:

Independent Black Filmmakers and Africana Cinema, Oral History and Public History. She has taught African-American history at Northeastern University, Brown University, the University of South Florida, Rowan University, Camden County College and other institutions of higher education. She is the author of My Name is Oney Judge (2010), her first children's book and Feeding the Soul: Black Music, Black Thought (2011). She has published articles in scholarly journals and essays in anthologies. Her forthcoming is Our Grand Pop is a Montford Point Marine, co-authored with Corporal Thomas S. Turner Sr. by Third World Press. She is president of the Montford Point Marines Association, Philadelphia Chapter, Ladies Auxiliary. Turner is currently working on a history of jazz in Philadelphia, entitled Been Here All Along: Jazz in Philadelphia, PA.

22

BLACK PANTHER AND THE
BLACK PUBLIC SPHERE

Keith Gilyard

The film *Black Panther* has ascended to position of first provocation in the universe of Black cultural politics. Debates will continue to be plentiful and effusive, as they always are when large-scale intellectual and artistic products speak to Black lives. By now, if you follow the media or have friends like mine, you are familiar with the discursive battlefield. You know that some people are upset that Killmonger is the stereotype of the thuggish African-American male. Even grooming at Annapolis and MIT has not refined him. As Christopher Lebron has pointed out, Killmonger appears to be "a receptacle of tropes of inner-city gangsterism." Of course, I contend, like Lebron, that Killmonger is not merely a thug. I like that while he is certainly overconstructed as gangster, he is unreconstructed in his righteous rage. His passion to fight White supremacy is too powerful to be watered down simply because he can excel within institutions of the dominant culture. So the question that naturally follows, and my friend Earl Brooks quickly posed it, is why not a movie in which the Killmonger-T'Challa opposition is resolved into a coalition for the best transformation of the world order? That is not a bad ending. It is even a glorious one, though not satisfactory to my sense of the epic, the dramatic, and the tragic. My appreciation for the aesthetic requirements of a truly sinister and genius villain as well as for the sometimes warping and uncontainable effects of racist oppression–the irrational often breeds the irrational–outweigh on this occasion my concern with nice, neat, respectable representation. This is the lesson that Richard Wright learned from the reception of Uncle Tom's Children that led to the greatness of *Native Son*. He got rid of the shackles of sympathy and opted for raw depiction of depravity while yet anchoring that evil in its genesis, that is, White supremacism.

Some of my friends—and yours—read the film as a rendering of a Malcolm vs. King dispute with a world-house, beloved community, vibranium-sharing King emerging triumphant. My nationalists don't like this. Even my world-house people are not too eager to hand over vibranium to the White folk.

Some of my friends simply pine for a Wakanda of the mind. I get it. A place of presumed empowerment and benevolence, a sort of "Pan-African Dream," as Gary Anderson has described it. In a meme that I saw, you can get a jet from Hartsfield-Jackson International Airport in Atlanta and fly straight to Wakanda. I am in no hurry because I do not yearn for a monarchy. M'Baku and the Jabari Tribe do not seem to have fared all that well under a monarchy, and I am sensitive to M'Baku's critique. There is generosity in some of T'Challa's latter gestures but no offer of democracy. He isn't running for president. He is the king. And as Anderson knows, there really is no Pan-African ideal expressed in the movie. Although it had the means, Wakanda lifted no finger to stop enslavement or colonialism or to address any of their repercussions.

Everyone I know loves the women: Shuri, Okoye, Nakia. They stole the show. But discussion ensues about why such major displays of brilliance, strength, beauty, technological wizardry, skill, integrity, and fortitude by Black women are still surprising in a Hollywood film. Then there are the reflections about the racial climate of Hollywood, the decision-making, the exclusions. Close ups show diversity. Wide-angle shots not so much. Nonetheless, the accomplishments of director Ryan Coogler in that realm have been spectacular. Moreover, it certainly is not hard not to support someone who has managed this effort and previously wrote and directed *Fruitvale Station*, a film about the murder of Oscar Grant by a BART police officer. We should talk about that film more.

In addition to the overt and politically-charged responses, there are millions of apparent, on-the-surface, apolitical ones that can be teased out later. I watched *Black Panther* while seated next to the eleven-year-old son of a friend and colleague in my department. When it was over, I asked him how he liked it. He said with the preadolescent authority that he could muster, "best movie ever." We must always remember that youth are watching, having aesthetic experiences, and, even when they don't realize it, being persuaded. Way back in the day, how many of us rooted for the cowboys?

I offer this tour of responses not to resolve any of the issues that arise but to speak to the pedagogical possibilities before us. Given its widespread reach, *Black Panther* could be the centerpiece of a program of study both in school and throughout the Black public sphere. Potentially, it is the bridge that connects us renewed inspection of the central concepts, across disciplines of rhetoric, poetics, politics, technology, that affect how our lives are structured and suggest how they may be restructured. Imagine a curriculum or series of forums, therefore, spurred by *Black Panther*, which incorporate engagement of rhetorical criticism, of nationalism versus integrationism, of Malcolm and King—Malcolm and King, not Malcolm versus King. Imagine a curriculum or ongoing conference that promotes discussion of forms of government, of forms of political economy, of gender roles, of the relation of art to other everyday concerns, of the racial implications of technological advances, of the career trajectories of Black cultural workers, of art-for-art's-sake discussions. And there is much more. The question of images, social responsibility, and vision. What do we learn from a White-supremacist nation being born on screen about one hundred years ago to *Porgy and Bess* to *Colored Girls* to *Celie* back to *Colored Girls* to a filmic *Malcolm* and a Malcolm in autobiography to *Black Panther*? And more.

The value of provocation lies in what is ultimately achieved. If *Black Panther* leads to the sharpening of analyses, the heightening of Black discourse, and the spread of critical dialogue, while making reasonable even if flawed aesthetic contributions, then it is hard not to cast it in the plus column. This puts the onus back on Coogler. This is not his masterpiece. That's still out there, being buffeted on the currents of the Black Freedom Struggle, waiting to be claimed.

Notes

Anderson, Gary. "A Pan-African Dream." Webeblack.wordpress.com. 2/21/18.

Lebron, Christopher. "Black Panther Is Not the Movie We Deserve." Bostonreview.net. 2/17/18.

Keith Gilyard is *Edwin Erle Sparks Professor of English and African American Studies at Pennsylvania State University and the author and editor of numerous books, including Voices of the Self: A Study of Language Competence (1991), True to the Language Game: African American Discourse, Cultural Politics, and Pedagogy (2011), The Next Great Old-School Conspiracy (2016), and On African American Rhetoric, with Adam J. Banks (2018).*

23
DETERMINING A NATION

Allyson Horton

I am the Smoke King,
I am black!
I am darkening with song,
I am hearkening to wrong!
I will be black as blackness can—
The blacker the mantle, the mightier the man!
For blackness was ancient ere whiteness began.
—W.E.B. Du Bois, "The Song of the Smoke"

"You get to decide what kind of king you are going to be."
—Nakia to T'Challa, Black Panther

Imagine that African
superheroes soaring in cinematic motion
going where no camera
has ventured before

& if light travels at a finite speed
Black Light be an electromagnetic force all its own spherical illumination
centripetal "Power to the People"
"Wakanda Forever" the sequel?

transmitting fierce energy moonwalking
Marvel comics into a whole new
stratos-Fear of a Black Planet

diasporic continuum of a soul powered

nation of Black lives that matter
in all our Afrofuturistic
polyrhythmic vibrations
melanistic gradations shapes: sizes: plait-forms

"Speak the Truth to the People"
"My Black is Beautiful"
"It's Nation Time" "Think Black"
"By Any Means Necessary"
"Say It Loud ..."
"Wakanda Forever"

native tongues calling & responding
in the language that brought us here
transforming the silver screen
through liberation narratives
that can't stop won't stop
become living breathing soundtracks
break beats of self-determination
turning tables scratching surfaces
beyond mediocre step & stance exiting theatres
in salute to ourselves double fists
pressed to the chest in salute to ourselves

we inhale, exhale traverse the planet
in salute to ourselves crowning jewels
of civilization since time immemorial

an identifiable people wi-fi connected
to a continent of unprecedented
blockbuster appeal undivided
our mission is never impossible

spiritual vibranium shielding our diverse trajectories
capeless & courageous we take knees
& quarterback our own balls
choreograph our own protests
in salute to ourselves
direct our own survival stories
in salute to ourselves

a self-determining people
whose real life superheroes be tangible
as Malcolm, Garvey, Huey
Harriet, Martin, Fannie
hardly invisible men & women
emerging from the dust
like Black Smoke Kings & Queens

unbreakable Mandelas unshakeable Obamas
rising against present-day contradictions
beyond comic strip transparency
re(envisioning) revolutionary panels
of lost & newfound transitions

casting our Black Light at finite speed
upon next generations of modern Avengers
charting the future course

& if history dares to repeat itself
may the transglobal force be with us

Allyson Horton is a native of Indianapolis, Indiana. She received her MFA from Butler University. Her poetry has been published in the anthology Turn the Page and You Don't Stop! Sharing Successful Chapters in Our Lives with Youth, Not Like the Rest of Us: An Anthology of Contemporary Indiana Writers, The Indianapolis Review and It Was Written: Poetry Inspired by Hip Hop. Her work also appears in the following anthologies published by Third World Press Foundation: Brilliant Flame! and Not Our President. Her work is forthcoming in African Voices magazine (Spring issue, 2018). Horton currently resides and teaches in Indiana.

24

BLACK PANTHER IS A MILESTONE IN AFRICAN AMERICANS' SEARCH FOR HOME

Peniel E. Joseph

The search for home, both figurative and literal, has been a central focus and an enduring theme of black intellectual and literary production from the antebellum era until today. In speeches, slave narratives, fiction and journalism, Black folk have sojourned to find shelter from the unremitting storms of racial and economic oppression, sexual exploitation and the unceasing imperial dreams of western empires sometimes disguised as democracies.

"Black Panther" is an epic film that taps into a long history of Pan-Africanist desire for homecoming. From the slave spirituals of the 17th, 18th and 19th centuries to Marcus Garvey's panoramic Universal Negro Improvement Association (UNIA), which stirred enslaved Africans across the Western Hemisphere with distinct visions of homecoming, renewal and rebirth, to its modern expression of defiance and self-reliance during the Black Power era.

Directed by Oakland native Ryan Coogler and starring a bevy of chocolate-, caramel- and cocoa-colored actors, the film carries the fearsome weight of history as a badge of honor proudly worn, rather than a burden destined to be carried. Black Americans, from the instance of their arrival in a New World marked by forms of bondage including slavery in the colonial era and present-day mass incarceration, have longed for memories of a world before conquest, life before colonialism. During slavery visions of distant homelands were whispered by Africans in America who, even after generations in bondage, retained enough memory of their past to instill cultural, linguistic and food rituals that linger to this day.

Imagining home for Black Americans meant creating safe spaces — both real and fictional — that could offer refuge against the racial hailstorms of everyday life they recognized as racial weather patterns violent enough to lynch entire towns, like Rosewood, Fla., out of existence. The legendary black feminist Ida B. Wells imagined home as a place where Back women might be safe from racial terrorism, while W.E.B. Du Bois, the preeminent civil rights leader and Black intellectual of the first half of the 20th century, longed for homeland on two continents, reasoning that Black people's "double-consciousness" emanated from their dual heritage in America and Africa.

Garvey came tantalizingly close to upending America's racial hierarchy in the immediate aftermath of World War I through provocative and inspirational rhetoric that made the quest for black dignity synonymous with love and respect for Africa. The UNIA cast the widest net in history in its search for homeland, attracting exiled citizens of the African diaspora to a call to cultural and political arms. His movement identified descendants from the "dark continent" as the proud participants in the first wave of a global revolution destined to culminate in a restoration of ancient glories.

"Black Panther" imagines home as the fictional African nation of Wakanda, not so much an empire but a Pan-African paradise whose deft mix of dazzling vistas and natural waterfalls is balanced by technological wonders that remain their secret treasure. That secret both protects Wakanda and burdens it with the knowledge of having remained on the sidelines while much of the world suffers, especially their Black sisters and brothers living in America.

Michael B. Jordan's Eric Killmonger represents both a personal specter from Wakanda's past as well as the embodiment of black political anger, rage and pain at the loss of ancestral homelands and kinship ties. Killmonger's brash intelligence echoes an unsettling combination of Malcolm X and Stokely Carmichael, updated with a burning desire to eradicate the system of mass incarceration in the United States, end neocolonial policies that impoverish much of the world, and ignite a political revolution that will alter power relations between the global north and south. His anger well-earned, his desire for home overwhelmed by a need for a reckoning that imperils Wakanda and the rest of the world.

More than a movie, "Black Panther" has become a cultural touchstone in the age of Black Lives Matter, with black social media — and white and Latino and Asian and Native American allies —erupting in a frenzy of hope and joy at the sight of a comic book superhero who is not simply a well-received black guest in a house owned by whites.

This time he is the king of an entire nation, the wise young ruler of an African kingdom whose leading warriors, scientists and healers are Black women. "Wakanda Forever!" echoes historical clarion calls, "Up You Mighty Race!" and "Black Power!" precisely because it imagines Black life as worthy of experiencing joy, receiving and giving love, finding home. Social media now offer a window into the past in a manner that, at its best, amplifies and disseminates over a century of intellectual work on black history, helping to catalogue the importance of past social movements while shaping current protests, organizations and freedom dreams.

What might have simply been an exercise in branding for one of the largest movie franchises on the planet has suddenly morphed into a pop cultural phenomenon that mixes political substance with cultural subversion. The latter point is best realized in Kendrick Lamar's throbbing soundtrack, most poignantly the album's best track, "All the Stars," performed with SZA. The video has rightfully become a much-talked-about homage to a mélange of African styles, reflecting the breadth and depth of the continent's potent cultural, political and aesthetic influence on the world. The song's chorus imagines home as a world away that, on some magical nights, seem closer. "Black Panther's" major achievement is to make those stars appear closer to all of us who are still seeking a port in the storm, a way back home.

Peniel E. Joseph is the Barbara Jordan Chair in Ethics and Political Values and Founding Director for the Center for the Study of Race and Democracy at the LBJ School of Public Affairs and Professor of History at the University of Texas at Austin.

25
GOOD PANTHER, BAD PANTHER
Paul Street

"Black revolutionary consciousness is merged with white and bourgeois Urban Nightmare images of Black 'underclass' 'thugs' and 'Super-predators.'"

"They are often the kinds of kids that are called superpredators — no conscience, no empathy. We can talk about why they ended up that way, but first, we have to bring them to heel." – Hillary Clinton, 1996

The latest Marvel Comics science-fiction movie "Black Panther" is stealth ruling-class propaganda, consistent with its production by the great manufactory of mass consent that is the American corporate entertainment complex.

Did you expect something different? If so, why?

AFROFUTURISM IN ONE HIDDEN MONARCHY

The plot is a little complex. There's a secretly rich, technologically hyper-advanced nation called Wakanda magically concealed beneath the bush in the heart of Africa. This fabulous Afrofuturistic state has escaped the ravages of white colonialism and imperialism.

Wakanda hides in plain sight through *Star Trek Next Generation*-like cloaking.

It is run by smart, warm, attractive, and benevolent Black royals. Despite its technical hyper-modernity, it is not a democracy. It's a hereditary monarchy where the ruling family makes the decisions in consultation with a handful of elders from different tribes.

Its scientific wonders (far surpassing anything that exists in the rich white nations) notwithstanding, Wakanda remains wedded to absolutism, aristocracy, and tribalism. That seems fairly classist.

The everyday people of Wakanda are backdrops at best in "Black Panther." All the action in the movie revolves around the royals and their top warriors. Ordinary Wakandans do not merit any attention. It's all about the rulers.

The king periodically defends his throne from challengers through grand physical battle conducted before tribal leaders who chant and carry spears. Some might consider that a little racist.

The secret to Wakanda's greatness is its possession and use of a super-powerful natural substance – a mysterious and many sided form of mineral wealth called vibranium. It is vibranium that has made Wakanda exceptional.

"Wakanda remains wedded to absolutism, aristocracy, and tribalism."

We learn that a vibranium meteor hit Wakanda millions of years ago. Just exactly when Wakanda became a super-advanced vibranium-fueled state is not made clear in the movie but the impression is that goes back at least to the 19th century.

The film could have constructed a story about how Wakandan culture and society generated the nation's capacity to discover, activate, and deploy the powers of vibranium. No such narrative appears in "Black Panther," however. Perhaps it is implicit, or maybe not.

Wakanda could have used its great power to help Black Africa and the Black diaspora abroad (including tens of millions descended from people stolen from Africa as slaves) resist the ravages of white supremacism, colonialism, and imperialism. That is certainly the path that great pan-Africanists like Kwame Nkrumah, Ahmed Sékou Touré, Frantz Fanon, Patrice Lumumba, W.E.B. Du Bois, and Malcolm X (among others) would have counseled Wakanda to take. But Wakanda's royal rulers decided instead to build a technologically fantastic Black utopia (though the experience of ordinary Wakandans remains largely invisible) within just one country, their own. They kept the country hidden behind its cloaking devices, keeping the wonders of a vibranium-enriched life – glories that apparently don't include the democratic empowerment of the Wakandan masses – for itself.

SUPERHERO VS. SUPER-PREDATOR: "FIRST THEY MUST BE BROUGHT TO HEEL"

The plot revolves around the conflict between the young, handsome, dignified, and newly crowned Wakandan king, T'Challa, and a challenger to his throne – Killmonger.

Killmonger is T-Challa's cousin. His father, N'Jobu, was killed by T'Challa's father, King T'Chaka, in 1992, in a public housing apartment in Oakland, California.

(Oakland is the city that gave birth to the real-life Black Panthers, the Black Nationalist and Marxist-Leninist group headed by Huey P. Newton in the late 1960s. The real historical Black Panthers are never mentioned in the movie, but the choice of Black Oakland as the only U.S. setting to appear in the movie makes it clear that the script-writers know about the organization.)

The ill-fated N'Jobu was stationed in the U.S. as a Wakandan agent. He was killed by his brother T'Chaka as the king was trying to arrest him and bring him back to Wakanda to be prosecuted for selling vibranium to a white South African black-market arms dealer named Ulysses Klaue.

Killmonger is left behind to grow up in white-imposed misery and poverty in Oakland. (The movie doesn't show any images of U.S. race-class oppression other than small scenes of a dingy basketball court outside an ugly Oakland apartment building.)

As a boy, we learn, Killmonger learned from his father about Wakanda. It became his dream to reach the hidden African wonder state, to claim the throne, and to turn Wakanda into an open revolutionary agent of Black liberation by all means necessary, including military force. He wants to avenge his father and his own left-behind status. He also wants to reverse Wakanda's commitment to Afro-futurism in one hidden country. He wants to export revolution like an Afrofuturist Trotsky or Che Guevara.

"Killmonger dreams of turning Wakanda into an open revolutionary agent of Black liberation by all means necessary, including military force."

Killmonger developed advanced warrior and regime-change skills by becoming an elite Special Forces murderer in the employ of the American Empire. He totaled up hundreds of kills, each of them marked with a knife on his body.

Beneath and partly thanks to his imperial training, Killmonger is a menacing sociopath. He is pathologically scarred by the horrors of his ghetto upbringing and military experience. He has become every bit as evil as – the amoral equivalent of – the racist oppressors he hates.

In "Black Panther," there are no warm, attractive, and inspiring advocates of Black pan-African revolution like Nkrumah, Sékou Touré, Fanon, Du Bois, or Malcolm. There is only the cold and repellent Killmonger. The revolutionary is portrayed as a noxious urban gangster, someone to be hated and feared. Black revolutionary consciousness is merged with white and bourgeois Urban Nightmare images of Black "underclass" "thugs" and "Super-predators."

Killmonger arrives in Wakanda (how he broke through the cloaking is not revealed) with the corpse of Klaue and challenges T'Challa to a battle for the throne. Killmonger wins the clash and hurls T'Challa down a waterfall.

After dispatching (he thinks) T'Challa, Killmonger is given special royal ("Black Panther") power and tries to militarily initiate the export of Wakanda-led Black revolution against the global white oppressors. But he is stopped at the last minute by a miraculously revived T'Challa, who (it turns out) was saved from death by one of Wakanda's allied tribes. As he comes back to life in a vibranium-enabled resurrection, T'Challa realizes that his royal ancestors were wrong to turn away from the needs of the oppressed Black (and perhaps other oppressed) people of the world. He resolves to take back his throne and shepherd Wakanda's de-cloaked emergence as a progressive and benevolent force on the world stage.

A great high-tech Marvel Comics battle ensues pitting the noble and bourgeois (see below) T'Challa and his forces against the morally degraded pan-Africanist thug Killmonger and his gang.

It's another Hollywood update of white America's longstanding distinction between the good Black and the bad Black. The good Black pursues moderate ends in dignified and polite ways. He doesn't take to the streets. He is respectful and respectable. He can be trusted and included. He believes in law and order and the maintenance of existing hierarchies. He is mindfully at peace with himself and his surroundings. He's "constructive" – "someone you can work with" to "get things done."

The bad Black is angry, violent, and undignified. He is sick and agitated, out of control, malignant, and sociopathic. He burns shit down. He's destructive. He is unworthy of admiration. He is a bad guy. He is to be feared. He is to be put down and locked up. He must to "brought to heel," to use white racist First Lady Hillary Clinton's colorful 1996 language on what needed to be done with urban Black youth. "They are not just gangs of kids anymore,"

Mrs. Clinton said. "They are often the kinds of kids that are called superpredators — no conscience, no empathy. We can talk about why they ended up that way, but first, we have to bring them to heel."

The bad Black wants to wage war on the white oppressors.

The good Black wants to reassure the whites and knows that the war that must be waged is on the bad and unrespectable Blacks, who make the race look bad.

The prince-like T'Challa is Booker T. Washington, Sidney Poitier, Colin Powell, Oprah Winfrey, Eric Holder, and, last but not least, Barack Obama. He's good.

The frog-like Killmonger is Toussaint L'ouverture, Denmark Vesey, Nat Turner, Bigger Thomas, Malcolm X, Jeremiah Wright, Huey Newton, and the nightly urban crime reports all wrapped up together. He's an all-around bad Black. He must be chained and perhaps put down, brought to heel.

THE GOOD BLACK IS ENLISTED IN THE JOB.

It's Good Black Panther vs. Bad Black Panther. It's Black moderate Superhero vs. Black radical Super-Predator.

Gee, guess who prevails? Was there any doubt? Seriously?

As Hollywood knows very well, millions of white Americans love good, nice, moderate and measured "Guess Who's Coming to Dinner" Blacks who help them feel safe and better about themselves. (Morgan Freeman has made a lucrative film career out of that role to no small degree.) And part of being a good Black is helping white authorities keep and put down the bad Blacks. T'Challa kills Killmonger…

…WITH THE HELP OF THE CIA

At the end of "Black Panther," the Hollywood-approved Good Panther T'Challa defeats the demonized revolutionary thug Bad Panther Killmonger with the critical space age battleship assistance of, get this, a kindly white veteran CIA agent named Everett K. Ross.

We first encountered Ross earlier in the film during a shootout with Klaue in South Korea – a shootout in which Ross is gravely injured while protecting T'Challa's fiancé. T'Challa repays Ross by bringing him back to Wakanda, where Ross is healed by the nation's spectacular medical technology.

Portraying the CIA as a friend of an independent and strong African state is a great historical and imperialist insult – a longstanding Hollywood specialty. As Milton G. Allimadi reminds us at Black Star News :

"When Congo won its independence from Belgium in 1960, Lumumba became Prime Minister. All he wanted was for Congo to get a fairer slice of the profits from exports of its riches. The CIA worked with the Belgians to have him deposed in three months. The following year he was murdered and the notorious thief and dictator Mobutu was installed in power and supported by the U.S. for 37 years….One of Lumumba's mentors was Kwame Nkrumah who led Ghana to become one of Africa's first countries to win independence from Britain in 1957….it was Nkrumah's passion to help liberate the other African countries from colonial rule that contributed to his demise. He also tried to industrialize Ghana – this is the only way for Africa to break dependency from the West and to create prosperity. Nkrumah also was overthrown in 1966 with the involvement of the CIA.

"An African hero whom many consider to be Africa's T'Challa of T'Challas, Nelson Mandela, was also a victim of the CIA. In 1962, it was the U.S. spy agency that provided the South African intelligence services a tip about Mandela's hideout when he was underground and fighting the racist regime; this led to his arrest and later trial, conviction and 27 years' incarceration. Who knows, with Mandela actively involved in the struggle from outside apartheid may have collapsed earlier.

"If these African giants – Lumumba, Nkrumah, and Mandela – were alive today, what do you imagine they would think about a film that transforms a CIA agent into a hero on behalf of Wakanda an African nation, albeit imagined, of culture, high science, technological achievement and wealth?...This is akin to a fictional account of the FBI as savior of U.S. Black communities. After it's hounding of Malcolm and Dr. King and the destruction of Black consciousness organizations in the 1960s including the Panthers with COINTELPRO, who would buy this storyline?" (emphasis added).

But we are talking about Orwellian Hollywood, a critical wing of the American Empire and military-industrial thought-control complex, where real history goes down the memory hole. So what if the U.S. military police and intelligence state has been a critical, blood-soaked arm of racist and imperial anti-Black oppression within and beyond the U.S, undertaking the bloody repression of the U.S.-grown Black Panther Party in the 1960s and 1970s? So what if the CIA backed the racist South African apartheid regime that hatched Klaue?

"This is akin to a fictional account of the FBI as savior of U.S. Black communities."

The movie, to keep things a little bit real, has T'Challa's sister call Ross "colonizer." It tells us that the U.S. military trains its elite soldiers in the darks arts of imperial murder and regime change. And it has the tribal leader who saves T'Challa (after Killmonger threw him down a waterfall) hilariously shut Ross up, making it clear that the white spy has nothing to say to African people about African affairs.

Still, "Black Panther" absurdly portrays a white senior CIA agent as a friend of an independently developing and autonomous Black African state. Actual U.S. foreign policy (imperialism) has moved in precisely the opposite direction in Africa and across the Third World for seven-plus decades.

(Here, though, it is worth noting that Ross shoots down Wakandan air-ships heading off to foment revolution and punish white imperialists abroad under Killmonger's command. That part of the story is certainly consistent with how the CIA has understood its mission).

INTERVENTION WITHOUT REVOLUTION: A HAPPY BOURGEOIS ENDING

At the end of the movie, T'Challa reveals what his supposed spiritual conversion to Black peoples' internationalism is really all about – not much. As one of his futuristic spaceships stands nearby no longer cloaked, admired by inner-city youth, the young Wakandan king stands on Killmonger's boyhood basketball court in Oakland. His aristocratic sister sneers at the grubby neighborhood but T'Challa tells her that he is buying up and rehabbing some ghetto buildings there and will set up some social "outreach" networks.

No doubt he will be hiring some youth counselors to preach personal responsibility and Black self-help ala Booker T. Washington and Barack Obama. The underlying power and oppression structures of class and race remain untouched. Empire grinds on. "In the end," writes Osha Neuman:

> "with all his superpowers, his access to the technology of an advanced civilization, its unique mineral wealth and sources of energy, what does the Black Panther do (or rather what is he allowed to do by the script writers and script doctors and directors and producers and funders of this movie)? He comes to Oakland and rehabs a decaying high-rise into a community center. He does not empty the prisons; he does not open the vaults of the banks and distribute to the wretched of the earth the wealth stored there by the 1%; he does not storm Wall Street and send all the stock brokers off for rehabilitation; he does not send all the nuclear weapons into space to travel harmlessly beyond the galaxy; he does not take back the White House and paint it the colors of Kente cloth. No, what the poor kids of Oakland with their shitty schools and rat infested housing get is a better place to play basketball. #How sad."

So, at the end of the day it all comes down to capitalism, well Black capitalism. Can anyone say "Enterprise Zones"? Market forces – the very same forces that brought the world Black chattel slavery and modern racist imperialism – to the rescue.

Capitalism is the problem. No, scratch that. Capitalism is the answer, the solution. Call in the Urban League.

Barack Obama, a great fan of the profits system, wins. The democratic socialist Dr. Martin Luther King, Jr. , who was killed by fascist white America after writing (in accord with the teachings of the great Black Marxist and pan-Africanist Du Bois) that "the real issue to be faced" was "the radical reconstruction of society itself," loses.

The movie is a monument to the persistence of the old regime. It's all so bourgeois and neoliberal, so Ta-Nehisi Coates. The revolution will not be cinematized. The king is dead, long live the king.

OPEN FOR GLOBAL CORPORATE WHITESPLOITATION

Global capitalism, that is. The movie ends with the CIA agent smiling as he watches his friend T'Challa tell the United Nations that Wakanda is joining the international community to help the world move beyond tribalism and make the planet a better place.

Hey, maybe vibranium will be offered for sale on the world market and opened up for transnational corporate "development" (exploitation).

That's what good Blacks do after defeating bad Blacks: align their communities and nations properly with global capitalism, leaving the basic class and imperial structures intact – like what happened in South Africa after the end of the apartheid.

(Actually, the movie ends with a with a teaser after the full credits, when we see a forgotten white Marvel superhero – Bucky Barnes, a onetime sidekick to Captain America – emerge from a Wakandan hut while T'Challa's sister laughs at three Wakandan children startled by his white and one-armed presence.)

Perhaps a follow-up movie will tell us what sorts of glorious miracles of human liberation the predominantly white masters atop Boeing, Raytheon, Lockheed Martin, Goldman Sachs, Microsoft, Google, (Tony) Stark Industries, and their Pentagon and CIA partners can cook up once they get their hands on Wakandan vibranium! We know what a wonderful job the white-owned U.S. and the West have done with Congolese uranium, diamonds, gold, and coltan, Brazilian timber, Ecuadorian lithium, and Middle Eastern oil – look at the miraculous capitalist world system we inhabit today, where environmental catastrophe looms and thermonuclear war beckons, where millions of Africans and others face starvation, and where the five richest white people possess as much wealth between them as the bottom half of humanity!

OBAMA AS CONTEXT

Like the wildly popular Broadway musical "Hamilton" (where some of the United States' founding white slave-owning capitalists get to be Black), "Black Panther" is very much about the Obama years, when the American white and capitalist Empire was nominally headed by an elegant, silver-tongued, partly African, and drone-wielding Black prince. Recall that the good Black Obama killed "bad" people of color (Africans included) with drones and Special Forces. He took the U.S. military presence in African to new levels. He devastated North Africa with the Libyan assault, which unseated the pan-Africanist ally Muamar Gadaffi (the African leader whose ugly death the white imperial gang-banger Hillary Clinton recounted with grisly glee seven years ago). He lectured unruly and "bad" homeland Blacks on their own personal and cultural responsibility for poverty and on their need to respect "law and order" even as white-racist U.S. superpredator cops murdered young Black men from sea to shining sea.

Like the Obama phenomenon and presidency, "Black Panther" exploits Black people's understandable desire to see Black heroes and heroines (elite Wakandan females play key and leading roles in "Black Panther," to the delight of some feminists) on the big stage by insidiously embedding those heroes/heroines within the vicious and eco-cidal projects of white-supremacist and U.S.-led capitalism and imperialism. As Neuman notes:

"Just as during the Obamas' eight years Black people enjoyed and took righteous pleasure in seeing a fine Black couple in the White House, so now Black audiences take justified and righteous pleasure in seeing images of fine Black men and women, heroic and powerful, commanding a blockbuster film. The Obama presidency confounded those who took for granted there would always be a blanket of whiteness on the peaks of power. This film may have a similar cultural significance, confounding those who believed a film by, for, and about Black people could never be a blockbuster. And, just as real pleasure at seeing a cool, beautiful, intelligent Black President allowed some to overlook the just as real betrayal by that Black president of the struggles of African-Americans, so real pleasure at seeing Black power and beauty portrayed on the screen, allows some to overlook the message that good Blacks' mission is to do battle with angry Blacks hankering for revolution."

Hurray for bourgeois and imperial Hollywood, every bit as significant part of the "manufacturing consent" apparatus as the leading corporate newspapers and networks.

BACK TO REAL HISTORY – BRINGING CONGO BACK TO HELL

Meanwhile, there's the real world. The "real Wakanda" is the Congo. "Tragically," Allimadi reminds us,

"today Congo is still exploited for its riches, including coltan. In recent years as many as 6 million Congolese have been murdered. Western corporations no longer need European colonial governors or armies. They use neo-colonial leaders – Nkrumah warned of sellouts such as these in Neo-Colonialism The Last Stage of Imperialism – like Gen. Yoweri Museveni and Gen. Paul Kagame in neighboring Uganda and Rwanda, respectively. These two basically rent their armies to invade and plunder; they and some Western multi-nationals are beneficiaries of the loot."

Right before I walked over to the theater at the mall to see "Black Panther" I happened (at a Barnes & Noble) upon a depressing cover story (in the neoliberal but candid Economist) about the Congo's re-escalated descent into imperialism-imposed Hell. The solutions to the Congo's plight have nothing to do with what "Black Panther" imagines and recommends. The Good bourgeois African and American prince Obama had no answers for Africa and in fact carried the rapacious, wealth-stealing, development-crippling, and neo-colonial U.S. military presence to new levels on the Dark Continent. With the great white nationalist "America First" circus freak Donald Trump – a real-life orange-tinted character like something out a comic-book portrayal of supremely stupid evil – in the White House, the chances of a renewed decent into calamitous civil war (the last U.S.-fueled one took as many as 5 million lives between 1998 and 2003) is on the rise in the Congo. Meanwhile the nation's vast mineral wealth flows out of African soil into the hands of malignantly sociopathic, eco-cidal, and white-owned transnational corporations and banks, corrupt empire-captive and sold-out government officials, and tribal warlords.

Don't hold your breath waiting for Coates, Marvel, or Hollywood to create a new Black Superhero who merges the grace and attractiveness of T'Challa with the aims not of a Whitney Young, a Colin Powell, or an Obama but of a Nkrumah, a Du Bois, a Lumumba, a Fred Hampton, a Malcolm X, or, for that matter a Dr. King.

Paul Street *is a journalist, historian, author and speaker based in Iowa City, Iowa. He is the author of seven books to date: Empire and Inequality: America and the World Since 9/11 (New York: Routledge, 2004); Segregated Schools: Educational Apartheid in the Post-Civil Rights Era(New York: Routledge, 2005); Racial Oppression in the Global Metropolis: a Living Black Chicago History*

(New York: Rowman & Littlefield, 2007); Barack Obama and the Future of American Politics(New York: Routledge, 2008); The Empire's New Clothes: Barack Obama in the Real World of Power (New York: Routledge, 2010); Crashing the Tea Party: Mass Media and the Campaign to Remake American Politics (New York: Routledge, 2011); and They Rule: The 1% v. Democracy

(New York: Routledge, 2014)

Street is a columnist at Truthdig and also writes regularly for Counterpunch, Consortium News, and Black Agenda Report.

26

DID YOU EXPECT SOMETHING DIFFERENT AND MORE RADICAL FROM HOLLYWOOD? WHY?

Dr. Eric Curry

HIDDEN KNOWLEDGE: WAKANDA, THE VEIL, AND AFRICAN AMERICAN LITERARY HISTORY

Director Ryan Coogler's Afrofuturist vision of Wakanda in the historically successful film Black Panther (2018) is both a part of and apart from African American literary history. On the one hand, this vision is apart from such history because Afrofuturism cannot be subsumed under broad histories of African American literary nationalism. As De Witt Douglas Kilgore suggests, "Afrofuturism emerges from and is in conversation with the generic traditions of science fiction" (565). On the other hand, Afrofuturism can take the form of specifically African American or Afro diasporic interventions in the field of speculative fiction and futurist narratives, interventions that draw on long-standing traditions in African American story telling. As Kodwo Eshun reminds us, "The conventions of science fiction, marginalized within literature yet central to modern thought, can function as allegories for the systemic experience of post-slavery black subjects in the twentieth century," thus recasting science fiction "in the light of Afrodiasporic history" (299, cited from Kilgore).

Black Panther brings questions of race, representation, diasporic community, and the blind spots of imperialism to the Marvel Cinematic Universe. In this way, the movie intercedes in an established sci-fi mythology. However, as it joins this one group of stories, Black Panther draws on a tradition that has been crucial to African American literature since the late eighteenth century. Coogler shows his audience how an African geographic space and the people living there cannot be truly seen by outsiders, especially "colonizers," a repeated Wakandan reference to white outsiders. In this way, Black Panther represents the limits of white perceptions, and thus white knowledge. To do so, Coogler's cinematic narrative draws on an African American literary tradition in which the perceptual limits imposed by white supremacist culture cast a veil over the reality of black subjects and the possibilities in black geographic spaces. I want to draw attention to how we might read the hidden nation and people of Wakanda as a narrative representation of white epistemology and its self-imposed perceptual limits, what W. E. B. Du Bois terms "the Veil of Race" in *The Souls of Black Folk* (1903).

Wakanda exists behind a technological veil, and this veil could be a representation of the racial contract as an epistemological agreement. In *The Racial Contract* (1997), Charles Mills looks at white supremacy as a political system, requiring "its own peculiar…norms and procedures for determining what counts as moral and factual knowledge of the world" (17). What whites know about the world and its peoples is and has been colored by the imperatives of colonialism, imperialism, slavery, Jim Crow, and apartheid. Hence, "true" knowledge of non-white communities and geographic spaces would be impossible, because the epistemologies built to support the exploitation of peoples and places prevent it.

For example, our first look at Wakanda in *Black Panther* suggests a lush, undeveloped land, but T'Challa's ship, returning home, passes through what is shown to be a sophisticated cloaking system covering the entire capital city. The veil, a projection of dense foliage, parts, and an advanced, futuristic city is shown to hide behind ostensible simplicity. The veil is, most directly, a means of hiding Wakanda from those who would exploit its supply of vibranium and the technology Wakandans use it to create. However, the technological veil and its ability to hide the truth about Wakanda is echoed in the presumptions white foreigners have or make about the African nation. The movie's white protagonist, CIA agent Everett K. Ross, expresses disbelief that Wakanda could be the source of sophisticated technology when interrogating Klaw, an enemy of Wakanda. Yet, Ross's misperception is soon corrected when T'Challa's sister, Shuri, saves the agent's life. At the end of the movie, when our hero announces a Wakandan outreach program to the world, and to the communities of the African diaspora, his offer of help is met with disbelief at the United Nations, with one (white) world leader asking, incredulously, "what could a country of farmers offer the world?" T'Challa responds with only a smirk.

This scene from the end of the movie shows how science and story-telling combine to keep the true nature of T'Challa's home a secret from colonizers. A cloaking device hides the capital city, but the effect is enhanced by the ease with which white outsiders follow the epistemological terms of the *Racial Contract* and its "invented Orients, invented Africas, invented Americas with a correspondingly fabricated population…who attain a virtual reality through their existence…in the white imagination" (Mills, 18-19). If the digital foliage seen covering the city at the opening of the film keeps those who would exploit Wakanda from effectively seeing it, then the epistemological limits imposed by the *Racial Contract* keep Euro-American U. N. representatives from accurately perceiving it. As Mills reminds us, over the last few hundred years, colonial and imperialist perceptions of non-white peoples and places have relied on a "cognitive and moral economy psychically required for conquest, colonization, and enslavement" (19). In *Black Panther*, the epistemological dimensions of the racial contract find representation in a mainstream, major studio movie release and a science fiction narrative. The movie shows us how an Afrofuturist aesthetic can bring necessary perspectives on the past, the present, and any possible futures to the modern genre of superhero-science fiction movies. This Afrofuturist intervention in one of America's contemporary mythologies, the Marvel Cinematic Universe, adds a necessary dimension, one that reflects the historical and cultural realities of white colonialism and racial domination, to its Futurist landscape. Any possible future must recognize a history of white supremacist domination and exploitation of non-whites, and Coogler's Afrofuturist narrative does this in a subtle way, deploying the trope of a culture hidden by the veil of race.

Wakanda is not a country of farmers; it is a country defined as much by its inventors and engineers as it is the hero and king, T'Challa. The inability of colonizers in *Black Panther* to see Wakanda for what it is, the notion that it is covered by technological and perceptual shrouds inhibiting what outsiders see, is a narrative representation of white epistemology and its limits. While the movie brings something new to modern American mythmaking, the trope of a veiled black culture or people is not new to the history of African American literary representation. This type of figuration is a crucial trope in African American literary history. For example, Phillis Wheatley's 1773 volume, *Poems on Various Subjects, Religious and Moral*, the first volume of poetry published in English by an author of African descent and a canonical African American literary text, includes a poem titled "On Being Brought From Africa to America." The speaker in this poem begins by thanking "mercy" for the moral knowledge imparted by Christianity, but the second half of the poem uses that position of knowledge to question white perceptions of black spiritual interiority. Giving voice to racial limits on Christian salvation imposed by slavery and the requirements of systemic domination, the speaker tells us, "Some view our sable race with scornful eye, 'Their colour is a diabolic die.'" Then the poem shifts to a lecturing tone, "Remember, Christians, Negros, black as Cain/ May be refin'd and join th' angelic train," and the speaker instructs the reader in how to properly understand the Christian doctrine of universal salvation. Only a false moral knowledge, and thus a false Christianity, would deny black spiritual interiority and the capacity for the salvation of revealed religion, and Wheatley's "On Being Brought" casts complexion as a veil preventing whites from seeing the spiritual humanity of blacks, a "diabolic die" seen on the outside that suggests what does and does not constitute knowledge of moral interiority.

In 1853, Williams Wells Brown deploys the figure of black cultures, communities, and people not fully seen and thus misread by white in *Clotel; or, The President's Daughter*, the first novel published by an African American writer and another canonical literary text. The novel introduces us to the character of Sam, slave to a Southern Parson, who is initially cast as a minstrel-like figure in "A Night in the Parson's Kitchen." However, in a later chapter, "The Death of the Parson," Sam's façade is dropped. In this chapter, the Parson's daughter, Georgiana, goes for a nighttime walk with her love interest, Carlton, when they overhear slaves singing. Surreptitiously listening to what Georgiana calls "these unguarded expressions of the feelings of the negroes" (155), she hears Sam singing a song that celebrates the recent death of the Parson, his master and her father. Georgiana had presumed to hear the Parson's slaves mourn his passing because, as she saw it, he was a good and kind master relative to others. Carlton reminds her that this presumed knowledge of the content lives of her family's slaves is blind to the fact that slavery in even its mildest form is a system of "deception; and Sam…has only been a good scholar." Sam manipulates white expectations of black slaves, strategically affirming white supremacist knowledge of black people as a means of survival. He plays on the mythologies of the veil, the false narratives of black subordination, to protect his interests, just as Wakanda does in Ryan Coogler's Black Panther.

Perhaps the most famous antecedent to Coogler's narrative representation of the veil of race as a figure for white supremacy and the limits of racist knowledge is in W. E. B. Du Bois's *The Souls of Black Folk* (1903), a book that gave use two crucial paradigms in the study of African American literature and culture, double consciousness and the veil. In *Souls*, Du Bois declares that the color line will be the central problem of the twentieth century. This problem, he tells the reader, had earlier led to Civil War over slavery. In his time, it could be seen in Jim Crow segregation. Double consciousness is a sense of self as a human being and a sense of self as an object of racist misperceptions, a racial subject determined by the false mythologies and invented populations of the *Racial Contract*. The veil, what Du Bois conceptually formalizes as "the Veil of Race" over the course of his book, is the epistemological apparatus in which an "official reality," one requiring a separation of the races to insure the vitality of the U. S. nation, "is divergent from actual reality" (Mills 18); a "consensual hallucination...[in] real space" that obstructs whites from seeing anything that contradicts a perceived need for racial subordination. Writing in a context where white sociological knowledge was being marshalled to support Jim Crow racial control, and the threat of cultural degeneration from racial mixture was one form of such "knowledge," Du Bois ends his book, a study of African America behind the Veil of Race, by asking, "would America have been America without her Negro people?" (187). Souls thus highlights the limits of white knowledge as well as the secret truth of what lies beyond those limits: there is no America without African Americans, and cultural degeneration will only come from racial separation, not mixture.

Beyond the veil in *Black Panther* is some of the very stuff that has made and will make the Marvel Cinematic Universe what it is. Vibranium, Wakanda's miracle mineral, was used to make Captain America's shield in his introductory movie, *Captain America: The First Avenger* (2011), and used to form a body for the cyber-super-villain, Ultron, in *Avengers: Age of Ultron* (2015). The protector of Wakanda, T'Challa as Black Panther, serves as a moral compass in *Captain America: Civil War* (2016), helping to resolve an intra-party conflict among the Avengers. Wakanda promises to be at the center of Marvel's Avengers storyline in the upcoming *Avengers: Infinity War* (2018), and the technological secrets and individual innovation behind the veil will likely help to save humanity in this next installment. We might ask of the Marvel Cinematic Universe, which, because of *Black Panther*, must now recognize the reality of racial history and its influence on any possible future—what would this Universe be without the Afrofuturist Wakanda and her people?

WORKS CITED

Brown, William Wells, Clotel; or, The President's Daughter. Bedford Cultural Edition, edited by Robert S. Levine. Boston: Bedford/St. Martin's, 2000.

Du Bois, W. E. B.. The Souls of Black Folk. New York: Bantam Books, 1989. Reprint.

Kilgore, De Witt Douglas. "Afrofuturism." The Oxford Handbook of Science Fiction, edited by Rob Latham. New York: Oxford University Press, 2104: 561-572.

Mills, Charles. The Racial Contract. Ithaca: Cornell University Press, 1997.

Wheatley, Phillis. "On Being Brought From Africa to America." From Phillis Wheatley: Complete Writings, edited by Vincent Carretta. New York: Penguin Books, 2001: 13.

Eric Curry *teaches composition and literature at Kennedy-King College and Harold Washington College in Chicago. His composition courses at Kennedy-King have been studying Afrofuturism, students are using their research to analyze Black Panther. Along the way, we have made exciting connections between history, the present and contemporary issues, popular culture, and African American narrative traditions. His teaching inspired the essay included in this volume. Eric came to Chicago from Philadelphia, where he taught courses in African American and early American literature at Temple University. A native of New Hampshire, he completed a BA and MA at the University of New Hampshire before moving to the D. C. area to begin a Ph.D at the University of Maryland. His primary area of research is in late eighteenth- and early nineteenth-century African American pamphleteering, which he links to the rise of the African American novel as a discrete literary genre over the latter half of the nineteenth century. Other areas of interest include African American authorship and self-publication, book history, the Black Atlantic, and narrative studies. He has published on turn-of-the-century novelist Sutton E. Griggs as well as earlier, nineteenth-century authors such as William Wells Brown and Martin Delany.*

27

THE BLACK PANTHER:
Archetypal and Symbolic Conversations About
Carol Lee

On the one hand, *Black Panther* is an extension of the Marvel superhero cartoons. However, super heroes have historically served as archetypes of values held by societies (Campbell, 1981), often embodied in stories in various medium (Achilles among the Greeks, Shango of the Yoruba), most recently in cartoons and films. In addition, in many traditional historical societies, animals take on symbolic value, reflected in epistemologies that view humans, animals, plants, water, all elements of the natural world as connected and inter-dependent, meaning we as humans learn from our relatives in the natural world. The figure of the *Black Panther* sits inside both of these traditions – archetypal hero embodying our wrestling around good and evil, and totemic animal representation of values.

The power of popular culture, especially in this case movies and by extension classic cartoons, is that the products of popular culture open opportunities for we, the public, to wrestle with foundational questions about who we are, what we value and what challenges are before us. The film *Black Panther* has opened up powerful dialogue within Black communities worldwide and within broader communities, particularly communities that self-identify as white within the U.S. and across the world.

I choose to interrogate The *Black Panther* as a window into discussions and debates within African and African Diasporic communities, minimally since the African Holocaust and the colonialism that accompanied and followed it. I view the film as symbolic in its structure and power. I interrogate it using literary and historical lens and hope the propositions I put forward in this essay and the breadth of propositions put forth across this important volume will spark conversations in our community that are very much needed.

PAN AFRICAN THEME
The film is clearly Pan African in its scope and symbolism. This is evident in the several African languages spoken in the film - Xhosa from South Africa as well as Igbo and Hausa from Nigeria. The actors themselves come from or are descended from the U.S., England,

Kenya, Zimbabwe, Guyana, Tobago and Uganda. The dress of characters is inspired from across continental traditions. As Ruth Carter, costume designer for the film notes in a recent issue of the *Atlantic Daily* (Ford, 2015):

"My approach was the same as [it is] on a period film: I did a lot of research," she said. The textile production, hand-dyeing, and beading techniques of the Tuareg, Zulu, Maasai, Himba, and Dinka peoples helped inspire an eclectic color palette: deep aubergine and crimson, effervescent chartreuse and tangerine, rich jade and silver. Carter explained that she wanted to 'show the world the beauty of tribal dress and move that forward in a more modernistic way.' (p. x) Her team included African designers who worked to create designs that were both tradition inspired and contemporary.

The actors talk explicitly about how they researched African traditions in preparing for their roles (see https://en.wikipedia.org/wiki/Black_Panther_(film)). Chadwick Boseman who played T'Challa, the Black Panther, looked to the historical figures of Shaka Zulu and Patrice Lumumba, read speeches from Nelson Mandela, trained in Capoeira martial arts from Angola and Brazil, as well as Zulu stick fighting. Michael B. Jordan who played N'Jadaka, a.k.a. Erik Killmonger Stevens, says he studied Malcolm X, Marcus Garvey, Huey P. Newton, and Fred Hampton, likely to help him understand political ideologies that may be construed as informing, in part, the ideological stance of his character in the film. Lupita Nyong'o who plays Nakia, learned Hausa for several scenes.

The director, Ryan Coogler, and his co-writer Joe Robert Cole, the costume designer, Ruth Carter, are all Black.

While there are many debates over who will really benefit economically from the film (largely the production company, Marvel Studios, and the distributor, Walt Disney Studios Motion Pictures), there is no question of a major Black presence in the film, a presence that is Pan-African in its scope.

The Pan-African focus is intentional, a focus that is not intentional in the various comic enactments of the super hero character. This intentional focus is due to the commitments of the director, writers, and actors, most of whom have personal histories of political commitments to the Black community here in the U.S. and abroad.

The Pan-African focus is important because it informs themes that emerge explicitly and symbolically in the film. And this focus is important because of the centrality of relations between Africans on the continent and African descendants across the diaspora within our communities for centuries. There have been at least two lenses on the question of Pan-Africanism. One has been arguments around issues of cultural unity across the continent, despite shifts over historic time in the boundaries of nation states. Cheikh Anta Diop's (1978) classic work *The Cultural Unity of Africa* reflects this lens, informed in part by external efforts to separate the achievements of Kemet (ancient Egypt) in the north and contiguous states from Africa south of the Sahara. Positions informed by the ideology of white supremacy have sought to depict communities south of the Sahara as not having histories of achievement in science, technology and the humanities (Mills, 1997). Another lens assumes a cultural unity across the continent and examines the presence and continuity of African traditions – belief systems, family structures, ways of using language, music, dance and the centrality of the drum – across the diaspora, despite efforts from the enslavement of Africans to destroy also such lived connections (Asante & Asante, 1989; Carruthers, 1984; Clark, 1999; Hilliard, 1992). Both lens have informed persistent political and cultural organizing within the diaspora and within the continent itself.

Among the most powerful examples of the lived connections between African descendants in the diaspora and their homelands is the African Burial Ground in New York City (Frohne, 2015; Hansen, 1998). During enslavement, in the 17th and 18th centuries, Africans in the area buried their dead near the center of white dominated capitalism, certainly in the U.S. Led by efforts from the Schomburg Center for Black Culture in New York and the broader community, the area was in 1991 acknowledged as a National Historic Landmark in 1993 and a National Monument in 2006. The Schomburg Center is itself an exemplar of Pan-African ideology on the ground, founded to archive Black cultural artifacts. It is an evolution of efforts in the Black community in the 1920s forward to have books by and about Black people integrated into the New York public library in Harlem, efforts that came to include works accumulated by Black Puerto Rican Arturo Schomburg in the 1930s. A wonderful monument to the enslaved was built in lower Manhattan. They also invited archeologists from Howard University to inter remains. They found, as would be expected, that the people had been in severe ill health. However, what they had not expected to find is that bodies were buried in positions, with markings on the body (think of the tribal markings on the body of N'Jadaka who challenged T'Challa), and with amulets that signified 'I am Akan,' 'I am Yoruba,' 'I am Igbo', etc. At a time when our people lived under conditions that we cannot imagine, at a time when all visible and physical circumstances of their lives signified them as not fully human, the people asserted their fundamental understanding of their full humanity as Africans through the significance of the transition into being ancestors, ancestors who are esteemed across African cultures. These same commitments and understandings are reflected in the naming of the African Methodist Episcopal Church, the practice of Santeria in Cuba and parts of South America, the Pan-African Congresses beginning in 1900 with representation from the Americas, the Caribbean and Africa who set the frameworks that would lead to the de-colonization of countries in Africa, the African centered education movement in the U.S., the presence of African centered organizations in the arts, the Back to Africa movement in the U.S. from the 1800s, and historical leaders such as Edward Wilmot Blyden, Marcus Garvey, George Padmore, and W.E.B. Du Bois.

These Pan-African connections have been persistent, and yet knowledge of them has been certainly not publicly acknowledged and have been outside media attention (Esedebe, 1994; Ture & Hamilton, 1992; Walters, 1993). In the U.S., before official desegregation, these institutions were well positioned and recognized within the Black community. One of the ironies of official integration is that this history is under ground and not under the public guise. One might think of this history as symbolized in the archetypal meanings associated with the Black Panther – the panther hidden from view who is always posed to attack for self-preservation.

A Pan-African consciousness today is evident, I think, in the response in Black communities within the U.S. and across the globe, including in Africa, of Black people coming to see the film deciding to dress in an array of versions of African inspired dress. And the variation and creativity displayed in what Black people are wearing to see the film reflects both tradition and originality, both the historical and the contemporary. This integration of history and the contemporary is an important dimension of any culture, and embodies dilemmas both in political confrontation within our communities and political themes invited by the film.

ARCHETYPAL THEMES

There are a number of archetypal themes invited by the film. One is the representation of T'Challa as a messianic, Christ-like figure. In the ritual through which he proves his worthiness to become king, he walks on water. When he emerges, transcendent from a presumed death, he rises out of the ashes. He is spiritual in his ability to communicate on the other side, to see and speak with his deceased father. He is the son of T'Chaka, whose name is reminiscent of Shaka Zulu, who led his people against the Afrikaner inroads that would eventually lead to the apartheid state in South Africa (think of Ulysses Klaue, the South African smuggler who steals vibranium from Wakanda in the film).

Father to son. Transitions in leadership, in the family, in the state, from father to son are the stuff of archetypal themes across cultural communities. These transitions often reflect tensions between traditions and the demands of new historic, political and economic circumstances. They can also reflect – related to both personal characteristics as well as differences in historical contexts of socialization – differences in underlying value systems.

T'Challa, through ritual, twice crosses over to commune with his deceased father, the king T'Chaka. I think these acts represent symbolically a fundamental precept that crosses African cultural traditions, namely that the unborn, those living on top of the earth, and the ancestors are connected. This precept is reflected in traditions across the continent (although not all) of pouring libation to ancestors before important events. In the second transition, T'Challa learns the facts: that T'Chaka's brother N'Jobu had been sent to America on behalf of the Wakanda nation as a spy, but had become a traitor; that Zuri, the elder statesman and spiritual keeper of the sacred herbs, had been with N'Jobu when what one may think of as a fratricide act occurs when N'Jobu is killed; and that his father had made the decision to abandon his nephew, N'Jadaka (a.k.a. Erik Killmonger Stevens), then a child who would later return to challenge T'Challa. It is in this second re-incantation that T'Challa confronts the spirit of his father, literally and figuratively, raising the moral dilemma of weighing fundamental human morality (not abandoning the child) against what political leadership perceives as the political needs of the state (and in so doing not revealing both the traitorous N'Jobu and the circumstances of his death to the broader Wakanda community). T'Challa's decision in confronting his deceased father and in so doing confronting his father's political ideology of isolationism in order to protect the state in archetypal terms represents a rite of passage for the son.

CONUNDRUMS: THINGS FALL APART

There are a number of conundrums in the film that reflect deep seated issues with which the Black community, on the continent and across the Diaspora, wrestle, conundrums that are both historical and contemporary. They include the following: weighing what Maulana Karenga (1986) calls tradition and reason; what it means to respond to the impacts of racism; what meanings we impute to relations between Africans on the continent and Africans in the diaspora; and the role of women.

TRADITION AND REASON

Maulana Karenga talks about the tensions between tradition and reason for peoples of African descent. I read the tensions as wrestling with the demands of modernity, including the ubiquitous power of capitalism worldwide, trying to figure out how do we compete on the world scene on the one hand without losing the traditions and belief systems that have sustained us as a people over the millennium. I think these tensions are as stark on the continent as they are in the diaspora. The question before King T'Challa is whether Wakanda remains isolated, hiding its power from the rest of the world, or whether Wakanda reaches out to engage with the world. It is notable that Nakia, the warrior woman he loves, argues for the latter. His decision is reflected in the final section of the film, interestingly not coming until after the credits, when he speaks before the United Nations.

In the history of African Americans, these conundrums are implicit in our internal political debates over how to address the persistent practices and policies that emerge from the history of racism in the country; are we to consolidate our own institutions internal to our community or are we to aim primarily to integrate into existing U.S. institutions. Challenges between Booker T. Washington and W.E.B. Du Bois, between Martin Luther King and Malcolm X, between the civil rights movement and the Black Power movement, in the role of historically Black colleges and universities, between organizations such as the Black Panthers and the Republic of New Afrika and the Student Non-Violent Coordinating Committee, the Urban League and the NAACP. These parallel movements around separation and integration within the U.S. have persisted across the history of African-Americans. I don't think the film offers any insights into these conundrums, but I certainly think it invites us to re-visit and to think about the complexities.

One of the complexities has to do with how we maintain our own humanity in light of the oppression we experience. This conundrum is represented in the character of N'Jadaka. N'Jadaka has lived, so to speak, in the belly of whale, not only experiencing the racism endemic to life in the U.S. but also ironically serving as a warrior for the U.S. in Iraq and Afghanistan. Interestingly, even in these warrior roles protecting the interests of the U.S., underneath his outerwear are the ritualistic markings of a Wakanda warrior, perhaps symbolically representing what Du Bois (1903) referred to as double consciousness. While on the one hand articulating goals for the liberation of Black people around the world, he also seeks world domination, saying "The sun will never set on the Wakandan Empire," reminiscent of the mantra under British colonialism that the sun never sets on the British empire. Rightly so, T'Challa says to N'Jadaka "You want to see us become just like the people you hate so much." One can think of this dilemma in remembering the response of family and church members after the massacre in 2015 of 9 in Charleston at the Emanuel AME Church, where members publicly forgave the killer, Dylann Roof, an avowed white supremacist. And one can think of the moving rendition of Amazing Grace, led by then President Obama, during the public memorial, Amazing Grace written by in 1779 by John Newton, who made his living on ships full of Africans, stolen from their homelands, being taken to be enslaved; a hymn which has ironically become a staple in African American spirituals:

Amazing grace! (how sweet the sound)
That sav'd a wretch like me!
I once was lost, but now am found,
Was blind, but now I see.

Historically, who is the wretch and what does it mean to see, these are the conundrums figuratively embodied in the differing conceptions of the role of the nation state Wakanda between T'Challa and N'Jadaka.

A third conundrum invited by the film has to do with relations between the continent of Africa and its descendants in the diaspora, again represented symbolically through the conflicts between T'Challa and N'Jadaka. While the role of the ideology of white supremacy used to justify the enslavement of Africans and the spread of colonialism across the globe is the clear and unequivocal culprit in the African Holocaust of Enslavement, less attention has been given to the role of political leadership in African nation states in collaborating with the European slave machinery. The Africa Human Rights Heritage group in Ghana and the Nigeria Civil Rights Congress have called for traditional leaders to acknowledge and publicly apologize for the roles of leaders historically in the African slave trade (https://www.theguardian.com/world/2009/nov/18/africans-apologise-slave-trade).

It is important to note that these roles of collaboration were played by political leaders, not by everyday people, reflected perhaps in how this dilemma is fought by the political leadership of Wakanda. It is interesting when T'Challa returns to Wakanda after his father's death to take on the ritual challenge of assuming the kingship, he passes over pastoral land where ordinary people look up and wave, as he proceeds in flight to the technologically advanced and modernist city where the leadership resides in Wakanda.

We can think of Queen Nzinga who led the fight against the Portuguese inroads into what would become Angola in relation to the women in the film. This leads to the fourth conundrum raised by the film around the role of women. The warrior women in The Black Panther, epitomized in the figures of Nakia and Okoye who heads the Dora Milaje, the women warrior force, represent an often unacknowledged tradition of women as political and military warriors, on the continent and across the Diaspora: The Mino, the all-woman military regiment of the Fon people of Dahomey from the 1600's through the 1800's, Queen Nzinga in the 1600's of the Mbundu people of what would become Angola, Queen Nanny who inspired by Marron communities in Jamaica would lead Africans out of slavery in the 1700's similar to the role of Harriet Tubman under U.S. slavery in the 1800's, to Carlota Lukumi, a Yoruba woman enslaved in Cuba who led rebellions by enslaved Africans. See http://atlantablackstar.com/2013/10/29/10-fearless-black-female-warriors-throughout-history/

The figure of the Queen Mother is important in traditional African political leadership, especially in societies with matrilineal lineage. Queen Mother Yaa Asantewaa (c. 1840–October 17, 1921) of the Ashanti of Ghana represents this tradition, leading the War of the Golden Stool in 1900 against British efforts to take over the monarchy of the Ashanti nation. The Golden Stool represented the historic Ashanti nation, linking the unborn, the living and the ancestors. The Queen Mother Ramonda of Wakanda represents the continuity of values of Wakanda. We can think of the high esteem with which mothers and especially grandmothers are held in Black cultural communities across the diaspora as a legacy of the import and power of the Queen Mother role. At the same time, historically the role of women in traditional African societies has been complicated, and not always reflecting equality in the roles and positions of men and women, certainly with regard to political leadership. One might view an epitome of these conundrums around the role of women in the recent kidnapping of hundreds of girls in Nigeria by the Boko Haram beginning in 2014. The film directly takes up this issue in the opening scene when we meet Nakia, the woman warrior who is loved by T'Challa, she is engaged in under cover espionage to free young women kidnapped by a group who are clearly intended to represent the Boko Haram. These conundrums around female leadership and power are also reflected across the diaspora. We have seen this play out in the U.S. in the civil rights movement (e.g. women not have public formal roles in the 1963 March on Washington) as well as in the Black Power Movement. It is interesting and notable that the Black Panther Party, as we find in the film The Black Panther, efforts were made to forefront the activist roles of women, perhaps most notably embodied in the figure of Assata Shakur, who was subject to the U.S. COINTELPRO program and escaped to Cuba, ironically a former colonial slave state, where she received political asylum.

CONCLUSION

The power of a film is not to give us answers, but to pose and help us imagine possibilities. Clearly there are many heated debates over the significance and meaning of this film. Some have argued it implicitly implies a colonial view of the continent. Others contest the decision of T'Challa to reach out to the rest of the world as problematic. I don't think the popular success of this film among Black people is because it gives us answers. Rather I think it's power is in helping us to imagine a world in which Black people are in charge, including at least some of the conundrums that accompany being in charge of our own destiny, namely then how do we interact with the rest of the world and with one another. I have seen the film twice. I know many people who have also elected to view the film multiple times, in part because of the many nuanced details that hold deep symbolic possibilities, but equally important because of the uplifting experience of Black people being in charge of our own destiny. I think of the figure of Shuri, the sister of King T'Challa, who is deeply sophisticated in science and technology. I love the scene when Shuri is healing the white CIA agent Everett Ross who cannot believe his wounds can be healed. Shuri says "another broken white boy for us to fix."

In some respects, we can think of the success of the *Black Panther*, especially its astounding financial success, as a public acknowledgement of the deep influence that peoples of African ancestry have had on the countries of the diaspora, especially the U.S. There are virtually no aspects of U.S. popular culture that are not influenced by Black music, dance, visual arts, other art forms and language. The economic foundations of the country have certainly been built on the enslavement of Africans. And virtually every advance in civil rights, human rights, bringing into fruition the promise of the Bill of Rights in the U.S. Constitution have come directly or indirectly as a result of legal, political and economic organizing by Black people. So in one sense, we might think metaphorically of the film, The *Black Panther*, as helping "another broken white boy for us to fix." The broken themes that populate our history are certainly not fixed by this film. But the possibilities of Black empowerment undoubtedly hold hope for our collective healing.

Carol D. Lee *(Safisha Madhubuti) is the Edwina S. Tarry Professor of Education and Social Policy and Professor of African-American Studies at Northwestern University. She is also a founder of several independent African centered institutions: The Institute of Positive Education (1969), New Concept School (1972), and the Betty Shabazz International Charter Schools (1998), all still in operation in Chicago, Illinois.*

28

BLACK PANTHER:
More Than Just A Wrinkle in Time, It Wrinkles Time

Eugene B. Redmond

Once when I was free
African sun woke me up green at dawn.
African wind combed the branches of my hair.
African rain washed my limbs.
African soil nourished my spirit.
African moon watched over me at night.

> Henry Dumas—from "Root Song," the whole of which
> Ta-Nehisi Coates used in Black Panther #3 (A Nation
> Under Our Feet). Marvel Comics, August 2016.
> (Original in HD's Knees of a Natural Man, Thunder's
> Mouth Press: NY, 1989.)

KWANSABA: PROLOGUE

We're Wakanda's Diaspora: Neo-Pre-Ancient African
Eye-Magi-Nation: Soular Ship wearin Benin
Mask & warrior-scentin Cosmogram. Black Panther
flashin Mojo Hand. Prime cut Vibranium
toppin Juju-Jav'lin. Conch-us-(K)night snippin
sail of Tri-Angular-Routed Slavers. Kwansaba
Crownin Dumas' Ngoma in East Saint Love.

ROUTES OF ROOTS:

Routed through roots of *Roots* (circa 1970s), *Black Panther* is enroute to Blockbuster attendance records; huge financial statements; high visibility/audibility on airwaves, magazine/newspaper stands and High Tech–e.g. Facebookings–hookups; and presence/s on the traditional "drums" and "grapevines" of our Soular System. *Roots* set TV viewing records, showcased the brilliance of Black actors, writers, directors and film technicians, and gave us Black History even if often via an operatic approach. But Black Panther, after accomplishing all of the above minus the operatic soap, carries us, in "giant steps," beyond *Roots*—like John Coltrane's "sheets" that go a-sound-steppin' over minstrelsy—Ntu *Pre-Ancient, Contemporary and Post-Future Black Modalities.* In *BP*, the Sci-fy, Marvel Comics, Euro-Surrealism and Make Believe cave under the wait/weight of Vodun-Juju-Folk Funk, Magical Realism (Dumas/ Reed/Morrison) and Interpenetrations of diverse elements of the Soular System. Including Life, Death and the Yet-to-be Born/e Life.

Proverbs—those mighty mental/poetic war horses of Africanity—are prevailing vehicles in both *Roots* and *BP*. But in the latter they're also ladders leading from roots up tree trunks to panthers that ("who") evolve Ntu conch-us-nests of humans: Who doesn't prepare "his children for his death has failed as a father." Or airways to space ships whose bellies have African masks carved into them. Now, let's "shout" for Prince Hall, David Walker, Yaa Asantewaa, Alexander Crummell, Marcus Garvey, Katherine Dunham, Elijah Muhammad, Olatunji, Billie Holiday, Felas (Kuti & Sowande), Kwame Nkrumah, John Henrik Clarke, Francis Cress Welsing, Sekou Toure, Yosef-Ben Jochannan, Maya Angelou, Asa Hilliard, Stokely ("Kwame Ture") Carmichael, Ivan Van Sertima, Amiri Baraka, William Keorepetse Kgositsile, and sundry other formerly "living" ancestors who strove to "reconstruct" the "mind" of Africa. To reassemble the "bones of Black Life" (Clarke). *Black Panther* undertakes such a Sankofa-like "fetch back" as it rolls through—and roils—oppressive forces within and without the Soular System. . . . And aims to "reconstruct" us.

Centuries, nay millennia, are compressed—artfully, in acknowledgement of African views/concepts of time (see M'biti)—as real Oakland, California and mythical Wakanda are traversed. And main characters (plus Soular Ships) appear in modern America and modern/ancient Africa. So do W.E.B. Du Bois' Pan Africanism and Fela Sowande's African Continuum . . . in everyday life and cultural-ritual practices. Backing up these presences are thousands of books, magazines, newspapers, stand-alone essays, and articles. All augment the important work that culminates in *Black Panther*. (Check out, for example, thoughts of painter-philosopher Oliver Jackson if you can get your hands on his notes from the 1970s when he helped dramaturge Paul Carter Harrison found Sons/Ancestors Players at California State University-Sacramento. Or my own notes on the *New Curricula* in the Eugene B. Redmond Collection at Southern Illinois University Edwardsville.

Today's "living" ancestors–walking/talking/writing kin like Maulana Karenga (Association for the Study of Classical African Civilizations), Morrison, Haki R. Madhubuti, Quincy Troupe (Third World Literature), Jackson, Harrison, Clyde Taylor, Jerry Ward, Angela Davis, Ryan Coogler and the BP family—continue seeding newer generations in the "Pan" Black/ African Continuum. Many, especially elder "living" ancestors, helped inform and form the New Curricula of the 1960's: Re: Africana, Pan African, Black, Multicultural/Ethnic, Women, Interdisciplinary, and Gender Studies. Entire new departments, schools, and divisions— like CSU-Sacrament's School of Social Sciences and Interdisciplinary Studies—have come Ntu being. The work of the generations, reaching taleologically—back or forward—to Pre-

Ancient Yesterisms-Morrowisms-Futurisms, upheaved America and the world. And now, through *Black Panther*, is re-upheaving newer world orders.

Epilogue: Black Poet Mari Evans (1919-2017)
Frame-work layer of 60s & 70s New Curricula
Taught that former slaves risk
Being re-Bondaged in New Packages [re-packaged in new bondages].
Her Remedy: That we keep looking Hard
Ntu Mirrors of Ourselves. Black Panther
Affords us another Opportunity to re-Begin Looking . . .
EBR April 23, 2018: 3:22AM

Eugene B. Redmond, *named poet laureate of East St. Louis (IL) in 1976, meshed "Arkansippi" sounds and beliefs with his formal training as a student at Lincoln High School in East St. Louis, Southern Illinois University Edwardsville, and Washington University (St. Louis, MO). He has held Professorships at Oberlin College, California State U-Sacramento and Wayne State University in Detroit; published numerous books including The Eye in the Ceiling and Arkansippi Memwars, both of which won American Book Awards; won fellowships like the National Endowments for the Arts; edited journals such as Drumvoices Revue; and received a Pushcart Prize. He retired from SIUE in 2007. Email: eredmon@siue.edu; Website: www.siue/ENGLISH/dvr/; EBR Collection: http://www.siue. edu/lovejoylibrary/about/digital_collections.shtml*

29

WAKANDA IS A BEAUTIFUL IMAGE, BUT WE DO NOT NEED A KINGDOM: A Critique Of the 'King And Queen' Narrative Underlying The Film, "Black Panther."

K. Tutashinda

ABSTRACT

The film, "Black Panther," as the highest grossing film of 2018, and tenth of all time, is undoubtedly the biggest major debut of an African American director in history. It has received only positive reviews and is a thrilling cinematic experience for all especially for African American viewers. Its aesthetics, storyline, and integration of futuristic technology are intelligent hooks revealing current thinking. Yet, at no fault to the director or writers of this particular episode, it has philosophically inherited ideas, that while not negative or extremely damaging psychologically, may nonetheless be inaccurate and not in our collective best interests in the future.

INTRODUCTION

The film, "Black Panther," directed by Ryan Coogler, an African American director from the Bay Area city of Richmond, California, is at present, the tenth highest grossing film of all-time-and, undoubtedly it will still be showing in the theaters for several more months. Its $1.3 billion sales so far includes only the United States. Theater and overseas ticket sales, including DVD and merchandise sales, could possibly be four times as much. (1.) The film has excited the passions and aspirations intergenerationally and has caused an upsurge in African clothing being worn and expressions of pride being shown. And, its accolades are well deserved.

In my over fifty years of viewing films, few have matched the positive portrayal of dark-skinned Africans, particularly women, in leading roles conveying the real life strength and determination of Black women the way this film does. It shows the power, grace, and sheer charismatic appeal of beautiful Black bodies, displaying subtle, yet smoothly choreographed movement. The costumes are very creative, mixing traditional African elements grafted onto athletically functional superhero or villain-wear. The music is basically a Kendrick Lamar album-and he just won a Pulitzer Prize in music. (2.) All around, "Black Panther" is and has been a positive cultural phenomenon of huge proportions.

Even the original character, created by Stan Lee and Jack Kirby in 1966 as part of the Marvel Comics Series, while not African American, per se', was a progressive force fighting evil in the form of the Ku Klux Klan in 1970. (3.) Said afterward to be the first superhero of African descent-an assertion which is challenged by those who believe the first Black Superhero to be John Henry 'the steel driving Man,' and coinciding with but having no association with the Black Panther Party, Black Panther may have been partly inspired by the usage of the Black Panther symbol by the Lowndes County Freedom Organization, the LCFO in 1965. Since its usage by the Black Panther Party of Oakland, the symbol has been infused with a grassroots militancy that has long entered into popular culture and the public consciousness of African American people. (4)

SO, WHAT IS WRONG WITH THE MOVIE?

While nothing is really wrong with the film, (well, maybe, the CIA agent being an ally, and Killmonger and T'Challa showing 'other' African attributes of competition instead of cooperation), the underlying assumption that 'Kings, Queens, and Kingdoms' are to be taken for granted as positive elements in our culture's collective past that should be praised and nostalgically longed for is a problem. While the film is excellent entertainment filled with more positive images than almost any film ever made, the continued perpetration of the 'King and Queen' narrative as being our greatest days needs challenging.

The "king and queen" narrative is in no way Coogler's fault. He, like all of us, has inherited, seemingly through osmosis the fact that we had kings and queens, and kingdoms too. There was Egypt, Nubia, Mali, Songhay, and Ghana. There was Axum, Monomotapa, Great Zimbabwe, and ancient Libya. Then there was Sokoto, Benin, Hausa, and the Zulu nation and many more. At Fisk University in 1974, my act of revolutionary defiance was taking African Civilization as opposed to the usual Western Civilization course-it was an eye-opening experience. Later, tracing the first migrations of early humans we realized that the Indus River Valley Civilization of Mohenjo-Daro in nowadays Pakistan, the birth-place of India, and Angkor Wat of the Khmer Kingdom in Southeast Asia, present day Cambodia were both African derived. (5.) In each instance, the knowledge of Great African Civilizations and their offshoots injected palpable feelings of pride in the face of blatant Jim Crow racism and white supremacy. And as descendants of enslaved Africans, this kind of knowledge became all the more needed. This information served and serves us today as a weapon battling low self-esteem, a remedy against self-hate, and a balm soothing the withered psyche constantly fighting against an onslaught of psychological warfare going back hundreds of years. Knowing we had 'kings and queens, too' made us feel better.

However, the assumption that just because we had 'kings, queens, and kingdoms,' in the past, it does not mean that we should view that or any other hierarchical living or governing arrangement as preferred or ideal in the future. Furthermore, we must challenge the personal attitude of an individual who goes around thinking "I'm a King" or "I'm a Queen." This attitude could easily morph into an egoistic tirade. This is not just semantics—words have power.

Probably originating in Abolitionist days, or before, the idea that we were 'Kings and Queens' was not without some substance, at least in a few cases. Olaudah Equiano, a captured African and enslaved in Virginia, was an actual Prince, who was expected to be the heir amongst his Ibo people of Nigeria. He escaped slavery and in 1791 wrote a memoir, The Interesting Narrative of the Life of Olaudah Equiano. (6.) With his situation being an actual example, a precedent of sorts was established, that was picked up on, most likely by African slaves who worked in the so-called master's quarters, and confirmed by the first African Americans to receive higher education. By the time the notion of 'Kings and Queens' reached the 60's and the Black Power Movement, it had seen many iterations-through the American Colonization Movement of the late 1800's, the Garvey Movement of the teens and 1920's, the Nation of Islam in the 30's till today, and the 60's activists on to the rap artists and filmmakers of today. The image has endured but it has rarely been fully examined.

In, "On the Subject of Kings and Queens: Traditional African Leadership and the Diasporal Imagination," Professor Al-Yasha Ilhaan Williams explores the use of the idea and term, 'King and Queen,' and its nostalgic appeal to the 'imagination' of African Americans. Williams writes:

> "Imagination plays a role in the conception of leadership identity and boundary or ideology that delineates a nation and that literature is often instrumental in creating these notions of group identity."(7.)

It is natural that a subjected people would idealize and fantasize when they too 'were in power.' But the power that they imagined we had in traditional Africa, even as a King or Queen, still had limitations, checks and balances, and clear features that we now call, democracy. Kings and Queens did not have unlimited power in Africa, and depending on the culture or tribe, could be killed or poisoned if the will of the majority of the people decided they had failed in their duties. There was in fact, according to Professor Al-Yasha Ilhaan Williams,

> "Harmonious marriage between autocratic dictatorship and popular democracy." (8.)

Only after European colonialism were there so-called Chiefs or Kings of unlimited power, often appointed by the colonial powers themselves, and they were often at odds with the will or wishes of the people. Having power concentrated only in one person's hands not only mirrored European customs, but made the negotiations for slaves, raw materials, and other merchandise easier. Therefore, the King and or Queen who many of us would have been proud of was actually an European version of an African King or Queen which in terms of self-determination, self-esteem, and self-pride poses not only serious contradictions, but hinders us socially and politically if projected onto the future.

Few question the true ramifications of living in a society with variously fixed levels of hierarchy, especially as experienced by those on the bottom. But in each of the societies and or nation states listed above—even if not following the European model—the poor and those at the bottom of the society witnessed untold suffering. Thousands actually died building the pyramids or died in the battles for Islamic Jihad in Sokoto or in building Angkor Wat, for that matter. More recently, American Jim Crow is a modern day example of hierarchical oppression. It should be noted that the very idea of civilization and its real value, has recently been called into question.

James C. Scott, in *Against The Grain: A Deep History of The Earliest States*, challenges the very notion of whether living in the so-called eleven thousand year span of civilization is any better off than living in the one hundred and ninety thousand year prehistory or in indigenous societies like the San, Aka, Hazda, Twa, or people in southeast Asia in a highland region comprising parts of eight nations called Zumia today. (9.) With regard to the fundamental questions of life, 'Are You Happy,' "Does Your Life Have Meaning," and 'Do you have peace of mind at the time of your death,' it could be argued that we, in so-called civilized societies are no further along than our hunter-gathering forebears one hundred thousand years ago and today. Have we as a species really progressed? Technically, yes, but culturally in terms of 'our humanity' towards one another? Almost all of the known infectious diseases originated in the overcrowded areas of the world's first cities. Organized more for taxation of grain, they began to symbolize the best of urban living as well as the worst. The concentration of humans more than likely increased the production of the arts, sciences, and organized religion, while eroding the free spirit nature of early nomadic humanity. STUDIES HAVE SHOWN, IN ALMOST EVERY CASE, THE DOMESTICATED VERSION OF AN ANIMAL OR PLANT IS NOT nearly AS HARDY, HEALTHY, AND well adapted as the wild version, and this goes for humans too.

Up until now, it has been assumed that the adoption of agriculture, living in fixed entities called cities and the domestication of animals in a linearly fashion was an evolutionary advance that was a natural improvement over the hunter-gatherer lifestyle. But, if it were truly the case, why do we still have today amongst us, people who still tenaciously cling to their own hunter-gatherer past? Did they not get the message that civilization is better, agriculture is better, cities are better, kingdoms with their kings and queens are better? Why didn't they get the memo? It turns out they may have gotten the memo and ignored it on purpose. In discussing the dichotomy between hunter-gatherers and agriculturalists, Scott explains:

"What is wrong –radically so, in my view– is not so much its depiction of the agriculturist as its caricature of hunter-gatherers. It suggests, by the implied contrast, that the hunter-gatherer is an improvident, spontaneous creature of impulse, coursing the landscape in hope of stumbling on game or finding something good to pluck from a bush or tree ("immediate return"). Nothing could be farther from the truth. All mass capture-gazelle, fish, and bird migrations-involve elaborate, cooperative advance preparation: the building of long narrowing "drive corridors" to a killing ground; building weirs, nets, and traps; building or digging facilities for smoking, drying, or salting of the catch. These are delayed-return activities par excellence. They involve a large kit of tools and techniques and far greater degree of coordination and cooperation than agriculture requires." (11.)

Elsewhere, Scott discusses the sophisticated use by hunter-gatherers of large scale fires, the first macro-technology of humans. Hunter-gathers long observed that fires herded animals in cordoned off areas making it easier to capture and kill them, while clearing the landscape such that certain edible plants could grow anew-thus attracting particular wildlife the hunter-gatherers wanted to kill and eat at a future date. It was not happen stance-they knew exactly what and why they were doing what they were doing. (12)

Additionally, in the 190,000 year old sojourn up to the dawn of the first settled enclaves that soon became cities-city/states-nations-kingdoms-empires, there were social values and behavior modification techniques that allowed hunter-gatherers, even today, to function, more or less harmoniously without police, jail, or capital punishment. (13.) However, it should be noted that hunter-gatherers also invented war, so it was not always peaceful.

The San Bushman, in the Kalahari region of southern Africa, are said to be humanity's' oldest inhabitants-culturally speaking. Their culture stretches back at least 80,000 years, where it is has been discovered that their ancestors had originated the world's first sacred ceremony-the worshipping of the python snake. In their long trek through history, and despite their present day existence being threatened through continuous land-grabbing and exploitation, they have devised methods that we might, even today, benefit from far more than a brief, feel good moment of remembering when we were, 'kings and queens.'

For example, the Ju/hoansi, a branch of the San living in Namibia, have a practice called, 'insulting the meat.' When a particularly skilled hunter brings in an impressive catch, be it gazelle, wildebeest, or kudu, he is subjected to light teasing and insults. Those gathered upon his return would say, "Look at that scrawny animal," or "what a small catch, you are not as good as you used to be," or 'that's a pitiful animal, look how small it is!' Everyone, including the hunter knows his catch is impressive, but he cannot acknowledge this fact or risk even more extreme teasing and insults. It is a game they play with real social value and meaning-the teasing and insults prevent any one member of the group from thinking they are special or more important than anyone else. All gathered know the particular hunter in question is the best in the village and he knows it as well but his 'ego' is checked such that harmony is maintained to make sure he accrues no special power or privilege as a result of being the so-called, 'best hunter.'

"Insulting the meat" was one of many tricks Ju/'hoansi used to cool hearts, discourage arrogance, and tear down any potential hierarchies before they formed." (14)

These skills as well as an increased appreciation of elders, childrearing without violence, and conflict resolution techniques that have now have evolved into 'restorative justice practices,' all are treasured cultural artifacts that need to be preserved and serve as real, time tested, social modifications that can be useful today-far more useful than imagining when we were 'kings and queens.' They are the seeds of real egalitarianism, and that is the echo from the past that needs to reverberate into the present of today. (15.)

CONCLUSION

As a film, the *Black Panther's* significance is more in the realm of economics, Black employment in Hollywood, and the empowerment of African American actors, directors, screenwriters, and producers, than its relevance as a cultural icon. Far more African American actors of all hues will now at least get a chance to show their skills and Black America in general, has flexed its collective economic muscles. It has been demonstrated that African Americans and others too will come out and support, financially, an African-centered project that is seen to promote positive values, images, and ideas, despite the criticisms of this paper or any other.

Yet, some intellectual fine tuning can still be done and hard questions can still be asked. It has been assumed all of these years by radical elements within the Black Liberation Struggle that we need our own nation. But do we? In most cases, what was really suggested was a 'national consciousness' that we as a people could organize around. And that would still be helpful today. But that does not mean a nation-state as they are presently formed. Those have arbitrary boundaries set by past European colonial powers that were incognizant of hundreds of years of animal, tribal, and intertribal migrations and movements. Is that the correct way to geographically view the planet? Do we, too, want the power to pillage, plunder, and murder those less powerful than ourselves? Do we want a Black nuclear bomb to compete with the 'powers that be?' Seven generations from today, would we still want the unequal distribution of wealth, including water, to be maintained by whoever is in 'power' at that time (even if it is us)? I think not. We are moving into an era where we must rethink what and how we envision the world. It is not a utopian fantasy (or maybe it is) to envision a world 'without borders'– 'without armies, police, jails, or prisons.'

Just two hundred years ago many of our African American people were still in chains. Could they look into the future and imagine us free today? As unimaginable freedom seemed in 1818-a future world without borders, inhabited by independent, autonomous peoples the world over working together in large, overlapping federations, alliances, and at times, confederations-is a true possibility if we envision it today. As beautiful an image as Wakanda is, we don't need it as a kingdom. And we don't need Kings and Queens either-even if they are as beautiful, charismatic, and Black as they are in *Black Panther.*

REFERENCES

1.Fisher, Luchina, 'Black Panther' crosses $1 billion mark in its first four weeks,' abcnews. go.com.

2.Felix, Doreen St., "What Kendrick Lamar's Pulitzer Means for Hip-Hop, April 17, 2018,

The New Yorker, newyorker.com.

3.Roach, David, Sanderson, Peter, https://www.britannica.com, 2018.

4. Rashid, Ali Abdullah, unpublished manuscript on John Henry, 2010.

5. Rashidi, Runoko edited by, African Presence in Early Asia, Transaction Publishers, New Brunswick, 1995. See also George Weber's Andaman Association, and Spencer Wells' Genographic Project..

6.Equiano, Olaudah, The Interesting Narrative of the Life of Olaudah Equiano: Written By Himself, edited with an Introduction by Robert J. Allison, St, Martin's Press, Boston, 1995, originally, 179.

7. Williams, Al-Yasha Ilhaan "On the Subject of Kings and Queens: Traditional African Leadership and the Diasporal Imagination," African Studies Quarterly, http://www.afric.ufl.edu/asq/v7/vt11a4:htm .

8. Ibid., p.61.

9. Scott, James C. Against the Grain: A Deep History of the Earliest States, Yale University Press, New Haven, 2017, pp 170.

10. The Art Of Not Being Governed: An Anarchist History of Upland Southeast Asia, Yale University Press, New Haven, 2009, pp. 1-40.

11. Ibid. pp. 65-66. Scott, James, Against the Grain: A Deep History of the Earliest Societies, Yale University Press, Hartford, 2017, pp 65-66.

12. Ibid. p. 170.

13. Diamond, Jared, The World Until Yesterday: What Can We learn From Traditional Societies, Viking, 2012, New York, pp 1-33.

K. Tutashinda, D.C. (*Brian P. Altheimer*) *is a Chiropractor, consultant, writer, and teacher. He has owned and operated Imhotep Chiropractic and Wellness Center since 1989, and taught in the Upward Bound Programs at UC Berkeley and Mills College for 32 years, 1984-2012. The author of eight books, he is a founding member of the Brotherhood of Elders Network (BOEN), and a Faculty member of The Healing Generations Institute. An elder at The Sons and Brothers Camp sponsored by The California Endowment, he also helps train the mentors.*

Dr. Tutashinda holds a Bachelor's Degree in Philosophy from the University of Arkansas at Fayetteville and a Doctor of Chiropractic degree from Life Chiropractic College West in Hayward, California.

He is the past editor and co-founder of Foresight: A Holistic View of African American Struggle, from 1981-1984. His adult activism originates from his involvement in the anti-Apartheid movement of the mid-seventies as well as Ahidiana Work Study Center and Collective in New Orleans in the late seventies. Since that time, his focus has been on healing, education and the development of independent, grassroots institutions. He is married, with four adult children and one grandchild, and lives in Oakland, CA.

30

BLACK PANTHER MEETS PINK PANTHER

Michael Dinwiddie

When World War II commenced just days after my Mother's eleventh birthday, she smugly informed her older sister, "We can't lose because we have Superman on our side!" Needless to say, her life was changed by the revelation that a cartoon character would be useless against the real-life threat of annihilation by the Axis Powers. My Mother is in her eighties now, but that story reminds me of how quickly we embrace action heroes as our saviors. In ancient times we had divine beings to watch over and protect us. All we had to do was intone the right prayer and perform the ritual sacrifice. Those gods and goddesses have been replaced by buff-bodied Rambos, Fantastic Fours, Avengers, Hulk Hogans, Rocks, and Wonder Women. All the evil in the world can be handled—and will be addressed—through super powers and cosmic forces so much larger than life that all we have to do is sit back and wait for good to triumph.

In fact we know that ordinary, regular people do heroic things. Human beings who empathize with others are the ones who lead revolutions and overthrow seemingly intractable regimes. Is this an optimistic view of the world? I should hope so. But I have role models to guide me along the way. Frederick Douglass instantly comes to mind. As you study his life, you realize that he freed himself—psychologically and then physically—from a slave system that had no intention of letting him go. Frederick Douglass was a real-life, human being. He was willing to risk everything. Mohandas "Mahatma" Gandhi was a small man in stature, scrawny and near-sighted. But his vision, shaped in apartheid South Africa, was large enough to unshackle a half-billion people from centuries of colonial rule.

So what is it about the Marvel-Disney film *Black Panther* that has intrigued and fascinated so many? Why do some view it as a symbol of liberation and empowerment, while others castigate and deny its potency? I suppose that it goes back to the symbol itself. In Lowndes County, Alabama, the black panther emblem was placed on ballots to contrast with the Republican Elephant and the Democratic Donkey. For first-time voters, many of whom were semi-illiterate and used to the chicanery of southern election officials, it ensured their votes would be correctly counted. A sleek, feline animal could never be mistaken for a brown mule or a gray elephant. It sent a powerful message to those tenant farm families: They had risked their lives to show up at the polls, and their votes mattered. Choosing the right symbol was a life and death decision, and the black panther was adopted as a symbol of all that the Black Power Movement of the 1960s would come to embody.

The panther's journey from rural Alabama to Oakland, California took on new meaning with the founding of The Black Panther Party, which stressed independence, self-reliance, and community control among other important goals in its 10-point plan. A militant, sinister image was manufactured by J. Edgar Hoover and his COINTELPRO minions as Gestapo-like tactics were instituted to destroy a party whose motto was "Power to the People." Hoover's greatest fear was that a "Black Messiah" would arise from the ferment of the 1960s to unshackle America's underclass from the oppression of what SNCC co-founder Rev. James Lawson aptly described as "plantation capitalism."

So we jump forward to 2017. Marvel-Disney released *Black Panther*, and it made film history. It had the largest box office gross of any film released in February (Black History Month) and it outperformed every other release in the ensuing weeks. It has buried—for the moment—the Hollywood myth that vehicles featuring African American protagonists will not successfully penetrate foreign markets. In fact, *Black Panther* is only the latest juggernaut illuminating an African American culture strictly policed at home but which continues to win widespread global acceptance in music, film, dance and other art forms. (Witness the power of Jordan Peele's Oscar-winning film *Get Out* in the previous season.)

Were they alive today, I have no doubt that the Harlem Renaissance "Negrotarians" would be proud and amazed at the success of *Black Panther*. From W.E.B. Du Bois and Charles S. Johnson to Walter White and Alain Locke, their belief that stories rooted in African and African-American cosmology would open up a racial common ground is borne out by ticket sales and positive mainstream press. While the women warriors of Wakanda are less genteel than those we would encounter in Nella Larsen or Jessie Fauset's novels, one knows that Zora Neale Hurston would heartily approve of this homage to the mythical Dahomeans (or Amazons, depending on which educational system in which one came of age). All in all, these Wakandans are respectable people of color under the gaze of a mass approving audience, controlling their own destiny and exercising agency at every level. They are peaceful and warlike at the same time, protective of their heritage and traditions—and of their extraordinary wealth.

So let us acknowledge that *Black Panther* is indeed a commercial success. It is a very well made Hollywood movie, exploiting the formula in an admirable way. It is, like the most successful film franchises today, based on a cartoon series. It is super-heroic and larger than life. Women are depicted as equals and in some aspects superior to men. It imagines a world where Africans have control of their own destiny. Wakanda is a rich, powerful nation sitting atop an element that came from outer space and is the most powerful energy source known to man. One cannot help but think of the devastation brought to Africa by the plundering of those precious metals that power our cell phones and microchips. How would the world be if Garvey's "Africa for the Africans" had become a reality? Again, I say, give the film its due. The movie is heroic and magnificent and artfully made. Its special effects are the best that Hollywood has to offer. Its cast is brilliant and the Afro-Futuristic world it creates rings true in all the production values.

And yet, there is an inherent problem in *Black Panther* that opens it to serious critique. In the story line, a Black man kills his brother and abandons that brother's child to grow up poor on the streets of the America. When the child Eric Killmonger returns to Wakanda, the horrible secret and internecine battles nearly destroy the kingdom as friends become foes and line up to fight to the death. It is only through more killing – this time, the first cousins in the royal family fighting (always) to the death—that the threat of a "race war" against the white world is averted. As the only character to have imbibed the African American experience, Eric Killmonger epitomizes an irrational hatred that is at the core of his bloodthirsty rage. Ironically, when he is finally defeated and dying in his cousin T'Challa's arms, the ability to heal any human's injuries (which we have seen utilized to save the life of a white man) seems to be unsought as a solution for this blood relative. Eric dies gazing out at the homeland that was held up to him as the most wonderful place on earth. In that profound moment, we realize that even in Wakanda, "Black Lives Matter" takes a backseat to a nationalist agenda. Only certain Black Lives seem to matter in this surreal moment.

I suspect that I am not the only person who experienced cognitive dissonance here. And it may very well be my fault. After all, I knew that *Black Panther* was based on a cartoon when I bought my ticket and walked into the theatre. Perhaps I arrived predisposed to view it as a palimpsest of deep desires—of a reclaimed African glory, a virtuous philosopher-king whose "420" trip takes him into the land of the spirits—but instead I was confronted with a terrifying fear: The only way to salvation as a people is to kill our brothers who have been warped and filled with hatred by the slave/plantation culture built on our ancestors' bones. I first had to recognize this subliminal message in order to reject it.

Perhaps it is more reasonable to think of *Black Panther* in the ways we think of *Batman* or *The Pink Panther*. There is always a place for a fantasy life. Bruce Wayne does not exist. There is no way that people mistake Clousseau for a real person, and a cartoonish holograph can never alter a real-life struggle for wholeness and wellness. Black Panther helps us understand that, in a war of attrition such as the one being waged in post-Obama America, imagery can only inspire us to aspire. No fictional character will advance our struggle for justice. We must never lose sight of the fact that orange hair is fake, whether on Batman's Joker or soaring above the clouds on Air Force One.

Michael Dinwiddie *is a playwright and associate professor at the Gallatin School of Individualized Study, New York University, where he teaches courses in dramatic writing, cultural studies, and African American theatre. His plays have been produced in New York, regional and educational theatre, and include The Carelessness of Love, The Beautiful LaSalles, A Guest of Honor, Dacha, Masque, Hannibal of the Alps, Original Rags and Northern Lights: 1966. Michael has been a playwright-in-residence at Michigan State University, Florida A & M University, La Universidad de Palermo in Buenos Aires, Argentina, and St. Louis University, among others. He was an Inaugural Fellow at Touchstone Pictures in the Walt Disney Writers Program and worked as a staff writer on the ABC-TV hit series Hangin' With Mr. Cooper. The recipient of a National Endowment for the Arts (NEA) Playwriting Fellowship, Michael also served as a TONY Nominator and received the "Spirit" Award from the National Black Theatre. Michael serves on the National Theatre Governance Task Force of the Theatre Communications Group and is chair of the Board of Directors of the Duke Ellington Center for the Arts. He is a past President of the Black Theatre Network, the preeminent organization of scholars, students, artists and educators dedicated to the study of the drama of the African diaspora. He has written articles and reviews for Equity News, Dance Research Journal, Crisis Magazine, Advertising Age and is a contributing editor to Black Masks Magazine. In 2018, Michael was inducted as a Fellow into the American Theatre College at Kennedy Center.*

31
TERRA FIRMA
Temple Hemphill

Dedicated to Ella, McKynna, Rylee, and Bethani,
future "bad as I wanna be" sisters

In the midst of breaking bread with my brother-friend, Dr. Lasana Kazembe, a historian and educator, I left with life-changing nourishment. Teaching colleagues in Chicago, we met to say goodbye as he prepared to embark on a new professorship in Southern Indiana. On the way out, Dr. Kazembe dropped several gems my way, including magazines and books to read, Chicago area artistic venues to support and a reminder to build Terra Firma. Detecting my ignorance to the phrase, he repeated it, "Terra Firma." He firmly added, "Solid Earth. Before you add a man, a baby or anything else to your life, make sure you have Terra Firma. That's what you need sis."

Solid Earth. After our meeting, I looked up Terra Firma's definition. *Merriam-Webster* defines Terra Firm as solid ground. Furthermore, when roots are deep and the base is strong, the sky's the limit; falls may occur but catapulting from solid ground makes rebounding workable. I know this first hand. Within a three-year span, I had survived a non-romantic stalking case that included the perpetrator's incarceration and the necessity for me to carry a GPS box on my person for almost a year and a semi-public divorce that included cyberbullying. I was in the throes of sho-nuff navigating multiple layers of pain. Romantic pursuits with a few clowns and nightly concoctions that included gin and juice could not permanently numb my pain that cut to the bone. Indeed, seeking solid earth sounded like a better prescription.

Nakia. Several months after my meeting with Dr. Kazembe, I found myself watching *Black Panther* minus companionship at an Evanston, Illinois movie theater. For the first time in several years, I attended a movie showing, solo. Matter-of-factly, while married to my filmmaker husband, we hosted several Oscar parties, including a couple at this particular theater. Needless to say, my emotions were scattered. Thankfully, I calmed my mind and witnessed a kindred strength in Nakia's character. She, too, fought to build Terra Firma. Watching her character's gracious and supportive spirit made sense of my past, present and future; she was I.

NEW VISTAS

I met with Dr. Kazembe in summer 2017. It's spring 2018, and I continue to reckon with just how to build Terra Firma that will not give way to life's venomous attacks. I am creating new paths to travel and to explore; my personal and professional travel schedules are abundant. I am cleansing spirits from my spaces and adding light to my life in the form of folks. I am committed to making things plain, in the form of truth-telling and living by integrity. I am minding my physical and spiritual health by entering 5K and 8K races with a half-marathon in mind and practicing mindfulness and yoga. I am creating a template for multiple streams of income that includes writing, speaking and consulting opportunities. Lastly, living a full life, while "cold-handling my business," as my mother calls it, sets me up for the nesting and mothering I desire. Surely, I see new vistas.

Time is the great equalizer. This slower, more deliberate pace was not always my race. The desire to establish my own family had caused me so much angst. Fear swaddled a lot of the Olympic breaking piss-poor decision making done in my 30s and 40s. Fast forward to my mid-forties and life had completely exhausted me; thaw my soul had become my silent mantra. Yet, here and now, I no longer make pocketbook room for fool's gold and wooden nickels that burdened my entire being. Furthermore, my go-to song has become *South African Black Coffee's Superman* featuring Bucie's voluptuous voice. But instead of begging someone to be my Superman, I decided to save my damn myself.

Covering. In the interim, as evidenced by Nakia and T'Challa's bond, I remain open to covering righteous brothers as and how the universe sees fit. One brother-friend relies on my business acumen to talk him through financial and business deals. Another brother appreciates my ability to speak life into him as he rebounds from his former life as a professional athlete to now living a low key, saner existence. As a freelance business writer and current health and wellness journalist and advocate, I am using my God-given gifts to bless these brothers; our steps are ordered. Let the chu'ch say amen.

Faith as a grain of mustard seed. As it stands, neither man is seemingly being positioned to be my romantic partner. Yet, as I sow into them, I expect nothing in return; karma is the payback. I have faith that Mr. Wonderful will eventually and organically take his rightful position in my life. In due season. Sorta like Storm and T'Challa. But first. Terra Firma. Because building one's own solid earth is what Storm, Nakia, Wonder Woman and other "bad as I wanna be" women do.

Temple Hemphill is a multimedia journalist, educator and health and wellness advocate. Hemphill divides her time among media ventures, teaching and speaking. Her journalism career includes doing interviews with Barack Obama, Stedman Graham, Gwen Ifill, Jennifer Hudson and Steve Stoute to name a few. A communications and media professor at the City Colleges of Chicago, Hemphill's forthcoming memoir serves as a cultural intervention and critique of the U.S. mental health system.

32

THE MASS APPEAL OF 'BLACK PANTHER'

Monica Moorehead

The movie "Black Panther" has financially taken the global film industry by storm since its official release in the U.S. on Feb. 15. Directed by the dynamic, young, multitalented African-American director Ryan Coogler and featuring a predominantly Black cast, "Black Panther" has accumulated more than $1 billion globally in ticket sales from Africa to China, including more than $600 million from the U.S. box office alone as of March 19. The movie shattered box-office records for the four-day "President's Day" weekend in February.

According to comscore.com which, together with Screen Engine, conducts exit polls of film goers on a global scale, the racial composition of those attending "Black Panther" during the Feb. 16-19 holiday weekend in the U.S. was 37 percent Black, 35 percent white, 18 percent Latino and 5 percent Asian. These are significant numbers, considering that the Black population is estimated to be around 14 percent of the general U.S. population.

The Disney-produced, Marvel comic book-based movie had a budget of $200 million. This is the largest amount of money ever given to a Black director to make a Hollywood film.

This is only the third feature film made by Coogler, who is a native of Oakland, Calif. His first was "Fruitvale Station," which focused on the real-life murder of Oscar Grant, a 22-year-old Black man, who on Jan. 1, 2009, was shot in the back by a white Bay Area Rapid Transit police officer as Grant lay facedown on the Fruitvale Station subway platform in Oakland. The murder was captured on cell phone video. Following a rebellion in Oakland, the officer was found guilty of manslaughter and served less than a year in prison.

Not only is "Black Panther" a box-office success historically. It has also been acclaimed by movie critics due to the brilliant acting and visuals.

The movie is based on a comic book character with the same name created in the mid-1960s by two white comic books writers, Stan Lee and Jack Kirby. These writers have been responsible for creating popular comic book characters like Batman, Captain America, Spiderman and many more. Movies based on many of these characters have made billions at the box office.

There was much speculation on whether a big-budget movie directed by a Black director with a virtually all-Black cast could become a blockbuster: Would white audiences pay money to see such a movie? "Black Panther" answered that question with a resounding Yes.

WHAT 'BLACK PANTHER' IS AND ISN'T

Before the movie opened, many Black activists had the misconception that "Black Panther" would focus on the Black Panther Party, a revolutionary, anti-capitalist, anti-imperialist formation founded in 1966 on the principle of self-determination for Black and other oppressed peoples against racist and state repression. This is understandable.

But nothing could be further from the truth. It is highly unlikely that any studio bosses, who are still overwhelmingly white, would fork over $200 million to a Black director to bring forth a positive story featuring a national liberation organization.

"Black Panther" is very much rooted in the philosophy of Afrofuturism, a term first raised by white critic Mark Dery in his 1994 essay, "Black to the Future." Since then it's been made universally popular by Black authors like Octavia Butler and Ishmael Reed and artists Janelle Monáe, Jean-Michel Basquiat, Sun-Ra and Jimi Hendrix.

Author Ytasha Womack states that Afrofuturism is "the intersection between black culture, technology, liberation and the imagination, with some mysticism thrown in, too. It can be expressed through film; it can be expressed through art, literature and music. It's a way of bridging the future and the past and essentially helping to reimagine the experience of people of colour." (theguardian.com, July 24, 2014)

While there are themes dealing with colonialism and the legacy of slavery, the movie takes place in Wakanda, a mythical African kingdom that, has been free from white colonial rule, able to control its own resources, most notably vibranium, the source of unimaginable technological advances concentrated in Wakanda. This kingdom is run by T'Challa, played by the multitalented Chadwick Boseman, who maintains his throne by fighting off challengers. Boseman's previous portrayals include Supreme Court Justice Thurgood Marshall, singer James Brown and baseball great Jackie Robinson.

T'Challa's security team is dominated by strong, powerful African women fighters called Dora Milaje and led by Okoye, played by dynamic Zimbabwean actor Danai Gurira. Rounded out by Kenyan/Mexican actor Lupita Nyong'o and Guyanese actor Letitia Wright, the characters they play have no problem pointing out T'Challa's weaknesses, despite Wakanda being a patriarchal society.

T'Challa's main protagonist is Erik "Killmonger" Stevens, played by another multitalented actor, Michael B. Jordan. This actor has appeared in all three of Coogler's feature films, including his breakout role in "Fruitvale Station," in which he played Oscar Grant. While T'Challa does not want to share the vibranium with other vulnerable nations, Killmonger, who is T'Challa's cousin, seeks to share vibranium with other African and oppressed peoples of the world in order to fight off colonial domination. Many will view him as an internationalist.

| 149 |

In his opening scene, Killmonger is seen in a British museum, admiring African artifacts. When a white woman curator approaches him, he asks her what country each artifact comes from. He corrects her on some answers, saying that each of the artifacts was illegally stolen, much to her chagrin. Complicating his motives, Killmonger allies himself with a racist, white, South African mercenary, played by Andy Serkis, who also wants vibranium — to make a profit.

Once again, the real issue of colonialism is brought before the masses of people in movie theaters, many of whom are unaware of how wealth was stolen from the African continent over the centuries.

Boseman stated that despite his character being portrayed as the hero, he related more to the Killmonger character, stating: "Killmonger is trying to achieve greatness ... but there's an expectation of greatness for me. I don't know if we as African Americans would accept T'Challa as our hero if he didn't go through Killmonger. Because Killmonger has been through our struggle, and I [as T'Challa] haven't." (cinemablend.com)

Boseman deemed his character as being "privileged," which is so true. Under this monarchy, he fights his challengers to hold on to his power while his "subjects" are onlookers.

Despite any political contradictions in this film, it has, with no doubt, resonated deeply with Black audiences in the U.S. and throughout the African diaspora worldwide, especially youth, due to its positive cultural portrayals of African peoples that run counter to Hollywood's historical and shameful racist movie stereotypes.

For this reason, "Black Panther" is worth seeing, along with the talented actors and the beautiful, stunning, African-themed costumes created by visionary costume designer Ruth Carter.

Serwer, Adam. "The Tragedy of Erik Killmonger: The Revolutionary Ideals of Black Panther's Profound and Complex Villain Have Been Twisted into a Desire for Hegemony." The Atlantic.com. February 21, 2018. https://www.theatlantic.com/entertainment/archive/2018/02/black-panther-erik-killmonger/553805/. Accessed March 22, 2018.

Washington, Booker T. Up from Slavery. Signet Classics, 2000.

Whack, Errin Haines. "Groups Affiliated with Black Lives Matter Release Agenda." AP News.com. August 1, 2016. https://apnews.com/41484b9f10884dfa87969a4231ba7697. Accessed March 28, 2018.

Woodson, Carter G. The Miseducation of the Negro. Africa World Press, 1990.

Monica Moorehead is a long-time national leader of Workers World Part¬y, a socialist organization. She is a managing editor of Workers World newspaper. She is the editor of the book, "Marxism, Reparations and the Black Freedom Struggle." Moorehead was WWP's presidential candidate in 1996, 2000 and 2016 elections. She is a founding member of "Millions for Mumia", which helped organized the largest demonstration in U.S. history to demnd the freedom of political prisoner, Mumia Abu-Jamal in 1999.

33
THE AWAKENING
Angela Kinamore

Over four decades have passed since I witnessed the success of a black film that took the nation by storm, while still having a positive impact on the Black community. Not since the airing of the unprecedented 1977 television miniseries *Roots*, based on the novel by Alex Haley, did many people learned what Africans suffered during The Middle Passage, and the realities of slavery in this country and abroad. As an African-American raised in the '60s, I am still present to the misconceptions that were taught in our schools, giving many people a distorted viewpoint of African people and African Americans.

When I first heard the title of the Marvel Cinematic Universe film, *Black Panther*, I didn't associate it with Marvel Comics, but rather the Black Panther Party of the mid-60s. It was the largest and most influential Black revolutionary organization of the time. Its original purpose was to protect African Americans from police brutality, a challenge that is still very relevant today. The consciousness of many African Americans was changed at a time when they needed to visually see black people stand up for themselves and take action.

Now forty years later, the film Black Panther, named after a character that existed before the organization or movement, accomplishes that task. The depiction of Wakanda, the fictitious, highly advanced African nation, represented a taste of Black Power and its infinite possibilities. I was pleased to see important messages and themes dispersed throughout the film that included: trust, loyalty, astuteness, spirituality, love, betrayal and the remembrance of our Ancestors. It was also extremely refreshing to watch a film cast with mostly blacks where profanity and the "N" word were not used.

Seeing the elders remembered and praised was another welcomed sight. It reminded me that we are here today because of the esteemed Ancestors who made it through The Middle Passage. When observing the genius of Shuri, T'Challa's younger sister who was knowledgeable of advanced technology, math and sciences—it was a reflection for me of who we truly are. Our Ancestors excelled in these and all academic areas, as well as sports and entertainment. Shuri's positive image was extremely important for young people to see and to emulate.

Black Panther brilliantly portrayed Black women through the character, General Okoye, played by Danai Gurira. It was amazing to experience the power of women and what they can achieve when they have the freedom to use their inner and outer capabilities to their fullest potential.

There is a critical need for more inspiring films and books to be developed and published. People worldwide are revealing the hunger for this kind of knowledge as well as entertainment that is heartfelt and fills an inner void. It's time for us to continue to write and tell our own stories. Because of the staggering box office success of this film, no longer can Hollywood use the excuse that black films are not profitable worldwide. Fortunately, today there are many talented writers and filmmakers who agree that the film, *Black Panther*, has kicked the door down for other stellar works to come forth.

It's easier to blame others then to look and see what we are not doing. For instance, there are those who feel it's not necessary to study spiritual or universal laws. This significant knowledge was also represented in the *Black Panther* film though the character Zuri played by Forest Whitaker. Africans know the importance of remembering the Ancestors, of being aware of spirituality and universal laws that govern this physical plane of duality.

It's critical that we strive to know our history, where we come from and our purpose in life. We need to raise our vibrations and concentrate more on the positivity in the world to help bring substantial changes. I say this because it is as if life is moving at an accelerated pace and we are being hit from all sides with unexpected and often tragic circumstances. The majority of airtime reporting the news is spent on accidents, corruption, murder and abuse. The threat of another war and the continuous terrorist attacks in various parts of the world and America is another major distress. Social issues that include healthcare, poverty, oppression of women, economic injustice, police brutality, child welfare and gender equality are other concerns on the minds of the masses. Still, there are those who envision a more peaceful world, an end to wars and other harsh conditions that make up Earth's current insanity. But it is required that we do our part and not blame God and others for the world's arduous conditions.

In the '60s and '70s the uplifting and healing energy of black pride, love of self and of our people struck a permanent core within that remains with me to this day. I'll never forget how our enslaved Ancestors were told that they would never be free, and that their descendants would always live in bondage. We must not believe the hype and propaganda that surrounds us about who we are as a people. Just as our Ancestors envisioned a better world for us, their descendants, so it is our obligation to continue the work and hold on to the vision of a better world for future generations coming behind us.

Now is the time to take up your Wakanda state of mind and go forth to bring out the innovative creativity and greatness within you. Trust Spirit and know that the Ancestors are with you. Immerse yourself in this awakening. Teach our youth on whose shoulders they stand, so they will remember and know that they come from a great people.

It is a new day. We must all strive to accomplish what we came here to do. In the words of John Henrik Clarke, who spoke of the incredible ancient Africans who built astounding civilizations, like them we too "will take that great and mighty walk one last time." *Black Panther* has placed the ball back in our court by showing the world who we are. Now we must take that ball and fly!

Angela Kinamore is current the Poetry Editor for African Voices magazine and is also the Features Editor and one of the founding partners of the online magazine, 50BOLD.com. It was created by her and three other former editors of Essence to inspire, empower and inform Black people 50 and older. Kinamore, who served as Poetry Editor for Essence from 1985 thru 2005, is co-author of the poetry book THREE WOMEN BLACK (Guild Press, MN). She has conducted poetry readings and workshops in New York, New Jersey, Philadelphia and Los Angeles, and has read her poetry at the Harlem Book Fair, Albany State University, and the Literary Arts Festival in Savannah, GA. In August 2014 she was one of the performers in Harlem who participated in a special tribute to Maya Angelou and her poetry in a 3-hour mayathon reading production called "Rising Still." Kinamore's articles and poetry have appeared in Essence and African Voices magazines and in the 35th Anniversary Issue (New Rain Vol 11) for Blind Beggar Press. She is current in the process of completing Rise of the Zakadarian Warriors, her forthcoming book from a new genre "Spi-Fi" or Spiritual Fiction, a term which she coined.

34
BLACK PANTHER–REAL AND REEL
Bill Ayers

I happen to know the Marvel Universe somewhat, and this one seemed to fit right in–hackneyed, predictable, and banal. It's a damned comic book after all. But at the same time the phenomenon of a Black superhero struck a chord in the young people surrounding us in the theater, and we were all like, "Wakanda Forever!" I don't underestimate the power of a cultural moment to elicit some sense of pride, history, and even agency. Of course my political head was gagging at the white CIA agent (!!!!) since they killed Lumumba and Nkrumah and lots of others, and never did ANYTHING good for Africa! I also have an abiding dislike of royalty, and I always remember Jimmy Boggs saying, "To me a king is always a son of a bitch." And then at the end, with all their technology and brilliance, the whole deal is to rehab buildings in Oakland? Charity not power.

While I feel unqualified to critique the film, I am comfortable discussing some of the events related to the real Black Panther Party and the Black liberation movement of the 1960s. It was a movement with an organic connection to anti-imperialist national liberation struggles exploding around the world from South Africa to Algeria and from Cuba to Vietnam—Malcolm X made the link concretely, beyond metaphor. The Black Arts Movement burst onto the scene at the same time, offering a fresh, revolutionary aesthetic as well as an opening to reimagine the Black struggle and to resist both complacency and cooptation.

There was, as well, a sad but steadily growing recognition that the important victories of the Civil Rights Movement (integrating public accommodations, passing national voting rights and civil rights legislation) had added up to neither freedom nor justice. The failure to seat the insurgent Mississippi Freedom Democratic Party delegates at the Democratic Convention in Atlantic City in 1964, and the willingness of the Democratic Party leadership to sell out the Movement and seat instead the white supremacist "regular" Democrats was pivotal—it showed many activists that any theory-of-change that relied on appealing to the consciences of good white people was corrupt and hopeless. People became clearer and stronger in their calls for justice, not optics, and for liberation, not integration. "I don't want to find my place inside your rotten society," one activist said at the time. "I want to create a world where my humanity is no longer a question."

When Stokely Carmichael, the charismatic and brilliant leader of the Student Nonviolent Coordinating Committee (SNCC) called for Black Power during the Mississippi March Against Fear in 1966, he both echoed and accelerated a sentiment that had been growing steadily within the Movement, especially among young activists, for several years. There was no sharp break or clear distinction between Civil Rights and Black Liberation, the "good 1960s" vs. the "bad 1960s," or the Beloved Community opposed to Black Power— Carmichael and many others embodied both. History of course is both what happened and the narrative of what happened, and so the contradiction lives on.

Stokely travelled the country after the Mississippi march, meeting with Movement organizers coast-to-coast, and his message was clear: the old strategies and tactics are exhausted and something new is in the air; freedom is not a gift from above, but an achievement of a self-activated community exercising its own agency; equality will never be won without first gaining self-determination for the oppressed; Black folks need to develop their own leadership; and, yes, Black is Beautiful! He argued that Black Liberation could never be based on changing white people's minds: "We need power over our own communities so that, no matter what the white man thinks, we can be safe and free."

SNCC organizers in Lowndes County, Alabama began to build an independent Black-led party, away from the scheming Democrats, and when, in order to appear on the ballot, they had to choose a symbol for the party, they picked a powerful image of a black panther in the wild. From then on the Lowndes County Freedom Organization was popularly called the Black Panther Party—and an enduring emblem was born.

When Stokely Carmichael spoke in Oakland, Bobby Seale and Huey Newton, two young nationalist organizers, adopted the panther symbol and formed a new organization: The Black Panther Party for Self-Defense. There was an initial formal relationship between Lowndes County and Oakland, but the alliance was brief.

The Oakland Panthers' first project was to build armed community patrols to follow the police in Oakland, and document their habitual abuses—exposing and resisting an occupying and militarized police force was foundational to everything the Panthers undertook. They analyzed the role of the cops and the courts in the Black community, and called for a United Front Against Fascism. Further, their Ten Point Program, too-often reduced to a narrative about feeding breakfast to kids, is built on a political base of organizing for self-determination, reparations, and socialism. The brilliance of the community service programs was precisely that they did not stand alone as some charitable Lady Bountiful, but lived in the bond between basic human rights and a revolutionary nationalist contestation with power. The revolutionary underpinnings of their organizing offer a profoundly different reading of basic needs.

We want freedom. We want power to determine the destiny of our Black Community.

We want full employment for our people.

We want an end to the robbery by the Capitalists of our Black Community.

We want decent housing, fit for shelter of human beings.

We want education for our people that exposes the true nature of this decadent

American society. We want education that teaches us our true history and our role in the present day society.

We want all Black men to be exempt from military service.

We want an immediate end to POLICE BRUTALITY and MURDER of Black people.

We want freedom for all Black men held in federal, state, county and city prisons and jails.

We want all Black people when brought to trial to be tried in court by a jury of their peer group or people from their Black Communities, as defined by the Constitution of the United States.

We want land, bread, housing, education, clothing, justice and peace.

Anyone who can reduce this to "breakfast for children" is either delusional or dishonest. These demands and the campaigns that followed—community control of the police, for example—were simply democratic petitions on the face of it, but in the context of colonial occupation each one took on a deeply revolutionary tone and tenor.

William Ayers, *formerly Distinguished Professor of Education and Senior University Scholar at the University of Illinois at Chicago (UIC), and founder of both the Small Schools Workshop and the Center for Youth and Society, is a graduate of the University of Michigan, the Bank Street College of Education, Bennington College, and Teachers College, Columbia University. Ayers has written extensively about social justice, democracy and education, the cultural contexts of schooling, and teaching as an essentially intellectual, ethical, and political enterprise. He is a former vice-president of the curriculum division of the American Educational Research Association. His articles have appeared in many journals including the Harvard Educational Review, the Journal of Teacher Education, Teachers College Record, Rethinking Schools, the Nation, Educational Leadership, the New York Times, and the Cambridge Journal of Education. His books include Teaching Toward Freedom, The Good Preschool Teacher, A Kind and Just Parent, Teaching the Personal and the Political, Fugitive Days, Public Enemy, and with Ryan Alexander-Tanner, To Teach: The Journey, in Comics, with Rick Ayers, Teaching the Taboo: Courage and Commitment in the Classroom, and with Bernardine Dohrn, Race Course: Against White Supremacy.*

Behold your influences upon by life. Dr. Diaw

35
WHO ARE BLACK PEOPLE–REALLY?
Dr. Patricia Williams Diaw

The compelling Marvel Cinematic Universe's latest installment, *Black Panther* is resonating a question in the minds of millions, globally. Who are Black people–really?

Black Panther has been described as the jumpstart for advancement, the beginning of a process of Black empowerment, foretelling that a new black nation is on the rise, –a nation that will lead the world and shape the future of humankind. Africans and their descendants have already been there and done that. Thus, the change in the world that the film signals, begs for more knowledge on the subject. Motivated by the film's content, this paper offers a minuscule peep into the vast trove of liberating knowledge about Black people and their contributions to humanity.

An important theme of *Black Panther* is its insistence that all of humanity should view itself as one family and assume responsibility for each other. While the birthplace of humanity was discovered in the East Africa's Great Lake region, by the late Dr. Louis Leakey, it is renowned Senegalese scholar/anthropologist Cheikh Anta Diop whose analysis adds: "It has been shown that the first inhabitants of Europe were a migrating black" (1981, p. 13); Diop reiterates: "The Grimaldi Negroids have left their numerous traces all over Europe and Asia, from the Iberian Peninsula to Lake Baykal in Siberia, passing through France, Austria, the Crimea, and the Basin of Don, etc." (p. 15). Moreover, "the idea of race in the human species serves no purpose…. there are always nuances deriving from continuous migration across and within borders of every nation, which makes clear distinctions impossible" (Ruthstein, 1997. p. 3).

Are these commonly accepted propagandist beliefs about the inferiority of the African continent, cradle of civilization, true or false? "Africa has no culture of its own, was without science and technology, was without education, hence could not read or write, was without shelter, hence put up in tress, living by hunting and employing primitive methods to trap his kill" (Nangoli, 1988, p. 2)." Concurrently, at the core of claims of inferiority is the fact that, for centuries the institution of slavery consumed the aspirations and exploited the agency of millions dark skinned people.

The word "slave" giving a connotation of inferiority, is the preferred metaphor to describe Africans who were innocently and violently kidnapped from their homeland for four centuries. Like the words tables and chairs, slaves is a common noun, and can evoke feelings of shame, anger, or denial. In conversations, lectures, or social science texts, the word is dismissive of human identity, culture, language, geographical roots, and diversity. What or who will change this? In *Black Panther*, cinematography redeems rather than copies life, as five Wakandan tribes, strategically welding indomitable individual and collective power, unite through their culture, history, and values to portray African sensibility and social realism.

Early in the film's development, Wesley Snipes (and others associated with the film project) refer to the film's potential to reveal authentic true-to-life representations of ancient people and place. The humanity of African people is the theme entwined and embellished into the fabric of the movie's plot, in a film decrying violence, poverty, and oppression. On some level, Black Panther filmmakers must have realized a point discussed by Nathan Ruthstein. "[Dehumanizing practices of racism] will never be eliminated in America until its white citizens overcome their deep-seated belief that blacks are inherently inferior to whites.... Simply put, it is a matter of accepting blacks as full-fledged human beings" (1997, p. 51). Brilliantly depicted on the screen and instilled into dialogue and action is a story of struggle, honor, sacrifice, fear, anger, revenge, all human-like in quality and mood. Courageous African ancestors and millions of victims/survivors of the Middle Passage are referred to and gloriously honored by the film's existence.

Years ago, Snipes visionary comments were reported, "I think *Black Panther* spoke to me because he was noble, and he was the antithesis of the stereotypes presented and portrayed about Africans, African history, and the great kingdoms of Africa. Indeed, it would be no surprise, if research for the film included a study of African kingdoms such as: Ghana, Mali, Songhai (5,000 B.C. to 1901 A.D.).

Delicately infused into the film's setting and plot are remnants of African belief systems, values, traditions, philosophy, political institutions, economic structures, social organizations, arts, music, dance, and oral/written history, all of which has been perpetuated for centuries (Diop, 1974; Rodney, 1972; Rose, 1999; Williams, 1987).

During the time, hundreds a years ago, when five fictitious Wakandan tribes warred over a meteorite containing vibranium, what non-fictitious events were possibly happening on the earth? Was it the ending decades of the antebellum era, and Africans captives in America were the economic backbone of southern, northern, rural, urban, agricultural, and industrial American systems? Is the world now capable of embracing this truth, after Black Panther?

According to research, Africans were skilled craftsman and artisans, carpenters, masonries, architects, engineers, blacksmiths, coopers, teamsters, coachmen, gardeners, stewards, seamstresses, and nurses (Miller and Smith, 1988). They were engaged in every sort of agricultural activity, i.e., planting, raising, and harvesting of virtually every type of crop, animal husbandry, dairying, land improvement, use and maintenance of equipment and machinery, and the construction of buildings (Fogel and Engerman, 1974). Knowledgeable about the environment (both land and sea), unfreed Africans were also indispensable as pathfinders through the Southern wilderness and as navigators of the Atlantic Ocean.

Surprisingly, entrepreneurs used Africans called slaves as investment capital to support fledgling industrial enterprises or as stock equivalent to property (Miller and Smith, 1988, p. 362). Moreover, Alabama, Louisiana, Mississippi and other southern states, by forcing Africans to work under the condition of chattel slavery, developed strong economies (Miller and Smith, 1988), otherwise the cotton and tobacco industries in the antebellum south could not have existed.

In contrast to the inferior view of "slaves" in M. J. Herskovits's book, *Myth of the Negro Past* (1941), Peter H. Wood's 1974 assessment in "'It Was a Negro Taught Them,' A New Look at African Labor in Early South Carolina" is quite positive. His common-sense observation is that the easy transfer of African patterns of work and craftsmanship to a lifestyle in a similar environment proved profitable for the struggling new colonial settlement (p. 13). It can be noted that "On the eve of the Civil War, the slave South had achieved a level of per capita wealth not matched by Spain or Italy until the eve of World War II or by Mexico or India until 1960". ("Confronting our Past", n. d., p. 1).

While in the North, Africans arrived from Angola by route of Brazil and disembarked upon the shores between New York and Newark Bays. They lived among the Dutch settlers and Native Americans in a village called Communipau (located today in Jersey City, New Jersey). Washington Irving (1834), 19th Century author, essayist, biographer and historian describes the Negros of Communipau in his classical nonfiction, *The Complete Works of Washington Irving.*

Irving states:

"THESE NEGROES...BEING...MORE KNOWING THAN THEIR MASTERS, CARRY ON ALL THE FOREIGN TRADE; MAKING FREQUENT VOYAGES TO TOWN IN CANOES LOADED WITH OYSTERS, BUTTER-MILK, AND CABBAGES. THEY ARE GREAT ASTROLOGERS, PREDICTING THE DIFFERENT CHANGES OF WEATHER ALMOST AS ACCURATELY AS AN ALMANAC" (P. 126).

Communipau is the community that James McCune Smith (2006) African American, former slave, abolitionist and "foremost black intellectual in the nineteenth-century" (Smith, 2006, p. viii) describes in the third of his essays on wealth, "Human Brotherhood and Meaning in Communipau (p. 125). In 1853, Smith espouses a remedy for the problems facing enslaved Africans predicated upon a spiritual character, perhaps as displayed in *Black Panther.*

Thinking about the Wakandans' shockingly advanced scientific technological inventions, be it known that Black scientists and engineers have been in the forefront of creating scientific technologies and inventions for centuries (Thompson, 2009). In the United States, much that we know about the creative and intellectual capacities of Africans enslaved in America is documented by Henry Baker who worked in the United States Patent Office as assistant examiner for 50 years. Baker compiled four volumes containing records of inventions issued to Blacks from the period 1834-1900.

It is surreal to imagine what the world would be like without the countless inventions of Black people improving the quality of life today and yesterday. Imagine a world where only the rich could afford to purchase light bulbs, or there was no place to safely secure important documents from fire or theft. Someone in your family could not see because of cataracts. A cell phone did not exist. Think about the millions of lives lost if there were no face mask to protect rescuers. In his book, *Unheralded but Unbowed, Black Scientists: & Engineers Who Changed the World*, Garland L. Thompson chronicles the historical contexts of great scientific breakthroughs, discussing black scientists and corporate leaders in the fields of science and engineering.

Minds are sparked by the *Black Panther* phenomenon, but the answer to the question, "Who are Black People, really?" is more sensational than the film could ever be. Logically, "If no one ever shows the masses......how outdated their preconceptions really are...how can we put an end to the prejudice and discrimination that continue to thwart Blacks' best performances in many fields," asserts Thompson. Black people continue in the forefront of business, science, technology, the arts, and service to humanity. The entire world owes them a debt of gratitude, love, and respect. Each one, teach one; each one, reach one. Seizing this opportunity and fulfilling the responsibility to do so, this time can become a redefining moment in history. A time that inspires folks who have knowledge about Black achievement to teach, and encourages all to learn the truth about self, other, and human achievement.

This paper is lovingly dedicated to my mentor: Sister Alma Nomsa John, RN (1906-1986).

REFERENCES:

Diaw, Patricia. *My Ancestors Were Never "Slaves"*. Le Forum Festival Mondial des Arts Negres [Conference Paper]. Dakar, Senegal. 10-31 Dec. 2010. Retrieved March 18, 2011, from www.leforumdufestival.com/comm/doc14.pdf.

Diaw, P. W. (2011). *Mischaracterization of Africans in the United States (1619-1865): A Post-Modern Narrative*. In M. Kandji (Ed.), *Across Disciplinary Boundaries*. Dakar, Senegal: Itecom Academy Press.

Diop, C. A. (1981). *Civilization or Barbarism: An Authentic Anthropology*. Brooklyn, N. Y.: Lawrence Hill Books.

Diop, C. A. (1984). *The African Origin of Civilization: Myth or Reality*. Brooklyn, N.Y.: Lawrence Hill Books.

Herskovits, M. J. (1941). *The Myth of the Negro Past*. New York, N. Y.: Harper and Brothers Publishers.

Miller, R. M., & Smith, D. S. (1988). *Dictionary of Afro-American slavery*. New York, N. Y.: Greenwood Press.

Mullin, G. (1981). *The Seeds of Slavery and the Slave Community*. In R. M. Miller (Ed.), *The Afro-American Slaves: Community or Chaos* (pp. 19-22). FL.: Robert E. Kreiger Publishing Company.

Parker, Ryan; Couch, Aaron (January 29, 2018.). *"Wesley Snipes Reveals Untold Story Behind His 'Black Panther' Film"*. The Hollywood Reporter. Archived from the original on January 31, 2018. Retrieved April 25, 2018.

Rodney, W. (1972). *How Europe Underdeveloped Africa*. Washington, D.C.: Howard University Press.

Rose, W. L. (1999). *A Documentary History of Slavery in North America*. Athens, GA.: University of Georgia Press.

Ruthstein, N. (1997). *Unraveling the Fear*. Washington, D. C.: The Global Classroom.

Smith, J. M. (2006). *"The Works of James Mccune Smith, Black Intellectual and Abolitionist"*. The Collected Black Writing Services (1-340). Ed. J. Stauffer. New York, N. Y.: Oxford University Press.

Thompson. G. L. (2009). *Unheralded but Unbowed: Black Scientists & Engineers Who Changed the World*. Author.

Williams, C. (1987). *The Destruction of Black Civilization: Great Issues of a Race from 45 B.C. to 2000 A.D.* Chicago, IL.: Third World Press.

Wood, P. H. (1974). *It was a Negro Taught Them," A New Look at African Labor in Early South Carolina*. Journal of Asian and African Studies. 9(3), pp. 169-179.

Van Evrie, J. H. (1868). *White Supremacy and Negro Subordination; or Negro a Subordinate Race, and (So Called) Slavery Its Normal Condition*. New York, N. Y.: Horton & Company.

http://exploringafrica.matrix.msu.edu/activity-3-history-of-africa-during-the-time-of-the-great-west-african-kingdoms-expand/

Dr. Patricia Williams Diaw is author of two published books. Storyteller and Writing: Cognitive and Affective Approach to Teaching/Learning offers a broader perspective for designing student-centered writing instructional programs; Recipe: Thirty-Three Poems About Life showcases her wisdom and enlightened world perspective. Dr. Diaw recently returned from West Africa where she lived for three years and conducted research on African culture. Her paper, My Ancestors Were Never Slaves (which she presented at the Senegal, 2010 Le Forum Festival Mondial des Arts Negres), was one of fifteen papers posted on the conference's official website. Her peer reviewed article, Mischaracterization of Africans in the United States (1619-1865): A Post-Modern Narrative was published in 2011 (Across Disciplinary Boundaries; Dakar, Senegal: Itecom Academic Press). As a professional storyteller, she has performed for 50 private and public institutions in the United States, the Caribbean, and West Africa. She is the founder and director of Two Smiles for a Child LLC (www.twosmilesforachild.com).

36

THE AFROFUTURISM BEHIND 'BLACK PANTHER'

Brent Staples

The cultural critic Mark Dery galvanized a generation of artists and intellectuals when he argued during the 1990s that African-Americans whose histories had been obscured by slavery and racism were in danger of being written out of the future as well — unless they engaged the areas of art, literature and technology through which that future was being envisioned.

Mr. Dery coined the term "Afrofuturism" to describe the work of artists who used the tools of science fiction to imagine possible futures. The list of practitioners was relatively short at the time: It included black science fiction writers like Samuel Delany and Octavia Butler and the fantastical orchestra leader Sun Ra, who carried the name of the ancient Egyptian sun god and offered an allegory of salvation in which African-Americans were urged to escape tribulation by emigrating to the stars.

The ranks of the Afrofuturist creators have grown considerably over the last 25 years. They expanded in dramatic fashion with the release of the wildly successful film "Black Panther," the first major superhero movie to feature a black director and writers and a majority black cast. The film's most important distinction is that it is told from an Afrocentric point of view; it breaks with the spirit of derision that has always saturated Hollywood films about Africans.

The movie takes its title from a 50-year-old Marvel comic superhero who might easily have passed out of existence had he not crossed paths with the African-American comic book writer Christopher Priest, who broke into this white industry during the 1980s and achieved influence in time to keep Marvel from hollowing out the character that has now become one of its most lucrative properties.

"Black Panther" made his first appearance in a "Fantastic Four" comic in 1966, just as the traditional civil rights movement was giving way to black power. The comic has been inescapably identified with black radicalism, but it was clearly finished and ready for distribution before the now famous voting rights organizers in Lowndes County, Ala., adopted a snarling black panther as the ballot symbol for their new political party. And the issue reached stores months before Huey Newton and Bobby Seale founded the Black Panther Party in Oakland, Calif. — which originally was conceived of as a vehicle to protect black citizens from police brutality but evolved into a Marxist revolutionary group.

The comic, as first introduced, was not the least bit radical in the political sense — and not even self-consciously black — but it had a genuinely radical subtext. The Black Panther's alter ego was T'Challa, a highly educated king of the mythical African kingdom of Wakanda, which had never been colonized by foreign powers and was the most technologically sophisticated country in the world. (To underscore the country's prowess, King T'Challa introduces himself to the Fantastic Four by giving them a vehicle that runs on magnetic levitation.) This portrait begs to be read as a critique of both the western slave trade and the prevailing attitudes of superiority through which Westerners have long viewed Africans.

The public understandably conflated the comic book character with the radical political party that carried the same name. This association created ambivalence inside Marvel — which periodically tried to change the character's name — and clearly played a role in keeping "Black Panther" a second-tier comic that often teetered on the verge of cancellation.

Things stood thus in 1998 when Marvel, in the midst of financial meltdown, approached a brash African-American man named Christopher Priest with the prospect of revitalizing the withering "Black Panther" brand. Abraham Riesman wrote last month in Vulture that Mr. Priest was horrified by the offer because nobody read the comic, but he agreed to do it when the company insisted. Elsewhere, he spoke of being put off when colleagues suggested he make the character more "street."

Mr. Priest was known for a combustible temper, and he eventually stalked away from Marvel. But the resounding success of the new film, which draws heavily on his characterization, underscores the value of the contribution he made when he decided to treat T'Challa as more of a king than a superhero and gave him the internal life of a military and diplomatic strategist. The decision to immerse readers more deeply in Wakandan mythology also paid creative dividends.

Other African-American writers have followed in Mr. Priest's footsteps. The filmmaker Reginald Hudlin had a successful run at the helm. Ta-Nehisi Coates, who is currently writing the series, has brought the books to a higher level of public notice. Nevertheless, the sinews of the film reflect the continuing influence of the pioneering man named Priest. This legacy bears out the argument Mr. Dery made a quarter century ago, when he observed that black artists could use the tools of futurism to change how the world sees itself.

37
BLACK PANTHER–WE NEED A HERO!

Thabiti Lewis and Don Matthews

The tremendous reaction to a Black comic fiction figure suggests that the Black African American community is searching for a Hero at a time whereby it is clear that Black and Brown lives do not matter. Also, the demise of one male father figure after another in the wake of the #Metoo movement highlights the community's felt absence of real life masculine role models. The psychosocial need for a "Hero" is a very human need that transcends time and geography and is especially important for a community which finds it's males the prey of police, the criminal justice system and even in the mundane everyday tasks of going to a store for a bag of Skittles and a soft drink, an order of waffles, or a cup of coffee. Enter Afrofuturism, an intersection of African Diaspora culture with technology. It is a cultural aesthetic philosophy of science, and philosophy of history that combines elements of science fiction, historical fiction, fantasy, Afrocentrism, and magic realism with non-Western cosmologies in order to critique the present-day dilemmas of black people and to interrogate and re-examine historical events. The film is a perfect blend of Afrocentrism, fantasy, science fiction, and historical fiction that makes Black folk feel good about being Black and Africa and a hero fiqure that cannot be killed.

The reason there is a hunger for a hero is because little has been resolved since the 1960s and 1970s, which was a volatile moment. The post-race rhetoric that accompanied the Obama presidency was trumped by the election of Donald Trump. Ironically, the 1970s is precisely where the plot of the film begins—in Oakland, where the Black Panther Party was formed. To be clear, the 1970s tone was driven by the struggle for civil rights in the United States reaching a high point, the struggle for feminism making strides, and the resistance to U.S. imperialism, particularly in Vietnam and Cuba. Both Kennedys were murdered; so were Evers, King, and Malcolm X. The Black Panthers, whose core focus was food distribution, health education programs, and voter registration, was one of the many black organizations targeted in the late 1960s by the FBI and local law enforcement agencies. People forget about the social programs that were the core focus of the Black Panther Party, choosing instead to focus on its advocacy of self-defense. The truth is that this generation pushed back because the government and racism gave them no other choice. This generation launched adroit assaults at imperialism, capitalism, race, class, and gender. And, there were many male and female heroes that emerged, but they were either run out of the country, imprisoned, or murdered. The void for a hero in the 21st century is wide.

Anthropologists of African culture have long noted the importance of the male Chief in African society, the importance of the warrior class, and the revered status of the father in polygamous family structures. Since the writings of W. E. B. Du Bois in Souls, sociologists have understood that a major strategy of Slave Masters was to usurp the role of the father as protector and replace it with the powerless Black male whose family, and his life itself, was dependent on the prerogatives of White males. The substitution of an illegal polygamy headed by White males, in contrast to the legal polygamy of their African homeland, was Du Bois' polite way of talking about the sexual brutality visited upon the Black slaves by their White captors.

Hence comes T'Challa, The Black Panther, king of the fictionalized Kingdom of Wakanda to save the day. He is the hero that we have been looking for, even if he is only found in the very sophisticated "funny pages" of our day. His creation is a part of the utopian wish of which only the oppressed can give it proper expression. Tchalla's Kingdom is simply the accoutrement that establishes the hero's status in the psyche of the masses of Black folks. The film offers us this glimpse via an increased representation of black feminism in pop culture as King T'Challa's greatest scientist and warriors are women. In order to do analytic justice to this archetypal need it is necessary to situate it in the Black Aesthetic of "Spiritual Wholeness and the Four Fs (faith, family, feeling and freedom) of Black Cultural life. (See T. Lewis "Spiritual Wholeness diss SLU and forthcoming, Wayne State U, 2018; and D. Matthews, "Honoring the Ancestors," Oxford, 1998, 2012).

It is our opinion that the major reason for the success of The *Black Panther* is because it addresses the core of a Black Aesthetic that expresses the values of Faith, Family, Feeling and Freedom. These are the core ethic that underlies the Black community and it's liberation praxis. Indeed, the praxis of liberation on display in this film is one that embraces the Four Fs and discards gender definitions. The Afro-futurism and liberation on display integrates feminism. In Wakanda this praxis of liberation for its women and men protects their freedom and is symbolic their advanced culture and technology. Women and men can challenge for the crown and women warriors protect Wakanda's throne – women are not marginalized nor are men marginalized in order for women to achieve a higher status. Thus, the spirit of the Four Fs creates the proper balance.

The Faith of Wakanda is seamlessly integrated in their communal life in the forms of rituals and mystical elements, such as the plant that gives the King his superhuman powers. The plant also helps him channel his true feelings that he must learn to trust and will guide him as he leads his nation. T'Challa is made in the image of The Divine King, who is to be worshipped and obeyed without question or doubt. The importance of family is at the heart of the movie. T'Challa's father's actions provide the dynamic that eventually leads to the crisis between T'Challa and Killmonger. The tragic nature of the Father-son relationship was emphatically emphasized in the fiction of the great Chinua Achebe (Things Fall Apart) and in the classic anthropological research.* The classical battle between fathers and sons as seen in the renowned Afrofuturist film "Yeleen," (Brightness) also revolves around the quest for Black males to gain familial power and recognition.

Yet, the aspect of freedom that has drawn the most intense discussion and debate in the Black community is the divergent political positions of the two male protagonists in the film. Much like the disagreement between Malcolm and Martin, T'Challa and Killmonger represents a Black Nationalism and the use of violence; whereas T'Challa looks for a more Integrationist position in which Wakanda can be of aid to the World community through its technological expertise. The movie invites a discussion of what liberation means and the forms of praxis that will accomplish the goal of liberation.

Feelings run high in the film and are easily expressed throughout the film. It is the perfect foil for the community response of a Black movie audience whose feelings surrounding the film are divergent. Whatever one feels the truth is that the film's appeal is a direct response to a starved Black community that has been forced to sustain itself on the reality of police brutality and entrenched systems of criminal, educational, and economic oppression. Whether good or bad, "Black Panther" gives them hope and something to cheer about when they feel like screaming in desperation.

Persons in the Black Queer community have noted that the queer identity of the Black woman's fighting corps, the Dora Milaje, was ignored in the movie. This heterosexual position continues to limit the possibilities of Black representation by the mainstream media.* As Roxanne Gay wrote in the Black Panther based Marvel comic; "The World of Wakanda," the Dora Milaje promise to "fight, work, learn and love together." Surely, the progressive attitude of Spiritual Wholeness as exemplified in the life and work of Toni Cade Bambara and of Blacks in the Diaspora would affirm this gender diversity as a part of the Black Aesthetic.

*https://www.wnycstudios.org/story/after-black-panther-whats-still-missing-marvel-universe/

Don Matthews is a scholar at large and the author of Honoring the Ancestors and Can This Church Be Saved?

Thabiti Lewis is an English Professor at Washington State University Vancouer and the author of Ballers of the New School: Race and Sports in America, and editor of Conversations With Toni Cade Bambara.

38
POWER TO THE PEOPLE!

Sadiki "Bro. Shep" Ojore Olugbala (s/n Shepard P. McDaniel)

As an advent reader of Marvel comics during my youth, I can distinctly remember great feelings of Black pride when the fictional Black Panther character debuted in a *Fantastic Four* issue during the summer of 1966.

Then, as with today's Marvel 'Black Panther' movie, there was and still is a need for more positive and intelligent Black images, which cannot only help bring pride of self to our Black youth but which hopefully will inspire them to do as I did at the age of 19, when I joined the Black Liberation movement in 1973 as a member of the New York State Chapter of Black Panther Party.

Therefore, because this "fictional" super hero" movie has already been over dissected, analyzed, criticized and praised I have elected in this writing to follow the then 1970s teachings of my Hunter College African Studies Professor, the late great historian Dr. John Henrik Clarke always to learn the struggles of the past in order to best to move it forward to the future.

In 1944, the All-Black soldiers of the U.S. Army's 761st "Black Panther" Tank Battalion entered into combat against the racist and fascist military forces of Nazi Germany. This heroic unit used the "Black Panther" as its logo and backed up its motto to "Come Out Fighting" by spearheading General George Patton's liberation campaign through Europe; which included the famous W.W. II Battle of The Bulge in France. If not for a combination of the Supreme Allied Commander Dwight Eisenhower's politics and good old amerikkkan racism, these "Black Panthers" would not been put on hold in Austria. A decision which ultimately led to the Russian army entering the German capital of Berlin ahead of the other allied forces. But this is only one of the many examples of our people utilizing the "Black Panther" as a Black Liberation symbol of struggle and resistance to oppression, imperialism, colonialism and genocide.

In West Afrika during the 1940s the warrior Leopard Secret Society of Bassaland spread fear and terror to the invading European by dressing in "Black Panther" leopard skins and utilizing steel claws to kill and mutilate White oppressors in what is now known as modern day Nigeria. These Black guerilla attacks also took place during the very same decade by "Black Panther" Leopard Men in Tanganyika. Even earlier, during the '30s, the Makanga of Central Afrika and the Anyoto in the Belgian Congo carried out similar "Black Panther" attacks against the European and his "Negro" sellouts.

Historically, our people can even go back thousands of years in the Afrikan Motherland to the Nubian Goddess Bastet. Because of both her gentle and fierce nature, this "Egyptian Black Panther" was worshipped in the ancient city of Bubastis as a great symbol of the Nubian Kings. Or as Huey P. Newton said: "the nature of a Black Panther is that it will never attack; but if cornered or provoked then the Black Panther will come up to wipe out the oppressor absolutely, totally and completely." Because she epitomized the protective aspects of motherhood, the "Black Panther Goddess Bastet" was honored by the ancient Nubians as the mother of Kings and the protector of the people.

As we return to this continent we find that throughout North, Central and South Amerikkka that the indigenous peoples, AKA as "Indians," also revered the Black Panther as a respected symbol of spirituality and struggle. First and foremost it must be understood that the color Black is respected and honored by the entire Red Race; and thus the Black Panther is believed to have great medicine powers for healing. Among Oklahoma's Caddo Nation, which was originally from Louisiana, the Black Panther Clan was also known as the Midnight or Black Jaguar. The Caddo believe that through dreams, the Black Panther teaches us to look inside of ourselves in order to embrace uncomfortable territory (Oppression) through self-discovery, and then courageously face the unknown (Struggle).

More recently, during the United States civil rights era of the 60's, when the Marvel Comics Black Panther character was created, the Black Panther logo continued its legacy as a symbol of struggle against the oppression for our people. First the Black Panther was used as the symbol for SNCC by the late Kwame Ture (Stokely Carmichael) from the Lowndes County, Alabama Freedom Organization's struggle against racist voter registration attacks by the White minority. That same Black Panther logo was then shortly picked up and adopted by the Oakland, California based Black Panther Party for Self-Defense, which was Co-Founded by Bobby Seale and the late Dr. Huey P. Newton.

This year, as with the very first fictional Hollywood *Black Panther* movie in 1995, which was produced by Melvin and Mario Van Peebles; I joined with other veteran members of the "original" New York State Chapter of the Black Panther Party along with comrades, friends, family and other concerned community activists organized both inside and outside of the Walt Disney/Marvel Comics produced *Black Panther* movie theater lobbies in order to pass out flyers and to inform the movie goers that there are still "real" Black Panther freedom fighters from the '60s & '70s who are still unjustly in political exile and being held captured by the U.S. Government as Black/New Afrikan Political Prisoners & POWs.

In the final analysis, as the fictional Black Panther super hero continues to generate billions of "non-returnable" dollars from the Black community; We need to seriously tap into the real Ancestral Black Panther spirit and bring about a true Revolutionary Pan-African Unity that will free the so called "Wakanda" aka Africa and take total control of our so called "Vibranium" aka natural resources... in order to use them for the benefit of both the African motherland and the entire Black diaspora.

Ukuthula Amandla Awetu – Peace, Power To The People

Sadiki "Bro. Shep" Olugbala aka Shepard P. McDaniel serves as both the Director for the Universal Zulu Nation World Department of Community Affairs; and as the Program & Operations Director for the Safiya Bukhari-Albert Nuh Washington Foundation which supports the families, medical needs, community projects and legal campaigns of U.S. government held political prisoners/POW's and political exiles.

A Bronx, New York native, he is a professional Child Care Worker and former Hunter College Black & Puerto Rican Studies Department major who studied during the 70's under such noted scholars as Dr. John Henrik Clarke, Dr. Marimba Ani, Dr. Luis Nieves Falcon and Dr. Yosef Ben-Johannan.

"Bro. Shep" also began his lifelong work as a community activist during the early 70's as a member of the New York State Chapter's Harlem/Bronx Branch of the "original" Black Panther Party where he worked both as a Black Student Union organizer at Hunter College and reporter/distribution manager for the Black Panther Black Community Newspaper.

At the age of 63 years old, he continues that work today with the Universal Zulu Nation in utilizing Hip Hop Culture as a tool for community building, organizing and youth advocacy as a counselor, lecturer and workshop facilitator.

39
A POWERFUL BLACK PANTHER AND A SUBTLE WHITE SHADOW

Nicole Mitchell Gantt

"How can I use Afrofuturism to end racism?" Author and filmmaker, Ytasha Womack was in a classroom on Chicago's west side, talking with African American 5th graders in an art class, as she reflected her experience in a lecture for Sonic Arts (February 26, 2017). She was shocked with her findings. Speaking about the prospects of Afrofuturism, she explained to them that with fantasy, they can imagine a new world, and even space travel. She asked what they wanted to see in the future. The children answered: "I would like to see a world without violence." After much effort to help them to imagine being safe, a student finally asked: "Are you saying we can use our imaginations and create the things we want to create and change the world around us?"

Womack realized that for Black children, imagination has become almost inaccessible without first establishing safety. Well-being is a state of equilibrium where one feels safe, knowingly surrounded by others who have their best interest at heart and who inspire them to achieve their fullest potential. Global reality has not promised a full day of this well-being in the life of a Black person without some annoying, painful or even dangerous moments where that equilibrium is invaded by some level of systematic racism. That said, one often hopes that relaxing in a movie theater can promise a place of escape at least and even empowerment at best. Yet, to experience two or more hours of peace in a movie has been a seemingly impossible feat for audiences of African descent. However, the highly anticipated Black Panther was met with celebration, as Black audiences proudly dressed in African regalia, proclaiming "Wakanda forever!" A sense of euphoria swept through Black social media that hadn't existed since Obama's first election.

Does *Black Panther* signal a paradigm shift in Hollywood's representation of Blackness, especially in science fiction? Over the past decade Afrofuturism has gained recognition as a vehicle for raising issues of social justice through fantasy, and perhaps the greatest success of *Black Panther* has been the global intensification of Black imagination. Black Panther, a crescendo to the global movement of Afrofuturism, offers a win for Black audiences, although with a closer look, one can detect Hollywood's remaining, if subtle, granular white shadow underpinning the film.

Black representation in Hollywood often requires a price, a poison for its exposure, normally manifested in a visual feast of Black suffering, struggle, the perpetuation of buffoonery and/or the killing of hope. *Black Panther*, for many audiences, flipped this script, as perhaps the first American film to continually center its lens on a positive African-diasporic image of Black wellbeing. Wakanda is the most technologically advanced society in the world, a functional community steeped in Black self-love, dignity, power, discipline, rooted in aspects of Black culture that audiences of African descent positively identify with. This image tipped the scales with a consciousness-bending image of Black well-being. It's as if a secret, the elegant secret of Black genius, romanticized by old stories of ancient Kemet, and coupled with a dry wit that nurtures Black survival, was suddenly amplified on the silver screen for the rest of the world to discover. While the movie avoids touching on the complex religious diversity within African culture, *Black Panther* does sensitively handle the importance of African ritual with care and respect, as seen in T'Challa's ceremony to kingship and his travel to connect with the ancestors through the support of the vibranium-rich heart-shaped herb. At the end of the film, a white member of the United Nations almost laughing at King T'Challa stated, "What can a country of (poor) farmers do for the rest of the world?" The audience was already in on that secret, having witnessed the immense power and brilliance of Wakanda. In a sense, the epic financial success of Black Panther is an answer to that question. Blackness in its total embodiment has been consciously undervalued in Hollywood and yet, the interest in a liberated image of Blackness can set forth a billion dollars or more. Surprisingly, Hollywood decided that playing this card of Black genius could be of mutual benefit — Black psychological empowerment in exchange for Hollywood's financial gain.

The film presents a game-changing expression of the beauty and power of Black women. Actresses Angela Bassett (Queen Ramonda), Lupita Nyong'o (Nakia), Letitia Wright (Shuri), Florence Kasumba (Ayo), and Danai Gurira (Okoye), shine in elegance, establishing the radiant chocolate skin-tone in its rightful place as a standard of beauty for film, bringing justice where this expression of beauty has long been dismissed in the history of films made by Black and White producers. To see this beauty embedded with natural hair styles, especially Gurira's fabulously bald head, was glorious. Wakanda, standing as an advanced society, exemplified a transformation in male and female relationships, although there was an absence in non-sys gender roles that could have easily opened new doors with the film. To have an army of Black women defending Wakanda was an awesome show of power, as was to see T'Challa's young sister lead in technological advancement for the city, and Nakia to be so focused on her work as a spy as to question her ability to commit to her love interest with T'Challa. Captivating was the moment Okoye, the Wakandan general, stood in front of the rhino and challenged her husband W'Kabi to stop what had become a battle between Black men and women. His submission to her was breathtaking, (minus the rhino licking her face), as W'Kabi, in bowing to his queen, did not submit his manhood, but showed the strength it takes to righteously correct a wrong.

The film delivered justice to Black audiences when white privilege, a norm that people of color witness in everyday 3D life, was constantly 'checked' throughout the storyline. Breaking stereotypes, director Ryan Coogler took the opportunity to bring thoughts to the global audiences that Black folks have been wanting to say for the longest, like when technology genius Shuri sucked her teeth, calling CIA operative Ross "colonizer," and on seeing him stated: "Eh, another broken white man to fix." Whenever a white character assumptively tried to pull his or her privilege card, it was revoked. The strongest example of smashing white privilege was when CIA operative Ross spoke up in Jabariland and Chief M'Baku and his army instantly silence him. Then, wiping out almost a hundred years of stereotypes about Africa in a single statement, M'Baku said: "Shut up, white man, or I will feed you to my children." (white man gulps). "Just kidding, I'm a vegetarian."

So, director Ryan Coogler cultivated an incredible mouthpiece for Black folks, but we have to shake ourselves to remember that this is film originated from Marvel Comics, was not authored by African Americans, and was produced by Disney. While landmark and a game-changer in many ways, a subtle 'white shadow' still lingers in aspects of the film.

Looking at *Black Panther's* music, its brilliant score is an African diasporic kaleidoscope, containing samples of musical essence found in the South African mbira, the West African talking drum and djembe, the harp sounds of the kora, the impassioned sounds of Malian fula fiutist Amadou Ba, woven with some 'bim bap' of African American hip hop, North African oud, and the soaring calls of Senegalese vocalist legend Baaba Maal, all intertwined into a compelling, yet traditional musical experience that movie-goers expect to hear. These samples of Black essence were essential to the success of the film, helping audiences to locate an experience somewhere in West Africa. However, as this essence is treated as a sample, echoing the African American compositional techniques in hip hop, the true breadth of the composition relies heavy on the orchestral writing. The music leans on sonic African samples in a decorative fashion, although these sounds are central to the film's validation of context.

For African listeners, the use of some instruments, including the mbira and talking drum, are not true to the real expression of music that utilize these instruments. Without the calling of Baaba Maal, the hollers of African women vocalists whose names we don't know, and the sounds of Amadou Ba's fula fiute, would the *Black Panther* have felt authentic? Would the ritual of kingship have been real without the Black voices of celebration? There is no doubt that the masterful composition, compelling in its heroic sounds, was essential to the success of the film, although there is a white shadow over its authenticity. What if some of these African artists were invited to truly collaborate and then credited for full songs within the score? What if the newly awarded Pulitzer Prize in Music winner, Kendrick Lamar, was given more than a minimal role in collaboration of music for the film? African American music has been long recognized for its incredible influence on almost every genre of contemporary music we hear around the globe. The casting for the *Black Panther* film score was delegated to young composer Ludwig Göransson of Swedish descent, who to his credit, immersed himself into the study of traditional music in South Africa and throughout West Africa to inform his composition. Göransson was chosen for his successful previous history working with *Black Panther's* director Ryan Coogler on *Fruitvale Station* and *Creed*. It is a traditional film score utilizing the tried and true classical compositional devices that have made composers such as James Newton Howard and John Williams famous. It is an interesting omission that Göransson did not choose from the African arsenal of sounds resonating from Islam. The sounds of calling to Islamic prayer normally permeate urban and village life throughout many African countries today, especially in West and North Africa. The absence of this sound in the film score seemed to make a statement, although I will leave that for the reader to decide.

Director Ryan Coogler insured that audiences were spared blood and gore in Black Panther. This softening allowed audiences to be energized by the film, and yet, Hollywood maintained its pact of Black carnage. *Black Panther* at its climax, presented a bloodbath of black bodies in civil war, much in resemblance to armed conflicts that are continually happening today in Central Africa Republic, South Sudan, Ethiopia, Nigeria, Rwanda and Mali. Neo-colonialism continues to compromise the sovereignty of African nations, fueled by Western interests in precious metals, diamonds, oil and the especially precious tantalum (perhaps symbolized as the film's vibranium). Tantalum is the metal essential to our cell phones and laptops that most probably fuel the raged conflicts in the Congo and Rwanda.

Wakanda is defined by the outside world as one of the poorest countries in the world, and yet it holds the strongest, most precious metal in the world — vibranium. Sound familiar? One question for African American audiences is: Who are we identifying with in the film? I'm sure that Black women other than myself asked: "Why did he have to kill her?" As the only African American woman, Linda, was killed by her lover, Killmonger, without hesitation, not far into the storyline. While on one hand, the images of Wakanda provide this beautiful notion of Black elegance, culture and genius, emotionally we are also compelled to connect with the more familiar African American representation of an impoverished Oakland, California (the original headquarters of the real Black Panthers) and Killmonger, brilliantly played by Michael B. Jordan. Killmonger is a truth teller, amplifying icy statements of Black thought that perhaps have never been expressed to non-Black audiences in film. Yet Killmonger, as a vessel of anger and hate can also easily represent an unconscious white fear of Black retaliation. European and American governments have propagated so much global violence on Black and Brown people that there must be a karmic fear that at some point the tables will turn. On another angle, if we use the lens of Wakanda to represent the Western world, Killmonger would then represent a lone Black hero who works to utilize Wakanda's resources to save the non-white world, yet because of his brokenness, he only knows destruction and is not fit to rule as king. Why did the only African American character in the film have to be so damaged? Who and where was his mother? Was there an intentional separation made between the African Wakanda and African Americans to further emphasize a real divide between these groups? In the film, Wakanda, supposedly the most advanced civilization on the planet, was not able to withstand its own checks and balances when the prodigal son, African American Killmonger, returned to take the throne, and within hours, the genius order of Black well-being toppled into chaos. Wakanda did not fall, but African Americans resonated with Killmonger's message, with hope that it sufficiently invaded Wakanda's policy of complacency — descendants of Africa throughout the world need Wakanda's help. Killmonger, makes for a fascinating villain as his struggle is so relatable to the African American experience, having suffered the loss of his African father and with it, his ties to his homeland. He was a clear symbol of African American ancestral distress.

Perhaps the most confusing aspect of Wakanda's strength is its ties to isolationism. Wakanda was able to thrive because of not being colonized by the Europeans, through disguising itself as an agricultural society with nothing of noticeable value to the outside world. While the film touts a visual Pan-Africanist cultural aesthetic, by showing images that celebrate a diversity of expressions from throughout the African diaspora. However, the idea of a prosperous Wakanda hiding under an invisible veil of isolation while surrounded on all sides by the turmoil of neighboring African countries, is far from Pan-Africanist. Yet this same veil that Wakanda hides under, could symbolize the enormous power of a real and possible Pan-African Union that hides just beyond grasp. What if each African country's wealth was managed without corruption and used to support and defend its citizens, while emerging out from under the limiting veil of neocolonialism? At the end of the film, King T'Challa proclaimed that Wakanda will no longer stand in the sidelines while there is injustice happening throughout the world, sparking Black viewers' hope for reconciliation and justice.

In Wakanda, vibranium has been used as the root element of their advanced technology, enhancing medicine, weaponry, transportation and even aiding in spiritual travel to the ancestral plane. In the wrong hands, vibranium can be misused for destruction, and yet it alludes to being captured. Perhaps Black imagination is symbolized by vibranium, an elusive, yet tangible source of great wealth and power. Killmonger, if representing the African American spirit, is broken as a result of his oppression into a most powerful force of destruction. Yet if he was healed and transformed to become N'Jadaka, a son of Wakanda, his potential and leadership ability would be seemingly limitless. What if vibranium represents the essence of Black imagination, and that in spite of consistent efforts to destroy the Black spirit, like King T'Challa's panther suit, the violent attack on Black people physically, spiritually and psychologically only results in making us stronger? That Black children, like those in the classroom on Chicago's west side, can find their way to dream even though we have failed to make their world safe. Black imagination is an incredibly valuable commodity that holds the key to the positive transformation of our lives and the globe. I believe that Coogler's brilliant shapeshifting *Black Panther*, deliberate in its imperfection, has repurposed a white framework from Marvel Comics into a powerful statement of Blackness, modeling realistic strategies for our stories to be told. If the pervasive white shadow cannot be discarded, perhaps it can be skillfully transformed. The film has us lit with the prospects of Afrofuturism, and hopefully we can keep that light burning.

Nicole Mitchell Gantt (NMG) *is a creative flutist, composer, poet, conceptualist, bandleader, and educator. A Doris Duke Artist and recipient of the Herb Alpert Performing Arts Award, she is most widely known through her work as leader and founder of Black Earth Ensemble, and through repeated recognition as the top jazz flutist by DownBeat Critics Poll and the Jazz Journalists Association from*

2010-2018. NMG's primary inspiration was her mother, Joan Beard Mitchell (JBM), a self-taught Afrofuturist writer and visual artist who was an early member of the Black Folk Art Gallery of Syracuse (now the Community Folk Art Gallery). JBM died before having the opportunity to satisfactorily share her work, so upon her death, Nicole as a teen decided she would continue her mother's path as an artist bridging the familiar with the unknown. JBM introduced Nicole to journaling and creative writing at an early age, which led to Nicole's attraction to work as a typist and graphic designer for over ten years at Third World Press (TWP), the longest running African American book publishing company in the U.S.. At TWP, Nicole Mitchell Gantt absorbed lifelong lessons in Black history, philosophy and institution building, and gained incomparable mentorship from TWP's founder and renown poet, Haki R. Madhubuti. Having started her musical career busking with her flute on the streets of San Diego and then Chicago, Mitchell eventually ascended from membership of Chicago's venerable Association for the Advancement of Creative Musicians (AACM) and co-founder of the AACM's first all woman ensemble, Samana, to become the first woman president of the organization. NMG's artistic work celebrates contemporary African American culture, centered in the belief that music and art has the power to be transformative, while narrative has remained key to her compositional process. Her greatest music mentors have included James Newton, Maia, George Lewis, Roscoe Mitchell, Anthony Braxton and Ed Wilkerson. Mitchell was commissioned to create three projects inspired by science fiction writer Octavia Butler, including Xenogenesis Suite (Chamber Music America), Intergalactic Beings (Museum of Contemporary Art) and EarthSeed (co-commissioned with Lisa E. Harris by the Art Institute of Chicago). Her project Mandorla Awakening, noted in the top five jazz albums of 2017 by the Village Voice, the New York Times and the Los Angeles Times, was partly inspired by the book Chalice and the Blade by anthropologist Raine Eisler and from NMG's own Afrofuturist narrative: Mandorla Awakening. Liberation Narratives (TWP 2017) is Nicole's tribute to Haki Madhubuti, which connects music of Black Earth Ensemble with Madhubuti's poetry. Meanwhile, Nicole's poems and prose can be found embedded in the lyrics and spoken word of her dozen musical recordings. As a writer, Nicole Mitchell Gantt has had articles published in Jazz Times magazine, Wire Magazine (UK), Arcana VIII: Musicians on Music (edited by John Zorn), and Giving Birth to Sound: Women in Creative Music (edited by Ranate Da Rin and William Parker). NMG is a Professor of Music at University of California, Irvine. She also enjoys being a wife, mother and grandmother.

40

WOULD-BE WAKANDA:
The Black Panther and the
Paradox of the Congo

Ewuare X. Osayande

With the arrival of *Black Panther* in theaters the world will witness a cinematic masterpiece, something never seen on the silver screen or even believed possible – a nation governed by Africans commanding the attention of the world and revered as a high-tech ecological paradise.

But we would not need to wait for February 2018 to witness this fantasy brought to life in film. Were it not for European colonization of the continent and US ambitions during the Cold War, the world might know of a real-life Wakanda: An independent and democratic Congo as envisioned by its first prime minister, Patrice Lumumba, a leader in every way heroic as T'Challa who defended his new-born nation with his life. Had he lived, and his agenda of economic reform executed, the Congo would have been able to realize its potential and be recognized as "one of the richest nations on the planet." [1] In his independence speech in the presence of their Belgian royal colonizers, Lumumba went off script and spoke passionately of the Congo people's suffering under the Belgians and their aspirations for a nation that will "eradicate all discrimination, whatever its origin, and we shall ensure for everyone a station in life befitting his human dignity and worthy of his labour and his loyalty to the country." [2]

Wakanda's political and mythical stature in the Marvel Cinematic Universe (MCU) is based in its treasured and protected resource, vibranium. This vibranium is arguably the most precious metal on the MCU's Earth as it is only found within Wakanda. Buried in the red clay soil of the Congo lies an assortment of the most sought-after metals and minerals on the planet. Valued at a staggering 24 trillion dollars, enough wealth to solve the problem of poverty throughout the world, let alone in Africa, yet the Congolese people are one of the poorest on the planet. [3]

This crisis of development does not originate in a lack of initiative on the part of the people. As Walter Rodney clarified, it was a condition of colonialism. "In addition to private companies, the colonial state also engaged directly in the economic exploitation and impoverishment of Africa." [4] He goes on the list three of the primary objectives of the colonial state with the third being, "To guarantee optimum conditions under which private companies could exploit Africans."[5] That exploitation continues today in the Congo enabling multinational corporations to gain access to these minerals at dirt cheap rates in transactions with militias that embolden regimes of rape and terror throughout the country.[6]

The truth that lies at the heart of that paradox of the Congo's poverty and wealth is what gives the story of Wakanda its life – Wakanda was never colonized. And it is that fictive fact that enables it to become one of the most advanced nations in the MCU. The story of the Black Panther begs the question: Given its over-abundance of resources, where would Africa be had European colonization never happened?

The *Black Panther* makes his Marvel debut in 1966.[7] Many have speculated if its creator Stan Lee was inspired by The Black Panther Party. Actually, the first appearance of the Panther in Marvel comics occurs months before Bobby Seale and Huey Newton initiated the party in October of that year.[8] A better source of inspiration for the African warrior king could very well be the assassination of Patrice Lumumba which occurred six years prior.[9]

Lee has long acknowledged that he conceived of the X-Men in response to the Civil Rights Movement.[10] It is therefore not a stretch to imagine that Lee's *Black Panther* might well have been inspired by Lumumba's short-lived yet heroic leadership and the will of his people to be unfettered by the colonial yoke. But whether Lee had Lumumba in mind or not, there are significant compelling comparisons between the world of Wakanda and the Congo of our own. Some of the main characters in the Black Panther narrative are mirrored in the historical arc that is the Congolese saga in ways that are uncanny.

Of T'Challa's numerous nemeses, none does he despise as much as the man known as Ulysses Klaw. Klaw is the one man responsible for killing his father T'Chaka, former King of Wakanda, and for stealing a stash of the treasured vibranium. Clearly, a most capable mercenary, what is intriguing about Klaw is that he is Belgian.[11] One need not look any further for a clear connection to the Congo. For it was that small European nation that would colonize a territory in Central Africa 77 times its size and rename it Congo Free State.[12] First taken in 1885 as his personal possession, King Leopold II would oversee the genocide of ten million Africans.[13] In the MCU, Klaw has his arm severed by Ultron in Avengers: Age of Ultron, but it was the people of the Congo who had their hands and feet butchered by the Belgians as punishment for not meeting the daily yield on sun-drenched rubber plantations that harvested millions for the Belgian king.[14]

Klaw as a Belgian mercenary responsible for assassinating T'Chaka follows the actual account of the Belgian mercenaries who were responsible for the execution of Lumumba in the Katagan bush in January 1961.[15] In The Assassination of Lumumba, Ludo de Witte recounts the role the Belgian government played in partnership with the United States and British governments to "eliminate" the prime minister of the newly independent Congo.

Klaw's Belgian identity signifies the imperative of merciless Western imperialists' continuing role in the looting and pillaging of the Congo and the elimination of its next generation of leaders.[16]

Eric Killmonger is to the Black Panther as Mobutu was to Lumumba. Killmonger is himself Wakandan just as Mobutu was of the Congo. Killmonger and Mobutu, both despising their rivals' ascension to power, pursued bloody paths to remove them and take their thrones. In Black Panther #35 (May 2008) Killmonger becomes leader of the neighboring Nigandan army and stages a coup backed by the United States government. This is a similar course of partnership that Mobutu took to power in the DRC.[17]

Killmonger claimed bitter disagreement with T'Challa's and T'Chaka's efforts to make Wakanda into an international nation. He intended to return Wakanda to its isolationist ways in the name of cultural authenticity.[18] This cultural nationalist approach was shared by Mobutu who changed his name and the name of his country to fit a culturally African aesthetic and crafted a national agenda that "was an attempt to legitimize his absolute rule by reference to supposedly African political values."[19] That "absolute rule" was granted by a US government that would keep him in power for 30 years as the Congolese people languished in poverty and strife. Mobutu's rule afforded no wealth for the Congolese people. But it did coin the term kleptocracy.[20] In the second trailer for the film we see Killmonger don his version of the Black Panther suit with leopard spots on his mask reminiscent of the leopard print hat that Mobutu was famous for sporting.

More than the personal bodyguards for the King of Wakanda, as the elite security force of Wakanda, the all-women Dora Milaje represent the entire nation's self-defense. That a nation's greatest warriors are women is a revolutionary proposition, in and of itself. It turns on its head long-held gender notions that continue to keep women's status the world over in dangerous conditions. Of all the stories that have been told about the crisis in the Congo over the past decade, no story gained greater visibility than the rape of millions of women throughout the various conflicts. As this article from Al Jazeera clarifies, "The DRC has long been exploited for its resources, from colonial times under King Leopold II of Belgium, and today by US, Chinese and European companies. The land is rich in raw materials such as rubber, ivory, gold, diamonds, uranium, coltan and timber. In return, it has suffered from war, corruption, death, disease, hunger, mercenaries, child soldiers and rape. Rape, sexual violence, and the abuse of women is the tragedy within the tragedy here."[21]

The current crisis of women and rape in the Congo represents what happens when a society has been fundamentally destabilized by corporate greed and war and their institutions corrupted. Whereas, the Dora Milaje represent what happens in a nation where women's equality is woven into the social fabric of every institution. As such, the Dora Milaje, as the Wakandan symbol of women empowered, is the revolutionary counter-vision of what too many women in the Congo know as the brutal face of colonialism's legacy of underdevelopment and exploitation.

Vibranium is not indigenous to Wakanda. Wakanda's vibranium supply are the remains of a meteor that buried itself deep within its core.[22] It is a finite resource with infinite potential for the Wakandan people. This sole resource and its mindful cultivation is the main reason for Wakanda's recognition as the most technologically advanced society on the planet. Within the red clay earth of the Congo lies an assortment of precious metals and minerals that are native to the very ground walked on for many millennia by Africans who would be the kings and queens of this world in every respect were they able to industrialize and realize the benefits accrued from the tremendous wealth that lies at their very feet. But this is not speculative fiction or the cinema of idealists. It is the bloodied stage of a drama that has not ended since Lumumba was gunned down. Dictator after despot and coup after coup, the Congo has become a looter's paradise where multinational corporations and stone-cold capitalists gather at the bowels of the nation's unprotected borders where Congolese youth dive deep into hand-dug mines and risk their lives for mere shillings to provide the world its laptops, cellphones, electric car batteries and jewelry.[23]

As an alternate vision of African reality, Marvel's Black Panther offers a radical critique of European colonialism and the current neo-colonial pillage of Africa. And through the magic of motion picture, it also presents in vivid color the vitality of the African spirit. May it inspire a new generation of would-be heroes to take on the mantle of Lumumba's unconquerable vision.

ENDNOTES

1.   Dan Snow, "DR Congo Cursed by its Natural Wealth," BBC News, October 9, 2013 http://www.bbc.com/news/magazine-24396390.

2.   Patrice Lumumba, "Speech at the Ceremony of the Proclamation of the Congo's Independence," June30, 1960 https://www.marxists.org/subject/africa/lumumba/1960/06/independence.htm.

3.   Esther Yu His Lee, "The Paradox of Congo: How the World's Wealthies Country Became Home to the World's Poorest People," Think Progress, May 28, 2016 https://thinkprogress.org/the-paradox-of-congo-how-the-worlds-wealthiest-country-became-home-to-the-world-s-poorest-people-d27cbdd1debd/.

4.   Walter Rodney, How Europe Underdeveloped Africa (Cape Town: Pambazuka Press, 2012,) 164.

5.   Ibid.

6.   Kieron Monks, "Why the Wealth of Africa Does Not Make Africans Wealthy," CNN International Edition, April 22, 2016 http://edition.cnn.com/2016/04/18/africa/looting-machine-tom-burgis-africa/index.html; Alberto Rojas Blanco and Raquel Villaecija, "Blood and Minerals: Who Profits from Conflict in DRC?," Al Jazeera, January 19, 2016 http://www.aljazeera.com/indepth/features/2016/01/blood-minerals-profits-conflict-drc-160118124123342.html#ampshare=http://www.aljazeera.com/indepth/features/2016/01/blood-minerals-profits-conflict-drc-160118124123342.html.

7.   Ta-Nehisi Coates, "The Return of the Black Panther," The Atlantic, April 2016 https://www.theatlantic.com/magazine/archive/2016/04/the-return-of-the-black-panther/471516/; http://marvel.com/universe/Black_Panther_(T%27Challa)#axzz52fQqsyGy.

8.   Garrett Albert Duncan, "Black Panther Party," Encyclopedia Britannica https://www.britannica.com/topic/Black-Panther-Party; "Black Panther Party Founded," African American Registry http://www.aaregistry.org/historic_events/view/black-panther-party-founded.

9. Georges Nzongola-Ntalaja, "Patrice Lumumba: The Most Important Assassination of the 20th Century," The Guardian, January 17, 2011 https://www.theguardian.com/global-development/poverty-matters/2011/jan/17/patrice-lumumba-50th-anniversary-assassination.

10. Bob Strauss, "Generator X," The Guardian, August 11, 2000 https://www.theguardian.com/film/2000/aug/12/features.

11. Ta-Nehisi Coates, Black Panther. No. 166, New York: Marvel Comics, December 2017.

12. Adam Hochschild, King Leopold's Ghost (New York: Houghlin Mifflin, 1998) 3.

13. Ibid.

14. Ibid, 164-166.

15. Ludo de Witte, The Assassination of Lumumba (New York: Verso, 2001); Agence France-Presse, "Belgium: Apology for Lumumba Killing," New York Times, February 6, 2002 http://www.nytimes.com/2002/02/06/world/world-briefing-europe-belgium-apology-for-lumumba-killing.html.

16. Rory Caroll, "Multinationals in Scramble for Congo's Wealth," The Guardian, October 21, 2002 https://www.theguardian.com/world/2002/oct/22/congo.rorycarroll.

17. Stephen R. Weissman, "The CIA, The Murder of Lumumba and the Rise of Mobutu, Foreign Affairs, July/August 2014 https://www.foreignaffairs.com/articles/democratic-republic-congo/2014-06-16/what-really-happened-congo.

18. Amy Giardiniere, "Black Panther: Who is Erik Killmonger?," ScreenRant, July 28, 2016 https://screenrant.com/black-panther-erik-killmonger-michael-b-jordan/.

19. Howard W. French, "Mobutu Sese Sekou, 66, Longtime Dictator of Zaire," The New York Times, September 8, 1997 https://partners.nytimes.com/library/world/090897obit-mobutu.html.

20. Ibid.

21. Marco Gualazzini, "The Slow Road to Recovery for Rape Survivors in the DRC," Al Jazeera, June 20, 2017 ‹http://www.aljazeera.com/indepth/inpictures/2017/03/children-violence-rape-recovery-drc-170321085151907.html.

22. http://marvel.wikia.com/wiki/Vibranium.

23. Todd C. Frankel, "The Cobalt Pipeline," The Washington Post, September 30, 2016 https://www.washingtonpost.com/graphics/business/batteries/congo-cobalt-mining-for-lithium-ion-battery/.

Ewuare X. Osayande (@EwuareXOsayande) *is a poet, essayist, activist and author of several books including* Whose America?: New and Selected Poems *and* Blood Luxury *(Africa World Press).*

41

BLACK PANTHER:
The Film Bobby Seale's and the Inner Office Staff's Review

Original Black Panther: Bobby Seale

In historical reality I, Bobby Seale, was the founding Chairman and National Organizer of the Black Panther Party for Self Defense. A year later via our chief council Lawyer, Charles R. Garry I told Huey in jail that I had extended the rules to twenty-eight (28) from our original ten Rules and I am dropping the "Self Defense" from our original title to stop people from confusing us as a paramilitary organization. That I have proclaimed to party members that we are political revolutionaries: that is, re-evolving more political, economic and social justice power into the hands of we the people.

Six Years later Huey Newton attempts in his Revolutionary Suicide book to imply that he started everything not Bobby Seale. In the early founding period it was I who personally had the monetary and organizing resources and the political goal objective dream of greater political electoral Black community empowerment. In 1965, through my demographic research, I had the top paying job with the Department of Human Resources for the City Government of Oakland, California. In the first year from October, 1966 to October, 1967, there were never more than fifty (50) people or so who joined my Black Panther Party. Huey Newton sat in jail in prison for three years while I structured multiple leadership and educated, taught members the fine particulars and methodology of effective grassroots community organizing.

After the first "Free Huey" rally with five thousand people in attendance at the Oakland Auditorium, [Feb 17th, 1968] I was contacted by phone and asked, by Dr. Rev. Ralph Abernathy of SCLC, to work with Dr. Martin Luther King, Jr.'s organizing for the "Poor Peoples Campaign" for greater economic rights. I enthusiastically told Rev. Dr. Ralph Abernathy to please tell Dr. King Yes! Yes! Yes! - My Black Panther Party would (and later did) definitely work with Dr. King's SCLC. Five weeks later the racist "pig" power structure assassinated Dr. Martin Luther King, Jr. on April 4, 1968. In the immediate aftermath of King's assassination, riots broke out all across the USA, but there was one headline in a major Oakland Bay Area establishment newspapers that read: "Bobby Seale stops riot in North Richmond, California."

Angry, upset youth soon flooded my BPP organization and seven months later, after Nixon won his presidential election in November 1968, I had pulled together a five thousand membership in forty nine (49) chapters and branches in cities and major Black community neighborhoods across the USA.

As party membership grew to five thousand plus, by November of 1968, sixty-five percent were sisters: women who in the middle of this rapid growth period I authorized security training that women would be a definite part of. I did this two months after Little Bobby Hutton was murdered by the fascist Oakland police. In this period I took former military party members and I set up party security training who I made sure half were sisters. These first ten women and ten men working out of my BPP central headquarters were trained to be proficient with weapons strictly for self-defense and emphasizing that women had rights, that no one male or female could force them to have sex. The average party member did NOT carry guns while they sold the party newspaper. Actually that policy came into existence while Huey sat in jail from October 1967 to 1970. During that period, I organized the Black Panther Party across the USA. Not only in political education but leadership structure.

In PE sessions, I taught BPP members the fine particulars, dialectics, and the methodology of effective grass roots programmatic community organizing. And in PE sessions with the application of my favorite specific dialectical principle that I called the Increase/Decrease factor of community organizing: The principal states that: "Quantitative increase or quantitative decrease causes a qualitative leap or change." At many of the PE classes I opened with: "Today we going to get down to the nitty gritty and we ain't gonna miss no nits or no grits!" There was general laughter, "It's all about addition and subtraction which is the basic function of all mathematics. I am waiting for someone in the PE audience to raise their hand and ask by saying, "Chairman I think you are wrong with the addition and subtraction. What about multiplication. And I would answer with, "Brother, multiplication ain't nothing but a fast way of adding. If you have the whole of something and you want to divide it then you are subtracting it from the whole of something. And I would conclude stating: "The increase amount of times, over and over every week, that you politely sell our BLACK PANTHER: Black Community News Service and you discuss with people the issues of "pig" power structure oppression of we the people, you are decreasing the apathy and increasing the consciousness." And some brother or sister in the PE session would say, "Right On!" and "Break it on down, Chairman!"

When California, Governor Ronald Reagan called me a hoodlum after I led the May 2, 1967 armed delegation to the state capital stating our first position against pending legislation to stop us from the legal right to observe the police I got my first lesson in being stereotyped as he stated that I was a "Hoodlum." I was pissed. "Damn it!" I worked the Gemini missile program. At Kaiser Aerospace & Electronics, in the engineering department. A NASA project. Electro-magnetic field black-light non-destruct testing inspection of all Engine frames for the Gemini missile program. In yet another early small PE sessions I would go on about how we must learn to base things on good proven scientific evidentiary fact.

Black history education sessions a few times.

When I discovered that Kwame Nkrumah had built a Bauxite (claylike ore from which aluminum is obtained) smelting plant in the country of Ghana it blew my mind.

I shouted out "Bauxite!" Everyone looked at me. I rapped off the fact that West Africans in Ghana ought to be rich with all the billions and billions of aluminum products marketed in the world.

I was lucky to be raised a carpenter and a builder and an architect. My father was a master carpenter, rough and finish. At age fifteen, working for my father and his contracting carpenter friend, I did the architectural lot plot three dimensional two story design for dens and upper level bedroom/bath addition to homes. After four years in the United States Air Force as a structural repairman for high performance aircraft also prepared me to be in the high tech world.

Along with constant voter registration my organizing technique was teaching party members to pay attention to all the specifics and particulars as our goal objective was to ultimately get control of thousands of political seats.

Today in 2018 through 2020 with the Ryan Coogler, fantastic, marvelous, profound block buster Marvel BLACK PANTHER movie, I am still involved and speaking at higher education institutions and teaching voter electoral organizing to community organizations. I am working with various ecological/social justice/economic justice organizations and have now, since May 2, 1967 when my name suddenly became a household reference: because I lead an armed delegation of thirty Black Panther people which included six sisters into the California state legislature to read for the second time my Black Panther Party's executive MANDATE number one: A statement in opposition to a pending piece of "Mulford Act" legislation to stop me and my Black Panther Party's very legal rights to stand and observe police and state, when a policeman first said to us, "You have no right to observe me," WE responded with, "No, California State Supreme Court ruling states that every citizen has a right to stand and observe police officers carrying out their duty as long as they stand a reasonable distance away. A reasonable distance, in that particular ruling, was constituted as eight to ten feet. We are standing approximately twenty feet from you. Therefore we will observe you whether you like it or NOT!" We were so legal it was a crying shame. We were reciting the law to the police and the thirty or more people standing in back of us had their minds blown. One guy said, "Man, what kind of Negroes are these?" Power to the people! Thanks!

TODAY: Mr. Seale's ecological program is Environmental Renovation Youth Jobs Projects. (A non-profit entity) R.E.A.C.H!

Reclaiming, Recycling and Re-Evolving.Ecological Economic Enviro-Empowerment Around All-Peoples Artistic & Active.

Creative-Cooperational.Humanism.

www.BobbySeale.com   ReachBs@msn.com   2016 Book-publication: "POWER TO THE PEOPLE The World Of The Black Panthers"

By Bobby Seale & Stephen Shames: http://bobbyseale.com/html/orderform1.htm

NOTE: {In all of our protest RESISTANCE to fascism we are REACHING to evolve a greater social justice, economic parity and earthly ecological humane liberation}

HERE IS THE BOBBY SEALE AND TOTAL INNER OFFICE STAFF'S REVIEW OF THE BLACK PANTHER MOVIE:

Evan Narcisse, a writer of "The Rise of the Black Panther" miniseries based on Marvel Comic's "Black Panther," commented on the recent "Black Panther" movie: "Wakanda represents the unbroken chain of achievement of Black excellence that never got interrupted by colonialism."

Narcisse also added: "We're in a political moment when the President of the United States calls people from countries like Haiti and Africa shit-hole countries. If you're a young person hearing that, you need to see a superhero that's smart, cunning and noble who looks like you. Granted it's fiction, but superheroes have always had an aspirational aspect to them."

The movie opens with a narrative, it's backstory: "Centuries ago, five African tribes war over a meteorite made up of the alien metal, vibranium; a warrior ingests a 'heart shaped herb' affected by the metal and gains superhuman abilities becoming the first 'Black Panther' and unites four of the five tribes and forms the nation of Wakanda. As time passes, the Wakandans use the vibranium to develop highly advanced technology."

The movie has an all-Black cast with the exception of two white men, one a pure villain, the other, an ally. A good portion of the cast are Africans who Ryan Coogler, the director, eventually auditioned after making many trips to Africa doing research for the movie.

Coogler grew up in Oakland, CA, very aware of Oakland's history relating to the Black Panther Party. He alludes to it at the beginning of the movie that takes place in an apartment in Oakland in the early 1970's where in a short scan of the apartment, the camera catches briefly on the iconic poster of Huey Newton in a wicker chair.

Coogler also showcases exceptional female power. Besides the regal Queen, played by Angela Bassett, there are characters such as Okoye, T'Challa's Chief General, the driving force behind Wakanda, or Shuri, T'Challa's sister, the backbone of Wakanda's technological infrastructure, or Nakia, a Wakandan Spy who successfully executes a rescue mission and last, but not least, the all-female Dora Milaje warriors!

It's no wonder that this "Black Panther" movie has ignited inner city black communities and organizations to mobilize and bus their Black youth to theaters around the country to see this movie.

Bobby Seale is the original 1966 Founding Chairman and National Organizer of the Black Panther Party [BPP], USA. Bobby Seale's most profound history of resistance was the 1969, Great Chicago SEVEN Conspiracy Trial in which, after seven weeks of Seale's contumacious defiance for judicial recognition of his six amendment constitutional rights. After seven weeks of the last three days of the trial Bobby Seale was chained, gagged and shackled to a chair, in Judge Hoffman's court room: with the SEVEN defendants, Seale was "The Eighth Defendant." Working Title to Bobby Seale's upcoming book, feature film and extended documentary. In the second court room trial before the hung jury Bobby Seale was actually found not guilty in the 1970-71 New Haven Conspiracy to Murder Trial: the charges trumpet up for the (Connecticut state prosecutors) by the FBI's cointelpro. Bobby Seale became the FBI's COINTELPRO sixties "PUBLIC ENEMY". Title to a 2001 documentary film by Jens Meurer and Bobby Seale. He was a special Negotiator at the 1971 ATTICA New York State Prison uprising. He won all political court room trials except the misdemeanor case of disturbing the peace at the California State Assembly, May 2, 1967. An extraordinary revolutionary humanist with his sixties/ seventies BPP organizers in forty [49] nine chapters and branches across the USA. Civil-human-rights protest resistance must organize with peoples Grassroots programs.

42
TAKE THE A TRAIN TO WAKANDA:
The Trailblazing Paths of
Luke Cage and the Black Panther
L.A. Williams and Lee Bynum

L.A. WILLIAMS: The *Black Panther* didn't become fascinating when his film opened in 2018; the first black superhero's been that way since inception.

By definition, adaptations adapt their source material and the *Black Panther* film is no exception, but for the most part, it's strikingly close to the comic book premise.

The Black Panther is T'Challa, king of the fictional African country, Wakanda, and thereby spiritually connected to Bast, goddess of protection and cats. This connection, plus training and some rituals, gives T'Challa extraordinary agility, senses, and tracking abilities. These abilities are amplified or downplayed, depending on who's writing him, but while he isn't super strong, he is consistently portrayed as one of the smartest, wisest, richest, and most honorable beings in comicdom.

To understand the significance of the *Black Panther*, it was reported that President Trump called African countries "$#i+holes" in 2018, when information is a mere Google or Siri question away. Now, just imagine what most 1960s' Americans thought of Africa. The best known African-based character was Tarzan, a white who regularly defeated black "savages." Images of Africans were usually of ignorant, inferior, poor and superstitious people. But in 1966, the legendary comic team of Stan Lee and Jack Kirby flipped those stereotypes when they introduced the Black Panther in "Fantastic Four" #52 in a Wakanda so wealthy and advanced, it had to hide from the rest of an unready world. They gave the world an exciting character and black readers a hero we could appreciate.

Like a relay team running on a roller coaster track, every long-term creative team that worked on the Panther over the decades added distinctive touches, strengths, and weaknesses to the mythos. Lee and Kirby laid the foundation, fabricating the villain Klaw and the impact absorbing metal Vibranium. Their king was formidable: a brilliant inventor, hunter, fighter and tactician. He's similar to Marvel's Captain America (also a Kirby co-creation) and DC Comics' Batman in that when he fights a super-powered foe, logic says the more powerful being should have the edge yet you know, somehow, T'Challa will win. Kirby and Lee's

T'Challa symbolizes sophistication and coolness while Wakanda represents Africa's potential had it never been conquered or unduly influenced by outside forces.

In the late '60s, writer Roy Thomas co-created nemisis M'Baku and transplanted T'Challa from Wakanda to Manhattan by making the king a member of The Avengers superhero team, exposing him to a wider comic fanbase. Thomas' actions had consequences under '70s & '80s writer Don McGregor, who returned T'Challa to Wakanda with some American phrases, foods (NYC pizza) and, most controversially, a fiancé, giving Wakandans… pause. McGregor established many of the elements seen in the film including the Heart-shaped Herb ritual, Warrior Falls fights, Queen Mother Ramonda, and Erik Killmonger. In the 1970s storyline that much of the movie is based on, Killmonger plans to overthrow T'Challa with a combination of foreign mercenary soldiers, dissatisfied Wakandans, and rampaging dinosaurs! The storyline shows the dichotomy between T'Challa and Killmonger. In the comic, T'Challa is unable to defeat Killmonger physically. But over time, Wakandans see that T'Challa is unorthodox, perhaps even clumsy, but is honest and truly cares about his people, while Killmonger is the opposite: smooth talking, but doesn't care about anyone but himself . Ultimately, Killmonger is pushed off Warriors Falls by a child he orphaned, symbolizing a leader can't succeed without the people's support.

'90s writer Christopher Priest introduced Nakia and the Dora Milaje (T'Challa's female bodyguards) and white CIA agent Everett K. Ross to the series. He also significantly increased the Panther's use of Wakandan technology as part of his arsenal, and elevated both T'Challa's (and Wakanda's) status in the Marvel Universe from minor to major. Reginald Hudlin continued that trajectory, while co-creating T'Challa's sister, Shuri, and deeply connecting him to other black superheroes, particularly Storm and Luke Cage. Ta-nehisi Coates followed suit, but also focused on T'Challa's relationship with African gods and traditions. The Black Panther has battled standard supervillains and would-be world conquerors; but because of his longevity, his fairly unique status as an African superhero, and various writers' priorities, he's also battled Apartheidists, colonialists, drug traffickers, gentrifiers, imperialists, nationalists, poachers, racists, rebels, terrorists, and xenophobes.

LEE BYNUM: In the 2015 initiative, "All-New, All-Different Marvel," the publisher made deliberate efforts to increase diversity on the page and behind the scenes. Engaging public intellectuals Coates and Roxane Gay, poet Yona Harvey, and acclaimed science fiction writer Nnedi Okorafor has imbued the world of the Black Panther with fresh narrative pathways for queer characters, a Black feminist undergirding, and nuanced perspectives on geopolitics.

WILLIAMS: The writers change, but what's remained consistent over the decades is T'Challa's struggle to balance the importance of maintaining Wakandan/African tradition and identity with the need to evolve.

BYNUM: The *Black Panther* film is at its most compelling when it interpolates Africana elements into the reliably Eurocentric superhero genre. Xhosa and Igbo form the basis of the Wakandan language. The Afrofuturist quality manifest in Kendrick Lamar's soundtrack sits comfortably alongside Senegalese-inspired leitmotifs chirped on a fulannu, against a backdrop of mbaggu rhythms. Ruth E. Carter's costumes reflect the visual influences of a dozen sub-Saharan cultures. The cast features Black actors from four continents.

WILLIAMS: While the Black Panther was the first black superhero, it took years before he headlined his own comic. The first black superhero with his own solo comic series was Luke Cage in 1972. There's an array of ideas and questions about black heroes' imagery, impact, trajectory and viability that will need to wait for another article. But suffice to say for now that there's an unprecedented number of black superheroes on store shelves and various screens these days, and most of them wouldn't exist, nor would the Black Panther film, had Cage not sustained a regular series from 1972-1986 with numerous subsequent revivals.

In many ways, T'Challa and Cage are a yin and yang. Because people are multifaceted, different types of heroes appeal to different parts of our personalities. Part of us wants to be suave and strategic like T'Challa. But another part of us wants respect "in these streets;" a macho part that doesn't need tactics because we can handle whatever comes. "The plan? These hands!" That's Luke Cage. He's essentially a super Stagger Lee or Shaft.

Carl Lucas is wrongfully convicted and then brutalized by prison guards. One tries to kill him by sabotaging a scientific experiment but the plan backfires spectacularly, giving Lucas impenetrable skin, superhuman strength and a prompt..."self-furlough." Lucas becomes a bulletproof Richard Kimble and adopts an alias.

BYNUM: Following his prison break, "Cage" devotes himself to coming to terms with his abilities and the responsibilities they confer: clearing his name and defending his neighborhood. There's a premium placed on the connectedness of territory and community in the Luke Cage TV series. On one episode, Luke even propounds, "I am Harlem and Harlem is me." In a similar fashion, place and space are at the fundaments of T'Challa's story as every inch of him is literally is covered in the fruits of Wakanda. (Vibranium, the country's most valuable natural resource, actuates the technology in Black Panther's super-suit.)

WILLIAMS: Their homelands impact them in other ways. T'Challa, an African king, is aware of most American social issues but they rarely affect him directly. But Cage embodies the African-American experience. Unjustly imprisoned. Brutalized by officers his tax dollars pay to protect him. Scientifically experimented on. Surrendered his birth name and took on a last name symbolizing his captivity. Lives in the 'hood. Has to work for a living . And is directly impacted by crime, politics, and race. Written poorly, Cage is a stereotypical buck or buffoon. Written well, Cage is one of comics' most honorable, most lovable, and funniest characters. He's also, to quote Ice Cube, "th' wrong ni**a to f#ck with…" and knows it.

For black readers and audiences, one of the thrills of *Black Panther* is watching African warriors armed with spears and shields repel the galaxy's most dangerous threats. And with Luke Cage, it's seeing a black man in a hoodie and t-shirt walk around the city fearlessly.

Since we routinely see videos of black men getting shot to death in reality, it's exhilarating seeing bullets bounce off one in fiction.

BYNUM: Some of the *Luke Cage* show's more stereotypic facets evince the comic's Blaxploitation roots. Certain mesages are dispensed with sledgehammer subtlety. Yet the writers weave a sometimes-impish, sometimes-recondite tapestry of contemporary New York City Blackness that serves as a forceful counterweight.

Luke's television archnemesis muses, "Black women have always had superpowers: turning pain into progress." In that black female superheroes tend to be few and far between in mainstream comics—with *X-Men's* Storm and *Justice League's* Vixen as the only marquee characters in the Marvel and DC Universes, respectively—the uncommonly daedal treatment of Panther and Cage leading ladies warrants special mention. One of Cage's strengths is the trio of black women—Claire Temple, Mariah Dillard, and Misty Knight—who drive much of the action. Claire, Luke's sort of-girlfriend, has proven to be as indestructible as he is. She's not a distressed damsel, but rather Luke's most versatile resource. Ruthless, louring politician Mariah cannot be deterred from taking control of Harlem, by any means necessary. Misty, who emerges a co-protagonist with Luke, wages a single-handed war against a corrupt criminal justice system that launches her from intuitive cop to bionic avenger.

Shuri has a sufficient number of *Hidden Figures* moments across *Black Panther* and *Avengers: Infinity War* that establish her firmly as every bit the scientist as avowed super-geniuses Tony Stark and Bruce Banner. Nakia exposes the vacuity of the submissive queen consort ideal, as well as the isolationist foreign policy to which T'Challa initially adheres. Okoye and Queen Ramonda are exemplars of dignity under pressure and patriotic dutifulness. The highly skilled, impossibly disciplined (and fully clad) Dora Milaje are unlike anything seen in a preceding superhero film. They are represented as exceptional in every way, especially without their comic book backstory, in which T'Challa ends the traditional practice of the Dora Milaje doubling as a harem for the king.

The creators of the *Black Panther* film and *Luke Cage* series are attentive to the iconographic potential of both works, and consequently, some of T'Challa and Luke's rougher edges from their comics are sanded down to the comfortably familiar levels of other unambiguously moral, unproblematically relatable mainstream heroes. The audience never sees in filmic T'Challa anything other virtue and virility; nowhere to be found is the often arrogant and recalcitrant monarch who has been the victim of a slavish devotion to his own inscrutable moral code. Similarly, Luke's teenage delinquent past and the oleaginousness of a savior who charges for his services are not probed.

WILLIAMS: But perhaps they will be in time. So far, we've only had one film centered on the Black Panther, which largely served to more fully introduce him to the larger public. But season two of Luke Cage clearly showed that its producers understand something critical from the comics: it's the combination of the characters' strengths and flaws that make them multidimensional, intriguing, and enduring.

L.A. Williams is a former comic editor, the co-writer of the comic book chapter of Forever Harlem, and a Dora Milaje groupie.

Lee Bynum is a historian who focuses on race and culture in America.

43
VIBRANIUM AND GAGUT
Clemson Brown

The movie "Black Panther" and the African world. Vibranium, Wakanda and Gagut, is there a relationship? Gagut, as I will discuss later, is a theory of everything and formulated by Professor Gabriel Oyibo. But before we engage Gagut, let's set the stage with some background information on Africa and its seminal place in world history.

African civilization is tens of thousands of years older than European history. All human knowledge has its foundation in Africa. Africa has had many golden ages before Europeans emerged from the ice of Europe. In a study called Global Distribution of DNA Series, copyright c 1996, by the American Association for the Advancement of Science stated that all people except Africans have 6 DNA series. Africans have 9 DNA series. They also stated that the greater the number of DNA series, the greater the probability of genius. In a video interview I did with Dr. Kenneth K. Kidd who headed up the study, he stated that the reason Africans have more DNA series than any other race is that they are the oldest humans and have more genetic material than any other human beings.

Dr. Kidd also stated that if you had a thousand whites and a thousand Africans, you would get genius from both groups, but, the probability is that you would get a greater number of geniuses from the Africans group.

I have stated the information concerning the African genetics because no European institution of education will teach the truth about the greatness and history of African people. The question is always asked "if Africans were so great, if they built the great pyramids of Giza, the sphinx and so on, why can't they do these things today?"

I want you to consider this phenomenon. If you take fleas that are capable of jumping 7 inches high and you put them in a 3in high jar and put a lid on it so that when the fleas jumps up they hit the top of the jar, after a while, the fleas will adjust their jump to only 3 inches or less. Even when you take the cap off the jar, the fleas will only be able to jump 3in. The phenomenon of this study is that the off springs of these fleas will only be able to jump 3 inches as well. Likewise, if you take the babies of a 15 foot long shark and raise them in an aquarium, they will only grow to be about 3 feet long. Likewise, when these sharks reproduce, their off springs will only grow to be about 3 feet long as well.

| 193 |

Consider this: African people having been removed from their traditional belief system, language, and history, and you have the jar and box that they find themselves in much like the fleas and sharks.

While Vibranium is a fictitious mineral substance, and Wakanda is a fictitious place somewhere on the continent of Africa, the movie "Black Panther" conjured up a mirror for us as a people to explore our ancient past and present day reality.

The noun "Vibranium "and the verb vibration are connected in origin. 'Vibration' meaning the movement of energy and Vibranium meaning a change in energy from one state to another.

The ancient Africans understood the nature of energy, that it could not be created or destroyed. They understood that this energy moves throughout the universe from infinity to infinity in waves. These waves move so fast that they are present all over the universe at the same time. There is nothing in the universe but this energy expressing itself in varying speeds. All things constitute this energy.

The ancient African world view was that everything is everything. They believe that the living, the dead and the yet unborn all share the same space. They see themselves as one with nature or God. In fact, some people called this energy God. Others call it nature.

The ancient Africans believed that when this energy condensed or slowed down, it formed the hydrogen atom which is the building block of matter. All physical bodies are made up of hydrogen atoms. No matter what it is, a tree, rock or human, it's made up of hydrogen. Energy moving at different speeds.

While energy cannot be created or destroyed, it can be changed. This is where melanin can have a direct benefit in this process. According to Bruce E. Bynum PhD., Why Darkness Matters. The Power of Neuromelanin in the Brain. melanin is the most important substance in the body when it comes to metaphysical and supernatural manifestation. Supernatural meaning "seeming to come from magic or God." Melanin is key to transmitting and receiving different frequencies just like a radio can pick up different stations. Melaninated people can pick up frequencies non melaninated people cannot.

This metaphysical state can be triggered by our subconscious mind and also by the consciousness we bring to bear on the matter.

Now let's explain Gagut. Gagut is a mathematical molding of the change in energy. Every change or movement in the universe is a mathematical equation. The language of the universe is mathematic. The language of God or nature is mathematic.

Professor Gabriel Oyibo, an African from Nigeria in 1990 formulated the equation for the unified field theory making it a theorem. Dr. Albert Einstein and all of the great mathematical physicists tried to formulate this equation, but could not. Professor Oyibo did. This is important, for two reasons, one. He is an African and two; he has given humanity the mathematics to molder energy into what every equation we need to solve whatever problems we have. All reality can be structured into a mathematical equation. Gagut is the mother of all equations. Any and all equations that can be structured properly are subsets of Gagut.

Some of the greatest minds in the field of mathematics and physics wrote letters to the Nobel prize committee recommending professor Oyibo be given the Nobel prize for formulating the equation for the unified field theory. I am including excerpts from two of those letters in this article.

From; Dr. Liviu Librescu, professor of Engineering Science and Mechanics. Virginia Polytechnic institute and State University. Distinguished Member of Ukraine Academy of Sciences of Ship Building, and a Fellow of the Romanian Academy of Sciences we have this statement: "Dr. Oyibo's creative mind went further to address very complex issues, and at the same time, unsolved problems of an enormous theoretical and practical importance. Among these, the formulation of the three-dimensional hodograph methodology solved by Dr. Oyibo, consists of transforming the full nonlinear potential transonic flow plane. This methodology that has far reaching beneficial implications was used by Dr. Oyibo to design 3-D shock free wings that operate in a transonic flow field, and also address intricate problems of the nonlinear quasi-unsteady transonic aerodynamics.

"However, Dr. Oyibo went further and developed powerful mathematical tools, based on group theory, namely of generic group theory, enabling him to investigate in a unitary way and get solutions for the first time, of a number of problem in which famous mathematicians and physicists have dedicated their entire life. Among others, these problems are;

1.   The exact closed-form solution to the full Navier Stokes equations,
2.   Closed form solutions to the turbulence problems in fluid and gas dynamics,
3.   Solutions for the various forms and hierarchies of the Boltzman's equations, and the formulation of the Unified Field Theory."

The second letter is from professor Edith Luchins, Mathematics Professor, Rensselaer Polytechnic Institute who has met with, written about and analyzed the work of Albert Einstein." I am thrilled that Gabriel Oyibo was the first to complete the test that intrigued and challenged Einstein and many other Luminaries in science; moreover, he did so in a mathematically elegant manner.

In closing, it is noteworthy to understand that the blood cells of Henrietta Lacks, a Black woman, are the only cells scientists have found that can live outside of the body and continue to grow in a petri dish. The cells of Henrietta Lacks are immortal and point to a time when African people could live for hundreds of years. Recently, scientists have found other Africans with these same immortal cells. While Vibranium and Wakanda are fictitious, they can be our reality through the mathematics of Gagut.

Minister Clemson Brown www.tapvideo.com email tapvideo@optonline.net
To read the full paper on vibraium and Gagut go to my website www.tapvideo.com

As founder and President of TransAtlantic Productions, **Clemson Brown** has dedicated himself to the mission that, never again, will the achievements, contributions and history of African people be "whited-out" of world history.

The journey of his mission which started over 30 years ago, has taken him all over the United States, the Caribbean, Panama, Cuba, El Salvador, Nicaragua, Europe, Mexico, and throughout the continent of Africa. He has traveled along with the leading African centered historians and activists of our time, documenting their knowledge and wisdom, as well as documenting the personalities and landmark events that have shaped and define the destiny of African people all over the world. In the process, he has created an archive of over 30,000 hours of raw and edited footage of film and videotape, making it one of the world's largest collection of African and African-American history on video.

His interest in young people led to the production of over seventy-five major documentaries, which have been used as learning materials in scores of community programs, schools and colleges across the country. Minister Brown has also trained uncounted numbers of young people in the use of media equipment and video technology. He has done this through apprenticeship programs and the establishment of media training courses in schools in the New York City area. A man of varied talents, Minister Brown has taught art, directed community activities, athletic programs and served as youth counselor, all while winning acclaim as a painter, sculpturer and creator of jewelry. His poetry has been collected and published and led to his inclusion in the "International Who's Who in Poetry" published by the International Biography Center of Cambridge, England.

His latest project is working closely with Professor Gabriel Oyibo and his milestone achivement in the solution to the Unified Field Theory, which he calls GAGUT - God's Almighty Grand Unified Theorem.

Minister Brown was educated at the City College of New York, where he majored in Fine Arts and also specialized in African-American Studies. He earned a Bachelor of Arts Degree in 1973. Clemson Brown was ordained as a minister at the House of the Lord Church in Brooklyn, New York, and presently, serves as a board member at the Temple of the Black Messiah in Philadelphia, Pennsylvania. He is married to Lady Viola Brown. They are the parents of Clemson R. Brown Jr. and Herlinda V. Brown, and the grandparents of Ashley and Latoya.